"What's your sign?"

can be the question that unlocks the door of understanding —complete understanding of yourself and those around you.

Let the stars guide you to the knowledge that will help you make the best of all your relationships—with friends, colleagues, and especially loved ones.

RICHARD N. BEIM

A COMPLETE ASTROLOGICAL GUIDE

PERSONAL RELATIONSHIPS

A TOM DOHERTY ASSOCIATES BOOK
NEW YORK

PERSONAL RELATIONSHIPS

A TOR Book
Published by Tom Doherty Associates, Inc.
49 West 24 Street
New York, NY 10010

Cover design by Joe Curcio
Cover photo by Doug Fornuff
Book design by Stacey Simons/Neuwirth & Associates

ISBN: 0-812-59408-8   Can. ISBN: 0-812-59409-6

Library of Congress Catalog Card Number: 88-51635

First edition: June 1989

Printed in the United States of America

0 9 8 7 6 5 4 3 2 1

CONTENTS

✿ III. GEMINI

🐘 IX. SAGITTARIUS

Introduction

What Is Astrology?

Consider a large party, filling up all three floors of the house. Downstairs in the living room, people are dancing; on the fringes of the dance floor, people are talking loudly and laughing. On the second floor, in one room, four or five people are having a quiet discussion about what makes the universe tick. In another, four people are raucously dissecting the foibles of all the other people at the party. On the third floor, one person sits alone in the library reading, while in a quiet nook across the hall two people are discovering a mutual passion. Everyone is having a wonderful time, but in very different ways. Why are people so different? Astrology can give you an answer to this and many other questions.

Astrology predates most of what we now call science. It is the earliest attempt to systematically explain how the outside world affects the personality of the individual, and it is one of the most extensive. A knowledge of astrology will give you a structure that can explain why you do well with some people and not with others, why some days are good and others are bad, and what to watch out for in your dealings with other people.

The basic premise of astrology is that the heavens affect what happens here on earth: the ancient philosophical dictum of "As above, so below." The positions of the relatively mobile objects in the sky (the "planets," from the Greek word for "wanderer," which include the sun and moon as well as what the astronomers call planets) against the relatively unmoving backdrop of stars (the wheel of the zodiac) at the time of your birth are a record of what influences are most likely to guide your life.

One of these wanderers has more effect than the others: this is the one whose light blots out the wheel while we can see it. This is, of course, the Sun.

Your sun sign is the most important factor in your astrological chart. You can easily figure out what your sun sign is from your birthday. The chart below shows what sun signs go with what birthdays. This is not a book of predictions, but is a guide to how the personalities associated with the various signs will get along with each other.

If you were born between:	Your sun sign is:
March 21 and April 20	Aries, the Ram
April 21 and May 20	Taurus, the Bull
May 21 and June 20	Gemini, the Twins
June 21 and July 20	Cancer, the Crab
July 21 and August 21	Leo, the Lion
August 22 and September 22	Virgo, the Maiden
September 23 and October 22	Libra, the Scales
October 23 and November 22	Scorpio, the Scorpion
November 23 and December 20	Sagittarius, the Archer
December 21 and January 19	Capricorn, the Goat
January 20 and February 18	Aquarius, the Water-Bearer
February 19 and March 20	Pisces, the Fish

How to Use This Book

This book is arranged into twelve chapters, each one of which describes a sign of the zodiac. The first sign is Aries, which the sun enters at the beginning of spring; the last is Pisces, which ends at the end of winter.

Figure out your sun sign. Turn to that chapter. The first

section is a short description of the character of people born under that sign. Read this to get a sense of what your astrological strengths and weaknesses are.

The next section describes how people of that sign get along with people of the various other signs in two very important areas: money and work, and home and family. Read this to find out how your daily life can be affected by the signs of other people.

The third and final section is the most useful; it describes how women and men of a sign get along with other signs. Read this to diagnose why a relationship is going wrong, by going immediately to a specific pairing; or read it to determine what sign you should be looking for to have the fulfilling relationship you deserve.

After you have read what you want to know about your own sign, you can go read about the other signs to improve your skills at dealing with all sorts of people.

A Final Note

Your sun sign is not the only factor in your astrological chart. If it were, there would only be twelve types of people in the astrological world. The other planets modify what your sun sign implies. You may find that you feel a greater affinity for another sign. There is nothing wrong with this; feel free to use the information about that sign to guide your search for fulfilling relationships. Remember that almost nobody is a perfect example of a given sign, but the guidelines will help you a surprising amount of the time. This book will serve as an introduction to the world of sun sign astrology. I know it will be of use to you in your search for the right person.

I. Aries 🐏

The Aries Character

Aries men and women plunge in fearlessly where others hesitate. They are courageous, daring people—undeterred by danger and threats. They will never be intimidated.

However, their physical and moral courage often lands them in difficult and awkward situations. Frequently they find themselves in the midst of disputes and arguments not necessarily of their own making. They are born fighters, modern-day warriors, and nothing delights them more than to be hanging in there battling for a lofty cause or for someone who has been badly treated.

Aries people will do a favor for anyone who asks. They are spontaneous, open-handed people. They give with an impulsive generosity. But no one can tell them what to do. They won't take orders or be bossed. Even in a working situation they invariably feel they know better than the superior giving the orders.

The Aries self-confidence is supreme. It is this that makes them so daring and bold, often driving them to recklessness. Behind them they leave a trail of victories and mistakes, but seldom do they look back. They are always moving forward. They never lose heart. Their enthusiasm and faith in their ability to overcome and survive is unshakable.

Aries people have tremendous physical energy. They use it to break new ground, to attempt what others think is impossible. They thrive on challenges and competition. They are pioneers and adventurers. In their lifetime they cover an enormous amount of ground and accomplish a great deal. But they don't dwell on their achievements. They are too intent on looking ahead for the next obstacle or challenge to bother much about what has been.

If an Aries person starts to live in the past—which is a negative trait of this sign—they become explosively emotional and very unhappy.

The typical Ariens meet their problems head on. They believe in confrontation and their power to seize the initiative in any situation. They are not the types to rehearse what they are going to say or do. They prefer to rely on their ability to respond in the moment.

These basically honest people don't try to duck out of their responsibilities. They grimace and bear them if the going is tough. They are not complainers. They are people of their word. They go after what they want in life and make no bones about it. In a word, they are go-getters. But they are not devious or deceitful. Their style is too direct and open for cunning.

Aries men and women are popular. Their optimism and sure-footed personality attracts others. They are often an inspiration to weaker and more timid people. Their social activities are numerous and are usually associated with their many projects. They seldom do anything without an objective.

These egocentric and fiery individuals are very out-spoken. They say precisely what they feel. They can be hurtful. They are too impatient for reflection and are often rightly accused of being tactless.

The Arien mind is quick and full of ideas. They are continuously seeing new opportunities for the action that is the wellspring of their being. They tend to tire of projects before they are finished—but mainly because they can see that a successful conclusion is inevitable. The Aries nature does not pursue success to bask in the glory, but to succeed because the task was thought by someone to be impossible. Aries people want only to prove to themselves that they can do anything they attempt.

With their cheerful, high-spirited ways, Ariens get along fine with children. But as parents they feel tied down by such responsibilities. Ariens are young at heart and children respond naturally and joyfully to this. Youngsters delight in the practical jokes and good-hearted teasing which Ariens can't resist.

The Arien parent takes considerable pride in his or her off-spring and endeavors to give them the best possible education. With an elevated opinion of themselves, they regard their children as some sort of affirmation of their good citizenship and worthiness as an example.

Aries people often walk over others who may be in the way of their ambitious plans. Slower-moving and slower-thinking types can be callously pushed aside. These and other inconsiderate actions result in fairly regular criticism and rebuke. The Aries person may seem to shrug off criticism without a care. But privately they are often appalled at their own thoughtlessness—once it is pointed out to them. But by then it is too late. They will do much in the way of kindness to try to make up. The biggest challenge they have to face in their life is to try to overcome their impatient and impulsive nature.

These people have a kind of one-track mind. Once an Arien decides on a course of action, that's it. They are not likely to heed any advice, even though it is obvious they are about to make a serious mistake. They seem to willingly tumble over the precipice just to prove they did it their way.

A quick temper and a tendency to sometimes hit out physically adds to the Arien problems. These people need almost constant activity to work off their excess energy. Sports or some sort of physical exercise is a must to keep frustration at a controllable level.

In their quieter moments, Aries people yearn to be more restful and less aggressive. But their sudden ambitions and impulses leave them little choice until with the years a mellowing maturity does it for them.

How Aries Gets Along with Others

Aries with Aries

Money/Job. Aries people do not make a god of money. They earn it and use it—giving a good share of it away in the process. They are not stingy people. They enjoy the pleasures and comforts that money can provide. But if denied it they don't complain; they make the best of what they have—and quickly set about making more. As they have the necessary drive, they are good money makers.

Jobwise, Aries people work well together. But the old problem of "who's telling who?" will arise if one of them is the boss and starts throwing his or her weight around. To be happy and efficient, Aries workers must be able to use their initiative without having a superior breathing down their necks. That's why so many of them go into business for themselves.

Home/Friends. Aries men and women are home-lovers and will work hard and well together to beautify the home and make it more comfortable. The home is the base for all their other activities, which usually require them to be in and out and often up late in the evening. Home is the one place where Aries feels really relaxed.

The home is used regularly for entertainment. This includes dinner parties for officials of clubs and associations for which the Aries person is helping to organize projects. More intimate dinners are held for close friends. These are likely to include at least one other Aries person. Aries like the company of suc-

cessful people and invariable there is at least one Aries among
their friends.

Aries with Taurus

Money/Job. These two will inevitably argue over money.
Aries spending will be too impulsive for Taurus. Taurus
loves good (expensive) things and will spend like crazy on
them, but only after giving each purchase a good deal of
thought and probably saving up specifically for it. Taurus
probably will spend twice as much on luxuries and comforts
in a year than Aries, and still complain that Aries is squan-
dering the income. It is the sudden impulsive buying that
Taurus frowns on. Also, Taurus is likely to indicate that
Aries' taste is lacking in refinement, and that will keep the
fur flying.

   Jobwise, Aries and Taurus can be a good combination. Aries
is fast and facile. Taurus is slow and thorough. Aries would
make a good salesperson working with Taurus who is responsible for making or acquiring goods. Taurus will work willingly
and conscientiously with anyone on a practical project, but if
Aries starts bullying or trying to cut corners, Taurus will not
cooperate.

Home/Friends. These two will make a lovely home together. Taurus will see that it has all the comforts and little
(plus big) luxuries which Aries might otherwise dismiss as
unnecessary. Taurus will be home to enjoy them a lot more
than Aries. Taurus never tires of sitting back and relaxing
in the lovely surroundings of his or her home. Taurus will
often get peeved at Aries being out and not sharing in this
pleasure. As friends, Taurus and Aries can be close but are
not likely to spend a great deal of time together. Aries hasn't
got the time, anyway. Taurus has the time but finds Aries'
impatience and restlessness a bit disturbing after a while. But
they will have many interesting discussions and Taurus will

teach Aries many things as he or she holds forth on a pet subject.

Aries with Gemini

Money/Job. These two have a hankering for financial security but it's deep, deep down. Especially in Aries, who just can't resist the impulse to spend when it's there. So Aries security is usually in the safety of the bricks and mortar of the house. Gemini is always on the lookout for ways of increasing income, increasing security. But his or her many changing interests keep Gemini buying and spending. It's a race to see which hand—the one bringing it in or the one pushing it out—works fastest. Together, Gemini and Aries are likely to have frequent money crises as their spending sprees clash. Once disciplined to economize and save, Gemini can amass money. On the job, these two work well together. But as a team they have to determine to finish the projects they start. Gemini is very easily distracted and often has too many irons in the fire even for his or her flexible mind to handle. Gemini finds it hard to reach decisions; Aries makes instant decisions all the time—many right, many wrong. Here, in business, the combination could get into trouble.

Home/Friends. Aries, who is in and out of the home for a good part of the day, will seem like an old stay-at-home compared to Gemini. Gemini uses the home like a tennis ball uses a wall. He or she bounces in and out at any time of the day or night. It has been known for a Gemini-Aries couple living together to not meet for a week except in passing at the door. But both love the home as a base and will make it as attractive and comfortable as time and money will allow. As friends they have a lot in common. Gemini loves variety. Aries likes intelligent and interesting people. Gemini knows a little more about more subjects than even Aries. But gradually they may discover that neither of them has a very deep knowledge of any topic, because they didn't ever have the time to study anything in depth.

Aries with Cancer

Money/Job. Cancer people are worriers and where money is concerned living with a free-spending Aries could give them a nervous breakdown. Aries likes to put on a generally luxurious front. They can be extravagant and careless, especially in investments. Cancer is careful with money, has modest tastes and dislikes extravagant display. However, Cancer has a flair for making money and Aries would do well to listen to their advice. Cancer yearns for security and Aries has to appreciate that without this there will be unnecessary emotional problems to deal with. Jobwise, these two may have some problems, especially Aries in trying to understand the changing moods of a Cancer workmate. But Cancer will appreciate and respect the ambitious drive in Aries. Cancer people are quietly ambitious and quite capable of reaching the top of the success and money tree even before Aries. They must never be underrated.

Home/Friends. Cancer people are real home-lovers and will establish a nest that Aries people will be proud of. They are devoted parents and will take much of the strain off Aries when it comes to dealing with the ties of children. They enjoy entertaining and Aries will be happy to bring friends to the home for some "good old home cooking." Cancer usually is a talented cook and will spend hours preparing for dinner parties. As friends, Cancer and Aries do not usually form close relationships. They can be dear friends but may not see each other regularly. The Cancer nature is a little too emotional and possessive for Aries comfort.

Aries with Leo

Money/Job. Leos can be lavish spenders as they like to make a big impression. Aries might at times get a little anxious about where the money is coming from, but as long as Leo does not gamble or play the stock markets all should be well as the two have an ingrained respect for security. Leo is frightened by the thought of poverty, more so than Aries. Leo is a hard worker and usually a good earner. Together these two with their energy and initiative could become wealthy. Jobwise, they will also get on well together. Aries will have to be tolerant of Leo's constant grandstanding and attempts to impress everyone with his or her many talents. The Leo nature is to take over control and in a close working association this could be a problem as Aries will not allow anyone to lord it over them. The exception could be Leo, whom Aries will tend to good-naturedly tolerate because they have so much in common at a deeper level.

Home/Friends. Together in the home there could be some problems. Leo, like Aries, wants to be the final authority. Roaring battles for supremacy could be fought every night. Yet when the dust has settled they will love one another just as much and neither will hold a grudge. The home itself will be very comfortable. Leo loves comfort. He or she also regards the home as a status symbol with which to impress their many admirers even further. Many friends will visit the home as both Leo and Aries like entertaining good company, but dinner parties may often develop into a contest between the two to dominate the conversation.

Aries with Virgo

Money/Job. Virgos are constantly looking for ways to become rich. They know the value of money. They are more inclined to spend it on necessities than luxuries. Aries will find Virgo a good restraining influence where money is concerned —if he or she can be persuaded to take any notice. But Virgo's love of security could also be irritating to the freedom-loving side of the Aries nature. Virgos are good savers but usually are too cautious to become wealthy. They also can lose their savings by being talked into speculating in dishonest deals. Jobwise, Aries and Virgo will work very well together. Virgo is modest and self-effacing, a conscientious worker whose main concern is to do a thoroughly good job. Virgo will have no complaint about being organized and directed by Aries as long as the work is based on sound, practical principles.

Home/Friends. Home life together could be a bit of a hair shirt. The natures are so different that in a close relationship these two could gradually start going their own ways. Virgo is either fussy about the home or inclined to let the place fall into untidy disorder. Aries won't enjoy either extreme. Virgo untidiness is usually due to feelings of insecurity or of not being loved. This an Aries partner should do their best to rectify. Virgo and Ariens are not the likeliest of friends. Virgo is a shy retiring type who can be put off by Aries loudness and assertiveness.

Aries with Libra

Money/Job. Librans are not money-hungry, but because they love beautiful and expensive things they get through a good deal of it. An Arien partner will be more interested in getting value for money and will not have the same desire for luxury. Librans can't help choosing the best. There will be arguments over money if funds are short but otherwise these two will co-operate. Working together in a job situation may be a strain on the Libran, especially if Aries is in charge. Aries wants quick decisions and instant action. Libra needs time to weigh up the pros and cons and then usually finishes undecided. Libra will welcome Aries' precise instructions and do a good job as long as there is no pressure. A Libran boss will appreciate an Arien employee's boundless energy and initiative.

Home/Friends. Aries like a nice home to bring their many business associates and community contacts to. Libra has exceedingly good taste in house furnishings and decorations and is a perfect host or hostess. Aries will be proud and Libra will be happy. Entertaining is very important to both. There will be many dinner parties for friends who will include successful and interesting people. Libra especially likes to be associated with celebrities. Both make friends easily.

Aries with Scorpio

Money/Job. Scorpios are more interested in amassing money than Ariens. They respect money because it helps them to achieve their goals, rather than for its power to provide ease and luxury. Scorpios and Aries will understand each other pretty well where money is concerned. Both can be big spenders when they want something. Scorpio is shrewd and more calculating than Aries in handling money. Both are hard workers and ambitious. Scorpio works tirelessly and steadily. Aries is always active in more than one direction and is inclined to work in spurts of energy. Together they can make a good team and will respect each other's talents. Both are strong, determined characters.

Home/Friends. Scorpio and Aries can clash in the home because both want the final say. But they are usually intelligent enough to work out a compromise that preserves the independence essential to their natures. Scorpio uses the home as an outlet for his or her creative instincts (which are considerable) and the home reflects this. Aries will respect Scorpio's artistic gift and give enthusiastic encouragement. Aries makes more friends than Scorpio. Scorpio is not so available. Both enjoy the company of powerful and successful people. Scorpio does not like light conversation so the dinner parties may tend to get too intense at times for Aries.

Aries with Sagittarius

Money/Job. Sagittarians spend a lot and usually go all out to make money, but they are not conventional earners: not the usual 9 to 5 wage slave on a fixed salary. They rely on their luck and ability to capitalize on opportunities. They are inclined to live too dangerously financially even for a sometimes financially reckless Aries who prefers a more steady income. Sagittarians invariably get involved in get-rich-quick schemes —but with surprising success. They have a keen business sense and are usually self-made persons. Jobwise, Sagittarians and Ariens will get along fine together. They will respect each other's skills, individuality and non-dependence. Neither is afraid to quit a job instantly if they feel imposed on or unappreciated.

Home/Friends. Sagittarians are usually too interested in the world at large to focus intently on their home. Aries, who spends a good deal of time away from the domestic scene, is an old stay-at-home compared with Sagittarius. These two will have a nice, large home as Sagittarius loves a comfortable base to return to. They will have many friends from all walks of life. The Sagittarian will be constantly bringing home new friends to dine and entertain them lavishly. Aries will enjoy this some of the time but will revolt if Sagittarius overdoes it—which is certain.

Aries with Capricorn

Money/Job. Capricorn can be very good for Aries where money is concerned. Capricorn is very correct and cautious and will always try to make sure that financial realities are faced, something that Aries may overlook when it suits them. Capricorns are good steady earners. They don't gamble or take risks. They are trustworthy and if given control of the finances will do a canny job and see that there's always enough in the kitty for vacations and emergencies. Jobwise, these two are both ambitious and determined to get to the top. Aries want to get there today; Capricorn will diligently slave away no matter how long it takes—and make it. An Aries employer will value his or her Capricorn worker. Capricorn will admire Aries' energy and ambitious drive, but may be caustic about Aries' tendency to take short cuts and overlook details. Aries will work happily for Capricorn who will allow him or her to use initiative within Capricorn's overall plan.

Home/Friends. The Capricorn person runs a neat, spotless and comfortable home but there is little emphasis on luxury. Everything is useful and practical. An Arien partner will provide the light, artistic touch. Capricorn people do not have many close friends, but when they are able to relax they enjoy socializing and entertaining. Aries is likely to find Capricorn a bit too aloof for a close friendship.

Aries with Aquarius

Money/Job. Aquarians enjoy wealth and status but are not likely to consider them worth toiling for. Aquarians would rather be involved in work they love even if it pays very little than sacrifice their life to make money. They are not extravagant or indulgent. It might be difficult for an ambitious, hard-working Arien to understand their Aquarian partner's take-it-or-leave-it attitude to money. There is bound to be some midnight discussions about it—but no arguments because Aquarians don't argue. They turn over or walk away. Jobwise, these two can work well together as long as one doesn't try to order the other about. This could be difficult for Aries who can't help trying to organize associates.

Home/Friends. Home life will be reasonably smooth as Aquarius will not be drawn into emotional scenes. This could at times leave Aries seething or stomping out and slamming the door. But their basic compatibility will allow them to interact fairly harmoniously most of the time. Aquarius enjoys human contact and this couple will have many friends and acquaintances. Some of them will be odd characters as Aquarius favors unconventional types whose ideas are often too far off the beaten track for popular consumption. Aries being a more conventional sign might not mix too well with some of these people.

Aries with Pisces

Money/Job. Pisces men and women love the material comforts that money provides. It gives them a sense of security which they badly need. When they do have money they give a good deal of it away. They love to share the pleasure others get from their generosity. They also feel a little bit guilty when they've got more money or things than someone else. Aries is also an open-handed sign. The two will need to watch their finances closely so that they don't suddenly find themselves in a jam. Jobwise, Aries and Pisces can work well together. But Aries has much more physical energy. Ideally, a working relationship will consist of Aries putting into action the very creative money-earning ideas of a Pisces partner, employer or employee.

Home/Friends. Pisces loves a beautiful home and on this score Aries will have no complaint. Everything will be as elegant, tasteful and comfortable as money allows. Pisces needs a good deal more quiet and solitude than Aries who may find it difficult to live with the long silences when their Pisces mate withdraws into themselves.

But the home will have many visitors and callers. Both enjoy human contact and friendship is especially important to Pisces. Pisces people are probably the most sympathetic listeners in the zodiac and there is usually a stream of friends turning up or telephoning to tell them their problems.

Love Mates

Aries Woman—Aries Man. These two people love action and adventure. She's daring, he's dashing and bold. Side by side they can zip along together in an exciting romance or partnership. All they've got to be sure of is that they're going in the same direction. It is easy for these two characters to get so involved in their own thing that they lose sight of each other.

But love—physical love—will help keep them together. Both are passionate. They communicate instantly through body contact. If words fail, lovemaking won't. She is looking for real love more than he is. He often can't distinguish between sex and love. He is sometimes just too physical. She has to teach him the finer side. And a typical Aries woman knows all about love and her body.

But she must learn not to try to be high-handed with this man. He won't stand for female domination. This is where the combination could come apart. Both are fiercely independent people, fiery and headstrong. There will be plenty of spirited arguments. Until they can agree who does what they will be fighting for supremacy every day.

But there will be a lot of excitement in their romance or life together. They will never stagnate and become indifferent and dull. Each will keep the other on his or her toes—frequently treading on them as well. These two are not strong on tact and won't hesitate to call each other nasty names.

There will be frequent changes of residence. Turnover of friends and acquaintances will be high. The pace of living will be cracking. He—like she—has tremendous energy that must be used positively. Otherwise they will take their frustrations out on each other and miss the magic that is possible in this mateship.

Aries Woman—Taurus Man. This is where an Aries female could meet her match—and love it.

In many respects the Taurus male is her exact opposite. First she has to understand that he is not going to be carried away by her enormous enthusiasm as people usually are. And he's not going to give in to her pushing, either. He is probably the most stubbornly unmoveable creature in the zodiac. He just won't be dictated to by this fiery and extremely self-possessed lady. He believes in a quiet easy-going life and (he thinks) he doesn't want it disturbed by any female dynamo. To get along with him and finally to win him requires some very special tactics.

The Aries woman must not try to shove or jostle him. He knows Rome wasn't built in a day. Like history, he believes in taking his time. So she must do the impossible for an Aries woman and be patient. He will be attracted to her if she makes a point of seeing his point of view. While he thinks he's in control he can be gently pushed.

She must avoid arguing, tears or pouting moods. He'll just walk off. Of course he wants a nice girl but he won't be pressured into anything. He's dead scared of making mistakes. His philosophy is that all good things come to Taurus people who wait. And he is Mr. Patience himself. His whole life is the proof of it. He has never yet done anything on the spur of the moment.

She, however, lives most of her life on the spur of the moment. And although she enjoys her quieter moments she can't bear to hang around. She likes to make things happen, not wait for them.

This man can be well worth waiting for. All she has to do is coax him along, humor his stubbornness and nestle up to him. She should rely on her considerable female magnetism. He is a very sensuous man and will respond to sex appeal but never to emotional tantrums.

Aries Woman—Gemini Man. A link-up between these two people will have many positive results: so many, that the partnership could endure for a long time. At worst, if a breakup should eventually come, both are likely to forget the difficult times and agree that it was very exciting while it lasted.

An Aries woman will provide most of the get-up-and-go physical energy in this mateship. The Gemini man lives mostly in his mind and his vibes have a nervous, insubstantial quality.

He's a bit hard to pin down, and even harder to keep tabs on. He can't proceed for long in an agreed direction. He gets too easily distracted. He needs a supportive partner and a strong female shoulder like Aries to cry on when he plays his sad little boy role. At other times he can be as hard as nails. He is a very changeable character.

Aries and Gemini have carefree natures. They both love to live in the moment. She delights in spontaneous physical action and he in thinking and analyzing. Together they represent a blending of body and mind and can achieve much in the way of success in the world.

But jealousy can be a problem for the Aries woman. The Gemini man is flirtatious. He doesn't usually have the stamina for a sustained second love affair, but he does enjoy using his mental and suggestive powers to stimulate women's interest. With his curiosity and impish mind he gets into some very tight corners, but extricates himself at the last moment.

This man falls in love with his mind first. She falls in love with her heart first. He needs a woman with a creative intellect and this the Aries female naturally provides. He is quickly bored by women who have nothing more to offer than physical intimacy.

Aries Woman—Cancer Man. Although different in so many ways, these two can make a wonderful romantic combination.

For the Aries woman, her first meeting with a Cancer man can be a rare delight. He has the ability to emphasize her feelings of femininity which are not always that strong in her. Aries women can appear so self-sufficient and enterprising that men shy away from them, preferring to concentrate on more helpless types. But not the Cancer male. He knows his stuff—and his women. His sign after all is ruled by the Moon, which represents the female principle. He is a male with female intuition and sensitivity. He knows that inside Aries is a real woman, and he knows how to reach her and please her.

He is gentle and respectful and quite old-fashioned by contemporary standards. He believes in actually courting a woman, charming her with his manners, gallantry and speech. A woman can be quite bowled over by such a courteous approach. He uses words like a poet.

The Cancer man radiates self-confidence. And his tough masculinity leaves no doubt that he is a man who can look after himself and his woman if she needs it. But it's mostly an act. This man is filled with doubts and anxieties. He is so deeply sensitive that he is terrified of being hurt, so he protects himself with a phoney macho image.

He is moody. One day he is outgoing and confident, the next withdrawn and uncommunicative. He is very easily offended. An Aries woman, with her tendency to be tactless, can cause him great distress and emotional instability. But if she loves him she can give him the support and companionship he so desperately needs. He in return will give her the devotion she wants, for once committed he is loyal and true.

Aries Woman—Leo Man. This relationship between two very strong characters will require them to take turns in giving up or climbing down—just for the sake of love.

And love it definitely can be between these two passionate, independent yet compatible people. With a bit more tolerance and understanding on both sides it can be the mateship of the century.

An Aries woman feels she can take pretty good care of herself. Her philosophy is that she will never be anyone's burden. She knows what she wants and who she is without anyone having to tell her.

But a Leo man can't help trying to teach and improve his mate. He does it for all the right reasons, perhaps—but invariably, it comes out in the wrong way. To an Aries woman he will sound arrogant, patronizing, self-glorifying, self-righteous and damned insulting.

Yet he is a deeply loving man. When he loves he really cares. But he is very stubborn and proud. He finds it difficult to apologize if he is in the wrong. Usually he rationalizes his faults and this can drive a straightforward Aries woman into a fury. She is impulsive. He is immovable. When they clash—and often they will—it is like a collision of two great wills or super egos.

But underneath, Aries and Leo are very compatible signs. Their frequent quarrels will usually end in fervent avowals of love—and rediscovery of the old magic in lovemaking.

This man likes compliments. And it is doubtful whether a down-to-earth Aries woman is going to feed his lion-hearted appetite for hearing how good he is. If she wants a favor all she has to do is soften him up with praise. Flattery will get one anywhere with Leo. That is one reason he may stray in a permanent relationship; if an Aries woman doesn't indulge his ego enough in this way, some other predatory female might. Leo the lion just cannot resist adulation.

Aries Woman—Virgo Man.

A relationship with a Virgo man can be a very rewarding experience for an Aries female. It may even last a lifetime. But if it doesn't she will still look back on it as a time when she found it possible to express a part of herself normally concealed from her other mates.

This man will not try to compete with her. He has an instinctive capacity for selfless love. He is not out to prove or defend anything. With his modesty, loyalty and understanding he truly gives to his woman.

This can be quite a surprise for an Aries woman. Usually she feels she has to assert herself, has to try to conquer the man to show her love. And of course this has the opposite affect, inflames the male ego and causes dissension.

But the Virgo man is often so uncompetitive that she can find love without feeling the need to fight for it. He is kind and considerate, devoted and faithful, sympathetic and tender— and will not stamp on her dreams. He is a different sort of man.

The trouble is his instinctive fear of marriage. He is difficult to get to the altar—not just on time but at all. And Aries women are not known for waiting around. Chances are that before he gets around to popping the question (or saying yes) this woman will have found a more nubile mate and taken the plunge. In her mind she will have rationalized the affair as just a beautiful friendship.

But if Aries and Virgo get it together on a permanent basis there are a few problems that will have to be faced. For one, he is very critical. Forgiving and understanding, yes, but relentless at finding fault. This he does out of a genuine desire to help. But to this woman who has a lot of hidden insecurities, it can be demoralizing or infuriating. Either way she will hit out.

This man loves to serve and when his woman is sick he tends her like an angel.

Aries Woman—Libra Man. This should be a fine love affair, but whether it can be made permanent depends a great deal on how hard the partners are prepared to work at it.

They are very well suited mentally. She wants an intelligent man with a good mind—and that's him. He is quick on the uptake, logical, fair, reasonable. He can discuss just about any subject. He is stimulating and challenging—just what the Aries woman needs and admires.

He is also a pretty cool customer, emotionally controlled and levelheaded. The danger is that an Aries woman, with her emotional nature, is likely to fly off the handle and become belligerent or aggressive. This sort of thing he cannot stand. He despises disharmony, loathes fighting. He will walk away, walk out, rather than stoop to a shouting match.

He is tactful and courteous. She is tactless and thoughtless. She doesn't mean to hurt but can't help speaking her mind. That will be accepted by her Libra man as long as she keeps her cool.

He loves beautiful things, including art, music—and women. This could be a problem for a jealous woman. Libran men are usually very attractive physically, sometimes strikingly good-looking. They are charming, amusing and fun to be with. They have many female admirers.

The Libran will be good for an Aries woman. He will gently try to make her see her mistakes. He won't come down hard on her, won't arouse her fiery need to defend herself. He knows instinctively how to handle people, especially partners.

She will help him too. An Aries woman loves excitement and has all the energy necessary to provide it. Libran men can be lethargic and tend to wait for something to happen instead of initiating action. This woman is all action and will spur him on to use his undoubted talents.

In lovemaking, he may be a bit lightweight for her. His mind is more on romance than on his body. She will have to use her passion to try to bring him more to life.

Aries Woman—Scorpio Man.

This could be a deeply satisfying relationship for an Aries female. This man wants everything a woman can give and in exchange is prepared to give—just about everything, just about. With a few adjustments on either side, it could be not only a love affair to remember —but one that can endure.

The biggest problem is that two very strong wills are involved here. The Scorpio man, like Aries, is a fighter. Both love to fight and both insist on winning. It would seem that one has to give in. But that is not how this combination works in reality.

Both signs are deeply passionate. The Aries woman is looking for an outlet for her passion, her love. She wants a man who has as much to give as she can take. And Scorpio, as long as he is the positive type, can do just that. This is the love-match where in lovemaking the independent Aries woman can give all without the feeling of losing. If she does give all, and he gives as much in return, they both win and live happily ever after.

The Scorpio man is often silent. In a love-match he does most of his talking with his body. The silences can be a bit trying on an Aries woman who likes to chat.

This man will be true to any woman who can give him sufficient passionate love. He is not interested in affairs as such; he is looking for just the sort of female that an Aries woman is. She will resist his attempts to dominate her otherwise, and he will in most cases understand this independence. They will have an understanding of each other deeper than most other combinations.

He is jealous. But she is unlikely to give him cause for resentment if he loves her. Both are ambitious and although he may not like her involvement in so many activities he will secretly admire her energy, enterprise and initiative.

Aries Woman—Sagittarius Man. It is easy for an Aries female to be great buddies with a Sagittarius man, but not so easy if she falls in love with him. A number of emotional problems are likely to arise which she will have to handle.

He is a flirt, perhaps only verbally but this can be very hurtful to a jealous Aries woman. He won't change. She'll have to. And that's not easy.

For happiness, this man has to have reached a point of experience where he's prepared to settle down. This doesn't happen until he's well over thirty. Basically he's a roamer, a good-humored, open-hearted friend to all. He loves adventure. He is restless and rarely content but usually happy and optimistic.

He is a big spender and leaves a lot to luck or chance. He gives expensive presents and always spends his last few dollars on his mate. But he is not too reliable. He changes his job regularly. He believes in freedom and the search for wisdom and both often come before his partner.

The younger Sagittarius man is hard to pin down. All of them are marriage-shy.

An Aries woman often suffers from an inner fear of being hurt or deceived in love. With a Sagittarius man she will have to come to terms with this in one way or another. Like her, he is honest and unlikely to deny the truth if she is prepared to ask.

Once the emotional problems are out of the way this can be a very happy and satisfying twosome. Both have much in common; they love sports, the outdoors and a busy active life.

Aries Woman—Capricorn Man. This is a romantic pairing which requires the Aries woman to take the initiative in a special way. This man needs help to get his feelings out. He's all buttoned up inside and it's quite possible for him to be in love with a woman without giving any indication of it at all.

Before an Aries woman who is interested in this man gives up and walks away from him she ought to make sure he's not writing love poems to her in his head.

But he must be coaxed very gently. He does not like women who are forward or throw themselves at men. The Arien approach is usually direct and uninhibited. This may confuse him and at first meeting can be misinterpreted by the Capricorn man. She's being natural; he's being careful. She's outward-going; he's introspective. There's a great gap between them. And it's all because he's terrified of revealing his emotions— because he might get rebuffed and be hurt.

This man is a contradiction. He is self-reliant, independent and ambitious—three qualities that will be admired by Aries. But his strength comes from rigid self-control, not from an easy understanding of himself. Inside, this rather aloof and serious-looking fellow can be quaking with uncertainty and self-doubt. Any love he receives he may at first seem to reject or be cynical about. He is not sure how to respond to affection. Outside of work he has a poor opinion of himself and basically can't believe that anyone would be truly interested in him, yet he is sensuous and a good lover.

An Aries woman can gradually bring him out, bring him back to life, with warmth and love. For there can be no mistake he has a great depth of feeling. This includes an intense love for nature and animals.

Aries Woman—Aquarius Man.
The more sensitive, openhearted Aries female is going to have some trouble trying to get it together with this man. To her sentimental heart, he will often seem cold and unfeeling. He will be friendly and kind to everyone. But sympathy of the kind that draws most human beings together is not his long suit. He is a different sort of human being from most.

The trouble is that Aquarians believe in a greater destiny than that usually limited to family attachments, normal friendships and even normal feelings. They believe more in the future of the human race as a whole than in the immediate expectations of individuals. They are a strangely detached kind of people.

An Aries woman may sometimes feel remote from her Aquarius mate. She is full of feeling and caring for those around her. He is more concerned with odd and eccentric people and collects them around him. She likes successful and competent people, whom he avoids.

He is a deep thinker, often a very original and inventive one. He is likely to regard an Aries woman's many activities and projects as having little real value or a waste of time. His aims are noble but that does not mean he ever actually gets down to doing much about them. He is a great observer and student of the human race—from a distance.

There will be plenty of high-spirited debates between them, but he loathes emotional displays and will avoid arguments. Basically however there is a deep underlying compatibility. If a love-match does not work out a good friendship might be the answer.

Aries Woman—Pisces Man. This link-up is going to present problems right from the start. But it's far from hopeless; success depends on the intensity of the love. If love is there the understanding will be present and the union could turn out to be a rich and fulfilling one.

Ideally, the combination normally works best when the man is Aries and the woman Pisces. Aries is a dominant go-getting sign. Pisces is a soft, dreamy and unworldly sign.

An Aries woman will have to tread softly here if there is going to be a permanent relationship. This man is not going to attempt to compete with her, or control her. He won't fight with her. He will let her have her own way. All this may not be very good for her. She really needs some sort of restraint on that self-confident, impulsive assertive nature.

But this man will do her a lot of good, even if the relationship is only temporary. To begin with she may feel she has met the man of her dreams. He will go along with all her romantic notions—and give her more. He believes in dreams, and if he has learned to cope with the world, can make them come true. But the danger is he will go along with her more inpractical schemes—which often are numerous—and this could be expensive for them both.

He is very emotional and easily disillusioned. The Aries woman will have to give him strength when he is down. She must understand that he is not a weak man. He is hypersensitive and in touch with a world that others know very little of. One day he will be meek and submissive and the next strong and independent. He will often seem cold and cut off from his partner as he retreats into his inner world.

He will never intentionally hurt anyone. He is a loving and kind man.

Aries Man—Aries Woman.
No man, not even an all-conquering hero like Aries, is going to take this woman over. She's her own person. She knows what she doesn't want—and that for sure includes a mate who tries to run her life for her.

Because she is so much like him, the Aries man will have to handle this woman very carefully. She can't be pushed or forced. But with love and tenderness she will give as much as any man could want.

However, she does like to give orders and can't help taking the initiative—both under the guise of an unquenchable enthusiasm which tends to sweep others along with her. As the Aries man uses much the same tactics, if they are not alert they may find themselves heading in different directions—with other followers but not each other.

Both are impulsive and quick-tempered. They will speak their minds and often hurt each other. But fortunately they are quick to forget and forgive. And the making up afterwards may even seem to make the arguments worth while.

Aries men and women are sensual. Being physically active people they know how to express their feelings through their bodies. The lovemaking should be very good. If it is not it means there is not enough love and there will be a danger of one or the other straying.

The Aries woman is a romantic idealist. She will do all she can to make the partnership work. She will be loyal as long as she feels she is truly loved.

For all his brashness and impatience, the Aries man can be tender and gentle. Although she may seem at times to be demanding a more demonstrative kind of loving, she will adore him for it.

Aries Man—Taurus Woman.

There will be many differences between these two, but most of these can be smoothed over and the partnership made a very rewarding one through their physical lovemaking. Here, they will communicate in a way that might be frequently lacking in their daily life.

The problem is that this woman is basically passive, calm, patient and reserved. He is aggressive, impatient, impulsive and bossy.

She doesn't have a great deal to say unless she's spouting forth about a pet topic. He seldom stops talking—and more often than not about himself. She will be a very good sounding-board for him until inevitably he notices the glaze of disinterest come over her eyes. There will be no mistaking this or the chill of her occasional negative silences which will exasperate him.

He likes to be continously on-the-go, busily engaging in numerous projects and organizing people. He's a typical city man who wants quick results. She prefers rest and tranquility, and pursuing sure and safe objectives. She loves the stillness of nature and the country. She can wait for what she wants.

She is likely to understand him more than he understands her. She will make sure his home is just as he likes it. It will be comfortable, tidy, clean and have many little luxuries.

She is a good mother. She will attend to a lot of the dull aspects of domestic and partnership life which Aries finds irritating and tends to neglect. With a willingness to give and take this man and woman could find something that keeps them together for the rest of their lives.

Aries Man—Gemini Woman.

In her love life, the Gemini female is looking for the impossible. An Aries man could come closest to providing it for her, but he must understand that before he met her this woman probably had done a good deal more searching than most among the males of this world. He might be appalled if he knew how many old flames she'd had. His innate jealousy could easily get the better of him. He might then upset the applecart and lose her. He would do better not to dig too deeply.

This woman values her freedom. Even in a partnership she insists on it. And she is prepared to give her man the same kind of freedom. That means not living in each other's pockets and being mature enough to stick to what you've got—once you think you've found it.

This will suit Aries. He will delight in her quick, versatile mind, her ability to discuss intelligently practically any subject. Her creative ideas will stimulate his thinking, so much so that the two of them could end up (or begin by) getting some kind of business enterprise going together. They can make a very successful team.

He is likely to get peeved quite often at the way she can beat him at mental games which both like to play. He thinks he's probably the cleverest mind around and living with a Gemini woman will remind him that as smart as Aries is, the creator didn't put all the mental gifts in one basket.

This man and woman are both youngsters at heart. If they can overcome their mutual tendency to be selfish their love also should remain eternally young.

Aries Man—Cancer Woman.
The main problem for an Aries man in this relationship is that after a while he could start to feel smothered. His light—his treasured freedom—may seem to be going out.

This will be due to this woman's very special kind of love. It is so intense that for a man who likes to put love in one compartment and the rest of his life in another, the effect can be suffocating.

A Cancer woman is sweetly feminine and appealing. At first meeting she can seem a bit helpless or confused and in need of some strong male guidance and support. This quality is likely to attract a self-confident and always-eager-to-help Aries man.

He will offer himself as the strength she needs. And he will be delighted with the way she responds. Their love-making will be delicious. Then he will discover that underneath she is a strong and tenacious woman. For this he will admire her more.

But by then he is likely to find himself staying more at home (with her) than ever before in his life; in other words, that he's losing control of his life.

This man will give up anything before he will sacrifice his idea of freedom. And that could mean splitting with his Cancer woman if her love becomes too clinging and restricting.

However, she is an excellent home-maker and mother. She is very much attached to her parents and these also could be another burden for him on the weekends.

Both will do well to make a resolution from the start: she to be less demanding in her love, and he to be less dependent on being independent. Then they have a chance of finding love that is a happy medium.

Aries Man—Leo Woman. This proud, dignified, attractive and somewhat hard-to-get woman born under the sign of the Lion is likely to surprise all her friends by falling for an Aries man almost at first meeting.

He of all the signs has a built-in understanding of Leo, and because of this can enjoy a special place in the heart of the Lioness.

Leo women love strong men, but not strong men who are mindless enough to try to destroy their dignity. She herself has the self-confidence and strength to give such males their come-uppance. A typical Aries man knows instinctively that this woman loves to be admired and flattered, and that for him to recognize and respect her obvious superiority over other women is a guaranteed way to her heart.

These are two self-centered people. Without the right consideration for each other it can be a tempestous union. Both partners want to be the sole authority. Both are born leaders. But their motivations are different—which makes harmony possible.

Leo wants to lead or to rule like a king or queen: purely for the adulation and adoration that royalty attracts. Aries wants to lead to prove that he or she can do anything better than anyone else. If the Leo lady gets sufficient recognition and praise from Aries she will be happy to let him feel he is boss of the household or whatever. Otherwise they will spend their lives fighting for supremacy—and usually making up by making love in grand style.

The Leo woman is often vain and arrogant. When they argue she will accuse him of the same things, for the two signs are very similar.

Aries Man—Virgo Woman.
This lady has a cool virgin heart. She's not very sure at all about love and what it actually means between man and woman. She needs warmth —the warmth of a man who knows that she's a very special person. It takes a special kind of loving affection to reach her, to convince her. Aries is the man who could do it.

But he must understand the subtlety of the situation. He can't use the old bull-at-a-gate approach with this woman. She's not easily impressed, not likely to be overwhelmed by the usual Arien self-confidence and enthusiasm. She relies on her highly refined intuition and analytical mind to reveal the truth.

She is gentle, silent, modest, undemanding. She is full of consideration for others and loves serving in helpful ways. What she does she does without expecting to be praised. She is bright yet unobtrusive.

The danger is that Aries may start to treat her as part of the furniture. In his concern for his many other activities he may forget to love her in the only way that she can really be reached—by praising her for what she does well and what she is. Not because she will demand it or even be looking for it, but because she deserves it and has a pretty poor opinion of herself. For the man she loves to express his gratitude or genuine recognition of her many qualities will help her to see herself in a more positive light. She needs affection, true warmth, and to be told frequently that she is loved. And no wonder. This woman is striving for a perfection in herself that just can't be attained.

Sometimes she will be fault-finding. But there will always be truth in it.

Aries Man—Libra Woman.
Aries men are so bull-headed, impatient and ambitious that they are often charging

blindly towards some sort of precipice. A Libra woman will act like a soft brake on an Aries man. She won't cramp his dashing style, threaten his freedom or try to undermine his self-confidence, but she will save him from many a fall.

This woman doesn't lose her cool easily. When an Aries man is angry or aggressive—which is pretty often—she will stand her ground. But in such a sweet reasonable way that he is likely to end up seeing that he is in the wrong and perhaps even apologizing.

She is tender, intelligent and wise, but she is a bit of a ditherer when it comes to making decisions. An Aries man who is constantly making instant decisions is likely to have a near-seizure while he waits for his Libran lady to decide whether she'll take the car or walk.

She is something of a manipulator, though. She is so naturally agreeable and charming that she works by suggestion. Seldom does she come straight out and ask her man to do something. She puts the idea in his head in advance—and lo, pleasant surprise, he does what she wanted and thinks he thought of it!

These two are well-mated. They are a good example of the masculine and feminine principles. He is all man; she is all woman. He will have to take the lead in their love-making as he does in everything else. But she must never destroy his confidence in himself as a lover or their life may fall apart at the seams.

This woman can be the best thing that ever happened to an Aries man. She can steer him towards the full and meaningful utilization of his enormous energies.

Aries Man—Scorpio Woman.
These two will bring out the fighter in each other. There will be many verbal clashes. But most differences between them can finally be solved in the physical contact of love-making, for these two signs have a deep sexual attraction for each other.

The main difficulty for Aries is likely to be the Scorpio woman's secrecy. He doesn't have many real secrets—not the extraordinary complicated ones that Scorpios have, anyway. He's too open and direct. And beside, he's usually in such a hurry to put his ideas into action that he hasn't got time to be secret about his secrets. There is little to hide in Aries.

Unlike him the Scorpio woman has loads of time. She can wait for ages to reach her goals. She loves to plan years ahead and to painstakingly manipulate people and circumstances towards her ends from behind the scenes. She is an intense, emotional woman. She broods.

An Aries man will never be able to work her out. He can't even hold a grudge for five minutes. Scorpio *never* forgets an injury. And she *never* forgives. She just gets even.

There is much that these two can learn from each other. She will teach him to be less selfish, rash and impulsive. She will learn from him (Scorpios have to learn from experience) that there is a freshness and rightness in being direct with each other without motive or design and that, without having to change her basic nature, this comes out every time as *straightness*. Scorpios are deep enough to understand this.

In lovemaking, the Scorpio woman will willingly submit to being conquered by her Arien man—as long as he is masterly enough and loves her enough.

Aries Man—Sagittarius Woman.
This woman prefers male company, but after she links up with an Aries man this could present some problems. He's a jealous fellow. He can't imagine how she could possibly want to be in any other man's company when he is so much all male and loves her so much. He must understand that she is not aiming to be unfaithful. She's only being friendly.

The Sagittarius woman will not tolerate unfounded jealousy. It implies she's dishonest and Sagittarians have an organic attachment to the truth. She may be disloyal if she feels she is badly treated. And she may have had numerous affairs previously—most probably disillusioning. But she would never engage in a sneaky affair without telling her man. She loathes deception.

Like him, she is very independent. And like him she enjoys being out and about. Some nights when he arrives home tired and looking for his woman to tell his troubles to, she may still be out and about.

He'll have to get use to the idea that she's not a dedicated housewife. She'll do her fair share around the place but no more. She likes a nice home. But she's not interested in making a career of running around with a vacuum cleaner, doing dishes and ironing. That's not her idea of love and partnership.

The Aries man's ego will frequently be wounded by her blunt speech. He himself is often tactless. But this woman's candid observations about people usually happen to be right—which tends to make them even more hurtful.

The physical lovemaking between Aries and Sagittarius should give a high order of satisfaction to both sides.

Aries Man—Capricorn Woman. The older this woman gets the younger becomes her attitude to life. She starts off usually being a very serious sort of girl, finding many men superficial and not liking those that are cocksure, arrogant and noisy.

A younger Capricorn woman meeting an Aries man around the same age in a social situation is not likely to be attracted to him. He is cocksure, arrogant, very noisy and obviously (in her opinion) too brash and a bit too glib with his answers to be anything but superficial.

If they meet at work, however, she may form a totally different opinion of this man over some months. She will admire his ambitious drive and efficiency (she is ambitious and efficient herself). And she will notice and respect the easy confident way he accepts responsibility. From then on, if they start dating she may even fall in love with him.

The Capricorn woman, young or mature, assesses everything on practical merit. That includes men. And as the typical Aries man is a good and ardent lover as well as an impressive worker and earner, she can find her heart's desire in him.

Her sexual desires are strong, but she often suppresses them because she's frightened of being emotionally hurt.

Although she becomes more flexible and mellow with maturity the Capricorn woman never loses her motivation towards power and security.

With his warmth and love an Aries man can take the coldness

of imagined inferiority from this woman and help her to glow like the delightful female that she is.

Aries Man—Aquarius Woman.

An Aries man attracted to an Aquarius woman won't waste any time beating about the bush. He'll plunge in and take his chances—which are as unpredictable as this lady. She might say "no." Five minutes later she might say "yes." Or she might even beat him to it and suggest they make love. It's not so much his passion and physical presence that she's interested in, but his mind. She wants to know what makes him tick.

Basically they are compatible. They love to talk and discuss. Friendship is very important to an Aquarian woman. In fact, she often has a problem trying to understand the difference between friendship and love. She will keep experimenting with love-making to try to find out.

She is not an emotional type. For her, everything is in the mind. She is distrustful of emotion, especially the kind that makes an Aries man make declarations of undying love shortly after meeting her.

The Aquarius woman's main occupation is trying to satisfy her curiosity. She sees the puzzle of life and is forever looking for the clues to work it out. Once she has experienced something (like love-making with an Aries man) there has to be something different about it to keep her interested. So he must never become lazy and habitual if he wants to hold her.

The danger for Aries is that her sexual detachment will make him feel rejected. This will be a blow to his ego and could increase his aggressiveness—which will make matters even worse.

If she wants a permanent union with this ardent man she should always welcome his embrace with enthusiasm and love.

Aries Man—Pisces Woman.

The lure of a Pisces woman is very strong for an Aries-born man. She is soft, cuddly, submissive, gentle and understanding. But most of all she obviously needs protecting from the horrible world, and that's where the Aries man is likely to step in with all the confidence and panache of a conquering hero. He will save her, he will protect her.

This woman will be impressed. How could she help it? He is so strong, masculine and full of action. But his sheer energy is likely to give her extremely sensitive receptive system a bad attack of emotional static. However, because she loves excitement and change she'll probably ignore the warning and go along with this ardent and passionate man. But it is doubtful, without a great deal of love between them, whether they will be able to sustain a long-time union.

Aries men are restless, boisterous and hyperactive physically. With their enthusiasm, driving ambition and competitive nature they throw out a lot of bow-waves.

The Pisces woman after a few exciting hours yearns for peace and solitude. She can't sustain any relationship for long that impinges on her sensitivity. She retreats into herself. Forceful personalities swamp her individuality. She is a delicate, emotional creature, although underneath very often is a strong spiritual woman. She is a contradiction, an enigma.

If an Aries man can appreciate her deeper needs and love her, she will pamper and spoil him, idolize and delight him, and for much of the time make him feel the luckiest man in the world.

II. Taurus 🐃

The Taurus Character

Not for Taurus the impulsive leap in the dark. They want to see where they are going and for what reason. Basic principles make the Taurus character in both man and woman. They understand cause and effect.

They are intelligent without making this too obvious. They will be putting two and two together quietly to be sure they are right.

Of all the zodiacal signs they are closest to Mother Earth. They do not abuse that which is natural. Their basic instinct about life in general gives them a head start over more rational people.

Once Taurus is sure of the course of action, there is a happy yet determined desire to get on with the job. They do things for a reason, so have clear vision and sound principles. Without an end product, time and effort will be wasted. Taurus won't have this.

Taurus is not a lazy bull. Once started there is no stopping him or her. They do things thoroughly and like to see something tangible for their efforts. Once they get their teeth into anything there is no letting up.

Obstacles have to be overcome. No quarter is asked and none given. The challenge of practical life is taken fairly and squarely. Their rule book says they must not chicken out when the going is rough. Their broad back will carry a heavy load for them and their dependents. They are always happy to lend a helping hand to those in genuine need. If Taurus offers you assistance, take it. It is meant sincerely and will be one hundred percent.

To Taurus a promise is a promise. Their firm commitment to undertakings makes them the reliable pillars of society. This obvious strength attracts the opposite sex, especially those who are looking for security. Taurus simply oozes the natural confidence to handle everyday affairs, come storm or fair weather. They make judgments by touch. They will never physically hurt that which they love. They are attracted by physical charms and are well aware of their own. They will try to make an impression by appearance or deed.

As parents they are considerate, firm, tolerant and apparently easy-going. They know their young have to grow up in a practical world, so they give them a good grounding in the facts of life. This will mean getting priorities right. For instance, a day's work cannot be done on an empty stomach! So Taurus' children will be well fed if not immaculately dressed. They will also know where they stand, be independent like their parents and will not feel that the world owes them a living. Pride is strong in Taurus and will often show in their children. The children will know they have certain standards to maintain.

Reliability means a lot to Taurus. They believe in their abilities and trust in that which has been proved good. They take on responsibilities because they have natural confidence.

They may not be bullish in appearance but they give the impression that they are not to be fooled with. Being practical people, they can take on anything or anybody. They will not be rushed, and are excellent planners and organizers. More to the point, they will know how things work and can do a job themselves if a colleague or worker drops out.

They respect the past: Rome was not built in a day and they are the world's greatest builders. They learn a lot from what has gone before.

They are here to stay and will leave something solid behind them when they eventually go. They like to be remembered. What they leave behind will be beautiful, for they have a great sense of physical proportion and harmony. This will show in their love of song and music as well as in the things they construct.

They can be their own worst enemy. Their unwillingness to give in or to make changes makes them obstinate. Sometimes they find it hard to find the right words and seem negative or moody. When frustrated they boil up inside till they explode. Everyone then will understand what is meant by "a bull in a china shop"!

They are never intolerant in their own eyes! They just fail to see what all the fuss is about.

Because they like comfort they need rest but are generally not lazy. They will take more time than is necessary to get moving. They would much rather stay put. Change without good reason just leaves them cold. They can freeze out those people they don't like. They are natural loners, so they seem to be anti-social.

Taurus people will give you a cuddle and enjoy yours in return if they like you. They are misunderstood because of their pride.

They "take it" to show they are strong. They are physical show-offs. Overdoing this will lead to exhaustion, their principal health problem. They need long periods of rest to recuperate.

They like the simple life and belittle the little people and smaller details of life when they are feeling nasty. This makes them appear to be snobs. Their love of material things can make them hoarders. They can set material values too high and lose sight of their more lovable qualities. They are likely to get in a rut; it is hard to move them when they do.

How Taurus Gets Along with Others

Taurus with Aries

Money/Job. Supply and demand mean a lot to Taurus. Work is essential but has to be productive. Aries can rub Taurus the wrong way. Aries lacks the staying power that goes with patient effort, yet Aries is honest and will face up to problems. They are a bit "pushy." They resent fitting in with the routine laid down by others. Even so, they will get on with the job in hand. They waste no time. This suits Taurus. They are practical with money. Like Taurus, they think of survival. While Taurus values money and will be careful, Aries always has a use for money. Taurus plans his budget and worries. Aries makes money quickly and uses it likewise. They accept each other.

Home/Friends. Taurus' home has to be comfortable. Aries loves home as a center of activity. Aries is adventurous with their home and will make changes. Taurus likes to feel everything is there to stay. Aries appreciates the Taurus hospitality, which will be generous. A meal or a drink is always on hand with Taurus. Aries homes are open to all who call. Both like a convivial drink, though Aries prefers hard liquor. It loosens guests up more quickly.

Friends come in all shapes and sizes. Aries brings a lively new experience. Aries will not sit back. They will be the life and soul of the party. Taurus enjoys this friendliness. Aries wins a welcome by getting things going.

Taurus with Taurus

Money/Job. Mutual understanding works well if it can stimulate or even antagonize the other occasionally. Both can get into the swing of work. They can both enjoy what they are doing. Common sense will stop them from making work into drudgery. They both appreciate the value of the end product so will cooperate.

They know how to use mutual resources. Both welcome comfort. They will watch each other like hawks to make sure money is used well. Money is not the root of all evil to them. They value it and take advantage of what it offers.

Home/Friends. A joint interest in the home means a calm, happy atmosphere. To both, home is a haven. It has to be good enough to make anyone feel welcome. Both like to have pleasant-feeling things around, or peaceful decor. The kitchen will be well stocked and wine will be available. Domestic animals are welcome if not necessary to them both.

Taurean friends know what to expect. Hostess and guest soon get settled. No word is needed to make the Taurus friend understand. The soft sentimentality of each makes friendship so simple. They will trust each other. They are always ready to help each other when in trouble, without a question being asked. They can share everything.

Taurus with Gemini

Money/Job. Gemini cannot abide being forced to stick to routine. Taurus can cope with routine. Gemini does not like to look too far ahead and plan for the future. Taurus likes to have things planned ahead. Both are practical. They can respect each other for doing a job in their own way. One will get on in one direction and leave the other in peace. Neither wastes effort.

Gemini can make money intelligently, possibly with no apparent effort. They believe in keeping it in circulation. If well off, Taurus is generous with money. Taurus then will make and use money on the grand scale. When less well off, Taurus will pinch pennies and save.

Home/Friends. Home to Gemini must include children. This appeals to Taurus. To both, home is a place of security. Gemini is in and out of the home but will always return. As neighbors they appreciate each other. Gemini keeps up with the local news and saves Taurus the effort. There is always plenty to occupy the mind in the Gemini home. Conversation is welcome. Music or video is a part of their scene. Taurus likes to be entertained.

Geminis are very friendly people. They seldom give offense. They are lively, ever young yet not childish. Taurus welcomes such a friend who keeps old age from the door. Gemini has a word for everyone and is such good company.

Taurus with Cancer

Money/Job. This can produce a mixture that is good for business. Both know the value of money and both know where they are going. Money will be used wisely and well, together. Each has a negative streak that can make them tight-fisted or mean, but Cancer provides that commonsense spur to make extra capital work for them.

At work they can fit in with each other. Cancer does not get in a rut but is careful. Cancer is ambitious but not careless. Both are sensitive to those around them, and can be caring, considerate and cooperative. Both can be particular about the way things are done.

Home/Friends. Home is the Cancerian stronghold. Taurus does not like to stray from the hearth. Together they will make a very special home. Cancer will be a bit finicky about the house. They notice things when visiting friends and make comparisons. With patience the domestic needs of both will be accepted, to their mutual satisfaction.

Cancer friends are welcome when Taurus has problems. Cancer is talkative and inclined to pry, so Taurus may be on the defensive till the caring side of the Crab is better known. They are both patient people. Friendship will not be hurried. That will make it stronger. They have plenty of scope for mutual understanding and will not waste a friendship.

Taurus with Leo

Money/Job. Leo is as firm as Taurus. Both accept realities. Both take pride in their work and handle business squarely. They both know the value of quality. Leo will stress the value of appearances, while Taurus understands output and productivity. They work together in top gear, each one pushing the other.

Money can go through Leo hands like sand. Leo likes to be seen as a generous person. Taurus knows that money has to be earned and is more prudent. Neither will sell themselves short. Both are professionals and can earn as much as they decide. Neither will be controlled by money. They will use it.

Home/Friends. The home of Leo is the castle. Leo makes this haven a special place, whether cottage or palace. Casual visitors may not be welcome. Those who visit should admire and say so! Leo is an excellent host or hostess. They give top quality service. Both Taurus and Leo know that standards can be set in the home . . . and show it.

Leos can be choosy about friends. Taurus has substance, and is therefore accepted. They have a respect for each other. While Leos can be very openly friendly, they can have reservations. This they can disclose to their Taurus friends, who will understand. They are honest with each other.

Taurus with Virgo

Money/Job. Both these types mean to do a job and do it well. Taurus wll lay down the main principles or guidelines and Virgo will attend to the details. It is a most happy and productive combination. Each is a professional in their own right.

Both appreciate the value of money. Taurus' clear aims will be accepted by Virgo. Both will make money work for them. They are both conservative in their habits but can spend when they have enough to go round. Each can accept the other's particular ways of making and spending money.

Home/Friends. The Virgo home will be comfortable. Both like the sensual human comforts. Each values material things. They will generally agree on food, both knowing that whole-some food is a must. Virgo can be a bit finicky around the home. This can irritate Taurus at times. Other factors can make up for this friction. Virgo will keep things tidy, saving Taurus the effort.

Virgoan friends are welcome for their variety. Many topics of interest will come to light through contact with Virgos. They take a wide interest in the practical world. They can explain clearly and will encourage Taurus to get involved with those around. As friends, Virgoans are so useful: they can fix anything and enjoy the chance to be of help.

Taurus with Libra

Money/Job. Both like the nice things of life. They get them in different ways. Libra may be more choosy but can handle a crisis. Libra uses intelligence and tact more than does Taurus. They will seldom quarrel when valuable work is to be done. They both like to see a good finish to what they produce. Standards of both are high.

Libras like to have money to spend. Appearances have to be maintained. They are not selfish when spending. Much is spent on others. They are not conservative and money is soon put to use once they have it to spend.

Home/Friends. Libras like a nice home. They have a flair for making things look beautiful. This is appreciated by Taurus.

The Libra home is airy, comfortable and decorative yet functional. The Libra is a natural host or hostess. This shows in the home.

As a friend Libra can lighten the Taurean heart. Taurus will become more sociable when in Libra company. Libra is naturally sociable and will make friends. They have great charm which is not just skin deep. This pleases Taurus who may at first feel the Libran is too good to be true. They can both enjoy the good life together quite happily. Each dislikes worry. They are happy lazing about.

Taurus with Scorpio

Money/Job. Pride in work can bring out the best in each. They will compete vigorously to prove their worth. Jointly they can produce on a grand scale. Mutual respect for each other grows with time. They can be co-workers or boss and employee and apply the same attitude to their jobs.

Each has a respect for money. Each will have a firm opinion on its use. One can cover the other's losses if necessary. Neither is going to waste hard-earned cash. They are whole-hoggers and can make a fortune together. Then they can get rid of it if they want.

Home/Friends. Scorpio friends are sincere. Like Taurus they like to be sure of their company. They hate superficiality. They know that good company is worth having and make this obvious. Their direct manner will suit Taurus. Scorpio will be a friend for life once the relationship is accepted.

In the home Scorpios are competent. They like a home that works well and is clean. They run a no-nonsense establishment and expect meals on time along with other parts of their schedule. They appreciate good food and drink, so join with Taurus in conviviality. They like order in the home and manage this without fuss.

Taurus with Sagittarius

Money/Job. Sagittarius has a way of irritating methodical Taurus. He can be a fly-by-night person. This makes working beside him a trial to the conscientious Taurean. Yet Sagittarius is a realist, so can work with a will when the spirit moves him. He likes to assert his independence and in the eyes of Taurus may seem to overdo it.

Sagittarius can make a lot of money. He is a natural speculator. He often has very good judgment. In this way he or she can impress money-conscious Taurus. The Archer may make Taurus feel envious.

Home/Friends. Home life is of little interest to Sagittarius. The wide open spaces appeal. They are not family people. They accept children but can take them or leave them. Home will be open, even to the doors and windows. This gets Taurus worried about comfort and safety.

Being naturally friendly, Sagittarius will have many friends. Foreigners are treated the same as anyone else. Taurus is conventional and likes to be sure of friends. Sagittarius will accept anyone till they prove themselves unreliable. Nevertheless, Sagittarius is often a good judge of character. His company can be most interesting. He knows how to tell a good tale and is welcomed into all sorts of company.

Taurus with Capricorn

Money/Job. This is an excellent combination for work. Capricorns are always management material. They are ambitious, and take little time off from work. Taurus appreciates this sort of dedication. Provided Capricorn does not push too hard, this pair will get on well.

Money will be made to work by both. Capricorns are not wasteful. Indeed, their grip on the purse strings can upset Taurus. Capricorn is conscious of social position and can spend money to this end. Taurus likes comfort and may consider that a waste of money, or just showing off.

Home/Friends. Home to the Capricorn can be a status symbol. It will be efficient but possibly colder than is the home of comfortable Taurus. They are never really settled when indoors. Their interest usually lies outside in the big world. Yet they will always have a home for entertaining influential friends or business acquaintances.

Their friends will reflect their desire for social recognition. Entertaining is the done thing. They make good use of friends and will return favors. In their best mood, Capricornians have a quiet dignity, so their friends are generally well behaved and conservative. This suits amiable Taurus. Capricorn is quite a social character and can get Taurus out and about.

Taurus with Aquarius

Money/Job. Both signs will stick to the task at hand. Each will recognize the other for their separate gifts. They are both independent types. They will work together amicably provided there is no interference. Aquarius may provide one sort of contribution and Taurus the other.

Aquarius often seems to have little interest in making money. Taurus should not try to take advantage of this. Aquarius has a firm set of principles and will expect the rate for the job. The work can be more attractive than the money to Aquarius. It seldom is so with Taurus.

Home/Friends. Neither will tolerate a fool gladly. They both can freeze out those they don't like. The friends of Aquarius will bring new insights into the life of Taurus. They may seem an odd bunch at first but they will grow on either him or her.

Home to the Aquarian can be a meeting place of friends or a center for social welfare. The friendly interests of Aquarius will impinge on all who live with them. Books, typewriters and other gear seem to be part of the Aquarian home environment.

Provided they do not get under Taurus' feet, they can be tolerated. Taurus knows these people are genuine. Like him they mean no harm or disrespect.

Taurus with Pisces

Money/Job. Pisces can cope with a variety of jobs. They may move around a lot. They have a way of getting on with people that makes Taurus feel happy. They want to be cooperative and will do little things to help. They are busy and not bossy.

Money may or may not interest them. They are a law unto themselves in this respect. Their own money may be used on things, or, as far as Taurus is concerned, wasted on risky causes or lazy people. They can be careless in the eyes of Taurus. Their intentions are usually good. They themselves will suffer any ill consequences.

Home/Friends. The Piscean at home can be comfortable or slipshod. They do not conform to the order that Taurus likes. Even so they are sociable and will leave Taurus in peace when they want to relax. Pisces loves to fuss around looking after others in the home. This will suit Taurus down to the ground.

The Piscean friend can be a tonic or a wet blanket. They are seldom the same two days running. Yet they mean no one harm; they are just naturally emotional. They have their highs and lows frequently. This can either amuse or irritate Taurus. The Pisces affection will be appreciated but their chatter when they are excited will annoy. They can be a source of great comfort to the domestic Bull who likes friends to visit him.

Love Mates

Taurus Woman—Aries Man. Both these people know what they are after. A Taurus woman has the confidence of the original Eve. She knows her charms can captivate.

An Aries man is out to make a conquest. He will try to make an immediate impression. He will try to convince her that there's no one like him anywhere. His self-assurance will be attractive to her.

A Taurus woman is not to be rushed. She has too much available to be won over in a quick romance. She will play it cool till she is sure he is all he says he is. She values substance. He has to prove he is not just hot air. Once she is convinced of his good intentions she will match all his ardor.

Physical contact is essential to loving Taurus. She enjoys the embrace of an honorable lover. She appreciates Aries more if he lives up to her hopes and stays the course. Once committed, her love is there to stay. Aries, too, is an honest lover when he feels he is secure. His lively approach to love-play is impressive. Deep down he will love Taurus because she takes no liberties with his affections and trusts him. He will be glad she is all woman. She understands him better than he understands himself. She listens with wide eyes to his exploits. She knows this makes him feel contented and eager to please her.

When settled as partners each will provide something the other lacks. He is a bundle of surprises. He will brighten her day. He will provide, and that is most important to a Taurus woman. She will show her unfailing love in the way she calms him down when he's upset. She knows the way to a man's heart is via his stomach. He will appreciate that.

Taurus Woman—Taurus Man. Both challenge and high hopes come with this combination. Each is aware of the other's need. They have a common understanding. They can come to terms either quickly, or, if they like it that way, at a leisurely pace.

Neither will be inclined to push the other into an arrangement they do not want. They are both mature, sincere people who know that they have a physical need. They will be patient with each other when any indication of irritation appears. When emotional tension develops, as it can, they will each have an instinctive desire to stand back and give each other space.

They each have very strong emotions. Demands on the other can be heavy but they each know those demands can be met. They will glory in each other's thoughts. A lot of happiness will be found in quiet. They are not bothered much about company. They can find enough to do together. When they are in company they will trust each other, knowing their love is forever.

Each has a great sense of humor. They can laugh at their failures and at the way they will get on each other's nerves at times.

The loving relationship will need to be productive. They each have a love of children. They have definite ideas about home life. Each knows what makes the other tick. Problems that come will be shared. They can lose all their fears and worries in the close embrace they both find means everything.

Their emotional life will never be dull if each gives the other the room to be an individual.

Taurus Woman—Gemini Man. Gemini may be attracted by the calm sincerity of the Taurus woman. She may not take to him at once. He is a bit quick off the mark. She will wonder whether his deeds match his words. He has a rather flippant manner. She will think he is out for a good time and may have her doubts about going with him. He is quite a nice man when she gets to know him better. He does not like to be too heavily committed. If she is interested in keeping his company, she will have a job on her hands.

He could be a flirtatious man. He likes lively company and will get her out into the social scene, take her to discos, introduce her to his many male friends. He is not jealous. She will be glad of this side.

He is a boy at heart. She will soon realize this and can get close to him by looking after him or putting him right. He will not resent her interest in his welfare. He likes to be looked after. She is strong enough to be able to help him get on in the world. His many talents are often wasted.

His perkiness will keep her amused. If he spends too much time chatting with others, she can bring him into line firmly, without hurting his feelings.

They have a mutual interest in the young. They will want to have children of their own when they are agreed partners. Home life together has many attractions. When it comes to the crunch they are both very nice, practical people with their feet on the ground.

She likes to be admired. He will take her around and show her off. She must never become too possessive of him or he will not forgive her. He may have his little nights out with mates, but will never forget her.

Taurus Woman—Cancer Man. This can be a very
productive union. He is a sensitive man. He is ambitious and could be looking for a mother figure or someone to make him a comfortable home. This she will soon realize.

He can be very convincing. He is dramatic. He knows how to trigger off her emotions. She will want a practical man and knows she would like to be secure. He has the ability and ambition to make his way in the world, so she may be assured of a comfortable home if they agree to live together.

She will have to put her foot down about domestic matters. He likes to run the home, so there could be arguments about who looks after what. He will want to have children around. They have so much on which they agree. Even cooking can be shared if they agree.

They will each have a common interest in family. They can strengthen their affections by getting to know each other's close relatives. They will get a lot of mutual pleasure from developing family ties. Their love will strengthen their home and family roots.

Neither is a social type. They will be happy in their own little nest curled up by the fire. This will satisfy her possessiveness and his desire to look after her every need.

He will be a tender lover. If he wilts in his ardor, she can give him all the womanly encouragement he needs. She expects a man to be a source of strength.

He will have to keep himself up to scratch. As long as he is ambitious and can provide what she needs there will be no disagreement. Adventure may be lacking, but they can go places together.

Taurus Woman—Leo Man. Leo thinks he is the answer to a maiden's prayer. He is attractive to most women and knows it. He will try to take charge of his woman by charm or strength of will.

The Taurus female is a strong woman. She understands men. She is as proud as he is. She, too, has charm which she will use. She will secretly admire him for the way he admires her. There is challenge between these two.

He may try to impress her by spending money on her if the charm does not have the full effect. She will soon realize that he may expect value for his money. She has more knowledge of value for money than he has. He will eventually realize that she is a very special person, very sure of herself.

Both are loyal, deep down. They have a lot to offer each other. Leo is a passionate lover. He will set his woman on a pedestal once she has won his love. He likes to show off himself, so will be proud to show her off. She can take this all in her stride. She can satisfy his passions. She can manage his home. She will be glad to have his children, in whom they will both take pride.

At times of tension they will each go their own way knowing that they both need space to live life fully. This is a sign of the respect they can establish in their way of living. Mutual trust will cancel all possessiveness. They cannot command each other. Loving means respecting each other as individuals.

Leos have an appreciation of beauty. This is the thing that attracts them in the first place. Taurus has an understanding of value. They make a fine couple. They can have a great future together.

Taurus Woman—Virgo Man. This can be a sound, enjoyable relationship. He understands her physical needs, being an earthy man himself. She will have to bring him out, because he can be a bit modest. Her charm will attract him strongly and his modesty will soon disappear.

They are looking for the same thing and will quickly get together to enjoy themselves. He will like her natural ways. She does not beat around the bush. This will help him relax enough to make her feel good.

He will make the first approach. She may be a bit quiet. In fact she will probably be weighing him up. Once she is sure he is a man who can give her what she wants, she will be more forthcoming. He has a lively mind as well as an active body, and thus is not lost for ways to convince her of his loving intentions.

Together they will get more intimate through doing things for each other. Both enjoy eating good food and enjoy a drink. He likes to be in company so will take her out to soft lights and sweet music. He is not a show-off, but will impress her with his knowledge of the many and varied aspects of everyday life.

Both have a keen sense of rhythm. Dancing is a natural outlet for their energies. They like to be close together but will not crowd each other.

It can take time for this relationship to come to marriage. Neither is in a hurry. He may be a bit shy of getting settled down. She must be quite sure that he has all she needs. They make a caring couple. He is excellent at looking after her if she feels low. He can fix all those practical problems. This side of his nature pleases her a lot. She cannot abide a man who is not practical. He can be an angel and she knows it.

Taurus Woman—Libra Man. This can be a tense relationship. He has a different way of looking at things than she does. He finds her practicality hard to swallow, for he is a rather intellectual type who likes to avoid the rougher side of life.

He has a lot of charm. He can make heads turn by his appearance and his manners. He knows just what to say to please and will attract admirers wherever he goes. This will intrigue the Taurus woman.

In her, he will see an attractive, soft, feminine woman who will listen attentively to his chat. They both have an appreciation of beauty. In this they are close and will find it easy to compare notes. They both like to take things easy. Comfort means a great deal to both. Given the opportunity, they can both relax in the sun and do nothing at all. This is the way they would both like to live.

He will always try to please her and make her days happy. He will have to pull something extra out of the bag to satisfy her physical desires. He is not a physical man, though he may spend a lot of time making himself look attractive. He is more interested in dressing the shop window than using the goods. She will want more than this from her mate.

He is a man who lives for today. She is looking for a man who is durable and can be relied upon for as long as she wishes. They can have a good, happy, flirtatious relationship, each being at ease in the other's company for short periods of time. It is not likely that a long-lasting relationship will develop, because these two are rather like ships that pass in the night. Nice people—but that's not enough.

Taurus Woman—Scorpio Man.

Here Taurus can meet her match. He could well be the real man she's been waiting for. There is a magnetic attraction between them both.

He is as strong as she is. He has a definite desire to dominate women. She will recognize this and will match his passion. This is a togetherness based on mutual respect and mutual desire. There can be no stronger tie between two people . . . and they both know it.

Though they both revel in their strength, they are considerate to each other. This is an honest link. Each is jealous of the other. Neither will give up this union without a struggle. He is extremely jealous of her as he will wish to possess her for himself alone. He will frighten off any other man who wants to go out with her. She is also possessive and will be on guard for any other woman who seeks his favor. Both are attractive people, so there is always the possibility of fireworks when either spots a possible rival.

With the true understanding that will come with a deep relationship, they should learn to trust. This has got to be the way they will love together. Too much emotion will be wasted if they do not trust each other completely.

He is the man who will give her the children she wants. Both have a great feeling for family and for home. They can be perfectly content with each other and their young in the coziness of the home.

They are both self-sufficient and confident. They will enjoy socializing when they feel like it but know that what they really appreciate is the warmth of each other's arms and no one else around to interfere. They have it made.

Taurus Woman—Sagittarius Man. With this woman

he has to prove his worth, right here and now. He will tell her the tale about his experiences. He may impress her for a while. But when it comes to the crunch there must be more than just talking a good line.

He likes to be on the move. She wants a man who will stay put and look after her. He has little time to concentrate on this woman who attracts him. She will demand attention. High-minded ideas cut no ice with Taurus. She wants to see results and know that she has his complete attention.

If he can stay long enough to make a deep impression on this woman and prove he is a man of substance, she will be patient and give him time. Otherwise theirs could be an interlude, an affair which is never meant to last.

He will be quite fascinated by this attractive, composed and affectionate woman who listens to his tales of masculine prowess. He should pay attention to her, or his self-promotion is wasted. She appreciates his manly love of freedom and his feeling for nature. She too likes to be free to enjoy the sun and the rain. Yet the need for security is strong within her. He considers security and stability to be a prison sentence. He hates to be confined.

She may be enthralled by his hopes and aspirations. On the

other hand she may quickly assume they are "pie in the sky."
Yet he is a realist and probably knows his weaknesses. He can
become impatient with her when she loses enthusiasm for his
tales of adventure.

There is a subtle attraction between these two. They could
be ships that pass in the night or could each totally reject the
other. The difference can outweigh the compatibility.

Taurus Woman—Capricorn Man. Here there is a
natural, instinctive link. He may be a bit superior until he gets
to know her better. He is inclined to look down his nose unless
her physical attraction is extra special. She will provide that
attraction.

He considers his reputation to be important. He is not going
to be seen around with just any woman, so he is choosy.

When he's being honest with himself, he will find she gives
him a lot of pleasure and knows him better than he expected.
She helps him to relax. She will make him feel young. She will
be considerate of his feelings, knowing that she has here a good
man if he'd only get loosened up.

He will be reminded, in her presence, of those happy and
carefree days of boyhood or youth (for he may be a late starter
in the romance stakes). He will be glad she takes him away
from social responsibilities, management worries and the more
serious things of life. He will be glad she accepts him as he is.
Her natural femininity will charm him and win the day.

Both are patient. Each knows that anything worthwhile is
worth striving for. They will each allow the other time and
breathing space. They are both practical people. He has the
determination and strength to provide for her. She knows how
to look after her man.

Once he is sure she is the right woman for him he can let
down his hair, in private or in company. Together the two will
go places. He will be glad to show her off in the best circles.
She will tell him that she expects love and togetherness as well.
They can climb the ladder together and never get in a rut.

Taurus Woman—Aquarius Man. To the Taurus
woman, this man may seem a bit odd. It can intrigue her. He

doesn't say a lot, which she does not mind, but he is not exactly physical either.

He admires her physical charm. In her he can see something out of the ordinary. He senses she is a strong physical woman and may feel a bit shy. Her direct gaze and honest answers to his sensitive approach can startle him. He is not naturally a ladies' man. Nevertheless he is glad she means what she says. He too is an honest individual.

It may take them both some time to reach an understanding. Once there is a decision to be together they will get on like a house on fire. They are equally sincere. Neither wishes to take away the other's independence. This is the one thing he cannot surrender completely and she must accept the fact. Her love will keep her from being too possessive. He will go off if he is pressed too far. Yet he will give her no qualms, for he is a loyal lover.

He is a highly sensitive, vibrant man. She is able to accept and comfort him in her own feminine way. She will let him simmer down gently after his intellectual enthusiasm. She gives to him something that is lacking in his nature. It is the differences that make the attraction so intriguing.

She will want to care for his physical needs. He can get carried away by some interest and forget all about such things. He will love her all the more for bringing him back to earth and making him feel at home and wanted. He is a gentle soul and so is she. They have a lot going for them, together.

Taurus Woman—Pisces Man.
The Pisces man has a sweet way with him. This relationship is highly emotional, largely due to the lively feelings expressed by Pisces.

He is not in the least pushy. She may think he can be managed and he likes to run about trying to please. He is a very sensitive man. He picks up the feelings she has not expressed to him and is way ahead of her. Though he is so very tender and loving, he does not wish to be cornered or tied to one person until he is quite sure this is the right one for him.

It may seem to her that he gets involved with everyone. Women in particular seek his company. She will naturally be concerned by this. She likes her man to look at her alone. If she tries to restrict his movements, she will lose a gentle friend if not a lover.

He can give her all the love and tenderness she will ever require, and still have compassion for many others in his daily life. This is something she will have to accept. He will be moody if his outlet of love for humanity is restricted. She knows what it feels like to be moody, so must remind herself that this attitude is totally negative. Fortunately, she may think, his moods come and go rapidly. He will raise her sagging spirits with his resilient ways. In his arms she will be able to let her emotions flow freely.

There is a mutual longing for deep-down love and security in both. He takes a superficial interest in much that goes on around him. He is glad to have this comfortable and loving woman there at his side to help him with his emotional problems after he has helped everyone else. He does need her support and is not too proud to tell her so.

Taurus Man—Aries Woman. She apparently knows what she wants. He will think she is pushy or just saucy. She will provoke his interest. She knows this, so she's going to make him take notice.

Life, to her, may be full of uncertainties—but she will never let others see she has doubts. She will lead him a dance and will call the tune. He will either go along with her at her speed or slow her down to his speed. She knows he can give her security, so she will keep with him part of the way. She will open his eyes to opportunities he has never dreamed of. She is straight to the point with him. She will hurt his pride if need be but he will know she is being honest and that means a lot to him.

She has a great love of life. Life is far too short to be wasted. So she has to get a move on and find out what is round the corner. She does not look back. What happend yesterday is done with. He will find new interests if he goes along with her. He can lose his hang-ups when he's with her. She has no time for sloppy sentiment but respects his honest and simple ways. She is an uncomplicated woman. He is an uncomplicated man.

He takes his time, is careful, considerate. Being a realist, she appreciates these manly qualities and will take advantage of them for as long as she needs them. The possibility of getting into a rut will terrify her, so she may go her own way at the drop of a hat.

She needs a man of action to match her own ardor. She admires his strength and positive desires to please her. But together they are never really at ease.

Taurus Man—Taurus Woman.

There can be instant mutual recognition. Common interest can get this relationship off the ground. If either is looking for something different there is no hope of togetherness. It's a well known fact that man will never fully understand woman or or that woman will never fully assess man. With these two there is, however, a great chance of knowing how the cookie will crumble. Neither is gambling.

To him she is all woman. Together they can be immediately in tune. Each knows the other's needs and has the ability to deliver. Physical attraction is the main thing. They both enjoy body contact, so they will not beat around the bush. They can either take time to enjoy the full ritual of love-making, or, when desire is strong, cut out the niceties and make an instant match.

Because she will know what he's thinking, she can be ready for his advances. They can have a courtship where little is said but there is no complaint from either. They are happy to be together and want no other distraction. This may lead to love becoming a routine. Intimacy can be fulfilling but can become, in time, a bore. It is then that the attraction of something or someone different will upset their happiness.

They are both possessive. Neither will tolerate the other seeing someone else once they are committed to each other. Jealousy can make both of them bitter and the nasty side of their nature can come to the top.

Provided they build on their togetherness, and have something to show for their joint efforts, there is no denying their great, abiding love. Otherwise they can be selfish and drift apart.

Taurus Man—Gemini Woman. He sees her as a lively little butterfly flitting from pollen center to pollen center. He will feel flirtatious and strangely alive in her company. He is intrigued by her personality and enthusiasm long enough to be interested.

She sees in him a man with potential who has to be livened up. She will tease him into action. She has a ready wit and knows what to say to get him going. She will lead him on because he is something different from other men, yet makes her feel she is a woman. He looks as if he will take care of her. She will bring out his lighter side, his sense of humor. She lets him see she does not want to boss him. She is quite happy that he should be the boss. This satisfies his vanity.

Courtship and casual love-making can be terrific for both. She is straightforward, he will find out. Even though she can relate to all manner of people, she is nice and does not push herself into company where she is not wanted. He will meet all sorts of pleasant people, just because she takes him along and shows him off to her many friends. This he likes. She can have him around and make him feel wanted without being in any way possessive. She will brighten up his day.

A lasting bond may be more difficult for either to maintain. There has to be a great deal of mutual trust. She knows his physical attraction to her sex and he cannot help, at times, feeling possessive. They can make a go of it, so long as they accept each other honestly. He must not tie her down or restrict her freedom. She must allow him time to feel settled and comfortable.

They can be lovers for life or just good friends.

Taurus Man—Cancer Woman. This woman is looking for her own home. She must find a father for her children and someone who will make a home to satisfy her needs. She is a great actress. Her sense of drama will attract him once she has decided he is her man.

She has all sorts of feminine ploys to trap him, and he is a soft, generous man who feels he must protect her. She will get to his heart via his stomach for she remembers all that her mother taught her about men. She sees that it is the physical man she should try to please as a priority and will make no bones about this.

He will be attracted by her total femininity. She also will please him by making him feel comfortable. She knows all about home comforts. She will manage things for him so that he has no need to worry about details. She will keep unpleasantness away from him. It may seem that she is protective of him, rather than the other way around.

He will realize in time that she is a very able woman. This will arouse his admiration. She needs his masterful reassurance but has a mind of her own. There are some things she has to reserve for herself. He can cooperate fully with her to get things they both want. She is very sensitive at times. When she's feeling good, she is loving and sympathetic. But she has the habit of getting up on her high horse and letting off steam. He will find this upsetting. He hates being told what to do, yet recognizes her business ability.

He must get used to her moods if they are to live together. She has to avoid nagging him to get a move on. They have to learn to give and take.

Taurus Man—Leo Woman.

She has an eye for quality. She thinks he is made of the right stuff, but he is quiet. She will make the first move if he doesn't seem to be impressed by her presence. She hates to be ignored.

She'll find he *is* a man of quality. He's also got a lot of substance. Like her he is on the level. He calls a spade a spade. He cannot abide people who put on airs and graces. If she's a snob, and she may be, that rebuff will put her off right away. She'll tell herself he is crude. If she's made of the right, regal stuff, she will know her judgment was right and will respect him for being a real live man. Once it is agreed that appearances are not everything they really enjoy life together.

There is no immediate need to get too serious. She wants to live life to the full. He will want to know her in a physical sense. She likes to feel strength and see beauty in a man and will encourage him to be a man full of passion and virility. A firm relationship is probable right from the word go.

They are both proud people. They can be fully committed to

each other. If either shows signs of flagging they are likely to part. Intimacy can bring out the best in both, for neither likes to be dominated. She likes to do things in the grand manner. He has the substance to treat her like a queen. He will be glad to show her off. They make a striking couple. She is no shrinking violet, so she will get him out and about. This keeps him alive, keeps him on his toes. They each do nothing by halves. No quarter is asked, none given. A lot of love and respect can come from these two.

Taurus Man—Virgo Woman.
In his eyes she is a female mystery. She teases him. There is an immediate link that both recognize but maybe don't immediately pin down. She may seem to him to be a diversion or a plaything. He will feel relaxed yet alive when she's around.

She knows he is a real man. She too is physical but as a woman knows she has to liven him up to get the best from him. She can be modest or bold. She will make him be gentle, yet will never challenge his authority. She makes him feel ten feet tall, yet he will not take advantage of her willingness to please or serve. There is mutual respect.

At times she can be quite prudish. He will see through this and still know she has a warm and caring heart. They instinctively know that the answer to doubt lies in a cuddle or caress. Together they are not inhibited. They are very conscious of their physical needs, so can be natural. They are both private people. They do not want to be watched, so they find their joy together more fully when away from the crowd.

She will be happy to play it cool when they are in company. He will be the man of the house. She has a lively mind and will prompt him when he needs a reminder. He will resent her if she interferes. Like him she is sensitive and can be easily hurt. He should be too big a man to cause her hurt but she can irritate him with her love of detail. He will show her what he expects and leave it to her to attend to all that's necessary. She knows how to retain his love and will not nag if he provides for her needs. They both are practical. Their love has to be productive or it falls short.

Taurus Man—Libra Woman.
This lovely woman attracts the Taurus as she does any other man. He will liven himself up to make the best impression. That is quite an achievement for both of them. She may not realize what she has stirred up. He appreciates beauty but it has to be more than skin deep.

Libra is an accomplished peacemaker. She knows how to cool fevered brows. If she is superficial he will eventually see through her charm and go off in another direction. She lives for the moment and does not want to keep up any long effort which will exhaust her. She is easily bored. Her affections can be here today and gone tomorrow. He is not of this nature. He persists if he feels he wants something. There has to be a compromise, on her part, if they are to get on together.

She wishes to please and can compromise to a certain extent. She will expect him to keep her in comfort and style as she requires. He may think she is worth the effort and expense. She will be loyal in her love. She is not very physical in expressing her affections, so he need not get jealous on that score. But she likes company and will not be confined to the home if they are living together. She likes the bright lights, entertainment and admiration. His passivity will exasperate her.

She can be bossy if her patience gives out. Her acute sense of balance means that she must stir things up if they are too quiet just as much as she will calm things down when they are too rowdy. She likes the pleasant and easy middle path. He is not a man to pussyfoot around. It is unlikely that they will stay together for long. An affair is more likely.

Taurus Man—Scorpio Woman.
He will feel she knows all the essential answers. She will recognize what turns him on. She knows she is a confident and mature woman and will see in him the answer to her prayers. Intuitively she will know that he has what is needed to make her complete.

There are no half measures with this couple. They are both proud. They can stand on their own feet. They are sure of their sex drive. He will know that he has to treat her as an equal. She knows she must respect his manliness or he will leave her. There is an immediate mutual respect running strongly.

She feels she knows how to handle such a man. Once the relationship is going she will not let any other woman come between them. He too, is jealous of his position and will frighten off any male who pokes his nose in. They can maintain this emotional tension through mutual desire and the strength of their physical and spiritual togetherness. Each expects a great deal from the other. They will not fail.

Theirs will be an honest love. Once they are secure in their love they will not challenge or criticize each other. They can quite happily live their lives in harmony without prying. Their pride makes them keep up the quality of their love, so they will never be out of love. They will be lovers all their lives. Their courtship will never end.

Should they get into a rut, they will know the remedy. Life together is too important to be wasted. They have the strength to lift it out of the mud. They are a permanent challenge to each other, a challenge they should both enjoy to the full.

Taurus Man—Sagittarius Woman.

To the Taurus man this woman seems to be looking for trouble. He sees that she pays little attention to what others say but has a definite opinion of her own. This is not his idea of the ideal woman. He will avoid her if he wants a peaceful life. If he is attracted to her for some odd reason he will try to straighten her out.

She is a tomboy at heart. Yet she has a serious side to her nature. She feels herself to be a mixed-up kid at times. This makes her, if anything, more inclined to travel her own path to avoid being misunderstood.

She sees him as a man of principle. He also seems to keep regular hours and has a regular routine. She is a realist. She admires a man who is brave and sets an example. She hates men who are complacent and self-satisfied. She has no particular material aim in life and can't abide men who have no vision. She is honest, to the point, outspoken and principled. She expects others to accept her principles but will not bind herself to theirs. She's a bit of a tartar when she gets on her high horse. There are some things about him she will accept.

He calls a spade a spade. He will be firm with her, yet gentle. She is a woman and lets everyone know this if they have any doubts.

She likes the wide-open spaces. He is close to nature. Here they are in sympathy. Each has a soft spot for animals, possibly for different reasons.

She can be biting in her comments, but has forgotten within hours. He is slow to anger and equally slow to forget. They are not really for each other.

Taurus Man—Capricorn Woman. She will be quick to see the potential in this solid, reliable man. He can give her a lot of love and comfort. She enjoys the physical expression of affection but she won't advertise the fact to everyone. She is a bit choosy about the company she keeps.

She likes him because he does not have a lot to say. She does not judge the contents by the wrapping! He strikes her as a methodical man who knows where he is going. She wants to achieve something in life and has a pretty shrewd idea she can get him to see things her way.

She is likely to make the first move. He will like the way she handles herself and seems to know what he wants. She is attractive without making a scene. He will see she has a lot of energy, yet is not going to disturb him. She doesn't bother with too much window dressing and strikes him as someone who values things and does not waste time.

Right from the start they will feel attracted to each other. It is a physical, emotional, instinctive and spiritual togetherness. They can have complete rapport. She is expert in timing. He has a lot of patience. Together they can plan, arrange and live their time together without fuss.

They each understand the formalities. They can enjoy all the stages in their togetherness from courtship to parenthood. They will see they miss nothing, as they grow closer together.

She may push him socially; this stops him from resting on his laurels. She may be hard to satisfy but he is the man who can give her the things she craves. She will be glad she has his strength behind her.

Taurus Man—Aquarius Woman.

To him she is attractive. She remains aloof yet is not unfriendly. He will see honesty in her eyes. He is naturally intrigued. There is, to him, no nonsense about this woman.

She is an honest, straightforward woman. She knows that men are attracted to her because she treats them all alike until she knows them better. She is rather naive in a way but can freeze anyone who tries to take advantage of her friendliness.

She will see in Taurus a nice man who seems a bit shy or lonely in company. She appreciates a man who looks like a man and is strong. Like him she has little time for half measures and calls a spade a spade.

She finds he is not a great talker. He communicates by touch. She will not resist his physical charm nor his embrace when she is sure he is not being flippant. She will keep him at a distance and make him sweat if she is not satisfied with his motives. She is never a pushover. She has ideals. He can satisfy some of these hopes at first meeting. Other essential points of their relationship will fit into place. Neither is impulsive, so they can take time to enjoy their love life.

She is not jealous or demanding. Once he's gotten used to her being sociable with men in general, he will know that she is loyal to him because he is special, yet she remains friendly to others. It may take him some time to grasp this.

Provided they do not crowd each other they can have a lasting relationship based on honesty and respect for each other. Each will accept the other's strength. Each is independent but can live for the other.

Taurus Man—Pisces Woman.

At first meeting he may think she is a bit much. She is highly emotional, and this can unsettle him. She seems to be very feminine and seems to have many friends who chatter or whisper together. She is openly loving, distributing her kisses around the place. He wants a woman for himself alone.

She is essentially a woman. She does not like crudity and will love a loving man. She sees in him the strong man who will protect her. This is fine. He is also, in her eyes, a man who wants her as a sensual, physical woman. She knows she must tame him to her own gentle ways, so she will work to bring out the sentimental side of his nature. She can calm this savage beast, she knows, by acting as a weak, defenseless female. He cannot resist a damsel in distress.

She knows the value of tears. Her emotions lead to tears of happiness and if she wants a helping hand she knows that her tears will bring him running. This is part of the game. They both will come to know it, yet when in love will both play it to the full.

She is intimate. The closer they become the better she likes him. He will be carried away by her love and devotion. She is not demanding and seems ready to do whatever he wishes. He may get a bit fed up with her being so self-effacing. She will then let him know that there is more to life than material things.

When he is under the weather she will look after him. She is remarkably resilient and seems able to come to the surface no matter how low they both may feel.

She may want to rely on him for manly things. He will appreciate that she has a lot to give and that she gives without counting the cost.

III. Gemini

The Gemini Character

The Gemini man and woman are both lively and quick-witted. They try to be one step ahead of the others all the time.

They are friendly and talkative as a rule. They have a word for everyone and a name for everything. They do not like routine, so they seldom get stuck in a rut. Others can set the guidelines and do the planning while Gemini will be content to carry out instructions. They will show their individuality by making some slight modification as if to prove they have that bit of extra know-how.

They are quite modest people. Their frequent comment when they call on the telephone is "It's only me." They accumulate a vast knowledge of all manner of things without apparently delving to the depths of any subject. They are happy to show their knowledge by giving a helping hand to anyone in need of assistance.

Everything that comes within their range will be investigated. They do this in a friendly way, so are not usually considered as being "Nosy Parkers." Having once gotten the hang of any operation, they are only too pleased to modify it. They usually can indeed improve matters and will be admired for their lightness of touch or cleverness with things that are mechanical or electrical.

Gadgets seem to fascinate them. They will try out anything new, get to know its function, then probably forget all about it. Their homes are often full of all sorts of interesting and weird decorations or knick-knacks that may work or may just be collecting dust.

They are easy people to get along with. Though they will

argue a point with the best, they are not offensive, nor do they wish to browbeat and dominate. They are happy to give their point of view and others can take it or leave it. Just to be sociable they will easily slip into conversation with people they do not know and are never likely to meet again. Their company is seldom turned down.

They have a great love of the outdoors. Open-air sports attract them. They are enthusiasts and will follow a sport or a hero all over the country. Nor are they lacking in skills at indoor entertainment. They are quick at anything they attempt. They appreciate the magician if they are not doing the tricks themselves. The theater and television attract them strongly. Many use their writing talents creating material for both forms of communication.

Children take to them like ducks to water. The Gemini never seems to lose a natural touch with the young. They make admirable parents who join in with their children in the formative years. It is never too much trouble for either man or woman Gemini to stay with a youngster and make them feel thoroughly wanted. The Geminian may never seem to grow up. They frequently look youthful to the end of their days and never have a gray hair. Children and animals seem to know they are in good company when Gemini is around. Despite the fertility of their brains, Gemini are not snobs and are simple, generous and genuine people at heart.

When Gemini is under the weather both man and woman can become a bundle of nerves. They easily become careless and forgetful in times of stress. They can be very unreliable. They will fail to keep a promise and have a way of making excuses that will infuriate those who have trusted them.

Their attitude to responsibility can be quite childish. They give the impression that they will never grow up enough to take life as an adult. Because of this behavior they can land themselves in trouble with all sorts of people.

They have an infuriating way of fiddling about or looking anywhere but where they should be looking when anyone is talking to them. They seem to be unable to concentrate. They get hold of the wrong end of the stick. They repeat things like a parrot.

One of their greatest failings is that of leaving loose ends. While they are happy keeping their nimble fingers at work, they seldom complete a job. So half-completed articles and tasks can litter the home or workshop.

Their quick wits can earn them a living. They seem to succumb to the temptation to cut corners. They will cheat or practice sleight of hand. They are expert at selling shoddy goods in a market as they mesmerize customers with their sales talk. They do not go in for a massive deceit. They seem to be content with petty roguery.

In many ways they are considered as lightweights. They can be quite petty and say all the wrong things. It is hard for them to keep a steady job, so they end up never having a skill or a trade to follow. Their friends are often as feckless as they.

They make a habit of interfering. Instead of mending things that have gone wrong, they will tamper with things that are working and mess them up.

They are the last persons in the world to whom a secret should be told. They will gossip and spread rumors all over the place. Frequently they will twist a story or an instruction to suit their own purpose and get others into hot water. Gemini at best will bounce and at worst will crack.

How Gemini Gets Along with Others

Gemini with Aries

Money/Job. Aries wants to get on with the job and Gemini will fan the flames. Aries can find Gemini off-putting because of the Gemini desire to improvise or interfere. But this will not stop Aries from making hay while the sun shines. They will not quarrel. They both have a good sense of humor that clicks.

Aries has no more intention of hanging on to money than has Gemini. They can both make money at high speed and get rid of it as quickly. Together they will always find the means of making what they require. They are never lost for an idea, either of them.

Home/Friends. Aries friends make good, intelligent company. They are not boring. They can keep the party going and this suits Gemini. They naturally generate activity and interest together, these two signs get on like "a house on fire." They never quarrel. To both of them life is too short to worry.

Both love their homes. They are naturally proud of home. Each sign has a love of children. They are both young at heart and make the home the center of life and activity. There is never a dull moment in the home when Aries gets together with Gemini. Neighbors will not take offense either and can become part of the scene. All manner of interesting things happen at home when these two are in top form.

Gemini with Taurus

Money/Job. At work, Taurus can exasperate Gemini and vice versa. Provided they are not doing the same operation, they will get along. Taurus likes to be left alone, so Gemini must not interfere. The Gemini "quick and easy" method of working can help Taurus if it works. They should not rub shoulders too closely or they'll fall out.

Taurus takes a dim view of wasting money. Gemini get-rich-quick schemes may not interest solid Taurus. Taurus like to pay bills and have no worries. Gemini is likely to be a bit careless. They are both simple and honest people at heart, but see things in a different light.

Home/Friends. The Taurus at home likes peace and comfort. While Gemini is kind, sociable and has simple standards, there will always be things happening in their home. Taurus will have to get some corner of the home set aside. The noise of children or talkative people will get on Taurus' nerves. Geminian meals may not be on time, either.

The friends brought in by Taurus may be few and far between. Gemini likes to have a variety of folk around and Taurus is much more selective. Friends of Taurus will be nice but have so little to say. Taureans will be bewildered by Gemini's lively friends.

Gemini with Gemini

Money/Job. At work these two will either work together intuitively, complementing each other, or continually get under each other's feet. They won't get too upset, possibly just make a few comments! As each is quick-witted, they can be boss and worker and treat each other as equals. One will accept the other's little quirks without getting upset.

Money has a deeper significance than either cares to disclose.

They are not close-fisted but appreciate money. So they will take a practical attitude to both earning and using it. Neither is hell-bent on making a fortune but they do like to have cash when it's needed.

Home/Friends. Home is an essential base for the Twins. They are both in and out like a jack-in-a-box but do appreciate their home comforts. They don't like to leave home for too long at a stretch. Together they'll make it a lively, friendly, comfortable and free place where all are welcome. They'll take turns at doing the chores and the cooking.

Friends come and go in all shapes and sizes. Neither is stuffy, so they will take a lively interest in each of their "instant" friends. Getting to know people is important to both. Anyone with a new line or a different interest is always welcome to both.

Gemini with Cancer

Money/Job. There can be a bit of friction over money. Cancer hates to let go of it and Gemini takes money as a commodity that has to be used. Cancer likes to have a good bank balance to feel secure, while Gemini does not look too far ahead. Both will earn. Neither is a scrounger.

At work they can get at cross purposes. Both are quick to see opportunity. Their methods of doing a job or working for promotion will clash. Cancer will want to be boss but may be a bit secretive or crafty in going about it. There can be mutual respect but some strain also.

Home/Friends. The Cancerian home is most important. It takes priority over all else. It can be a busy place or a very orderly place. To those who live in it all is provided. To them it is a haven and the beginning of everything important. Geminis are more casual, though they do love their home.

Their choice of friends will show the difference between the two signs. Cancer has few friends outside the family circle.

They can be hospitable to the Gemini-type friends for a while but will not agree with all who will, in their estimation, make a convenience of their home. Tension can grow which can lead to harsh words.

Gemini with Leo

Money/Job. It is natural that Leo should be the boss. If the positions are reversed things may not go as well. Gemini can take it either way. They will avoid the rut in which Leo can get stuck. Each expects recognition for their efforts but Leo is better at watching others work than doing a job himself or herself. They otherwise like to be self-employed.

Money is important to Leo. It opens doors to fame and approval. Leo may be tightfisted in order to amass money. Regal tastes lead Leos to live beyond their means. They are inclined to overdo things where money is concerned and Gemini is more modest.

Home/Friends. Leos have to be larger than life. They need comfort which has style. This can worry Gemini a bit, but not too much. Both like to have children around, though Leo will like them in their place and not climbing about everywhere. Gemini doesn't mind as long as they're happy.

Leo is, like Gemini, a sociable person. Guests will be made welcome. Friends have to qualify for the favors of Leo. Leo has not a lot of close friends but appreciate those who show appreciation of them. This may seem a bit farcical to carefree Gemini. There is a chance that Leo can be a bit stuffy or snobbish and this can show in their friends.

Gemini with Virgo

Money/Job. These two can cooperate and be a great success at work. Both are ingenious. Both can see a number of ways to do a job. They may get too complicated, though, and that will upset the applecart. Virgo, like Gemini, must be busy and on the move. They may find it hard to agree who is boss. Gemini may take on that role.

Virgo will make good use of money. Neither sign makes money their god. Each has feet on the ground, though, and will not waste money unduly. Perhaps Virgo is a mite more conservative than Gemini. Neither is a fool with money.

Home/Friends. The Virgo home is a lively place. They like comfort and good food. Virgo will be the cook, without question. The kitchen will contain no "instant" food, or very little. Each will make home interesting. Both like T.V. and talking. Little things about the home will be important to both. All will function well and be up to date.

Virgo has an interest in most things. Friends will, like those of Gemini, come in all shapes and sizes. Virgo, like Gemini, is a neighborly soul who will have the neighbors in for a chat and slip next door to return the compliment. Both have a happy knack for making friends, Virgo more quietly.

Gemini with Libra

Money/Job. There is common ground between these two. Libra is, like Gemini, rational and intelligent. They will readily resolve any differences, either on method of working or on principle. Each will try to please or help the other whether as boss or worker.

Money is a means to an end for both. Libra does not like to be without it, knowing that standards and personal appearance have to be maintained by practical means. Both will make money work rather than leave it lying around in a vault.

Home/Friends. The Libran home will be more highly organized than that of Gemini. Libras have a love of beauty that will be expressed in their home. It will not be ornate but will

definitely be tasteful. A lot of money can be spent by Libras
getting things exactly to their taste. They don't like it being
messed up. To some extent Gemini may upset the order, but
they share an interest in keeping up to date. This helps matters
considerably.

Both make friends who can discuss all manner of things.
There should never be a dull moment. Libra will be more
concerned or selective. They do not go for people who are
coarse or too blunt. Libra can control the more wayward
Gemini inclinations and lend refinement to friendship.

Gemini with Scorpio

Money/Job. Scorpio will have to be boss. Gemini, even if
disagreeing, will accept this. Gemini can live with anyone and
uses wits to get things done. Scorpio will watch Gemini to be
sure that nothing is being skipped. This watchful or tense situation can go on a long time, both considering work to be a
four-letter word.

The Scorpio attitude to money will not suit Gemini. They
can go their separate ways, becoming more and more selfish.
Scorpio can be really tight-fisted or just use money wisely. They
take their money seriously. More casual Gemini will not be
controlled by money and is more moderate.

Home/Friends. While Scorpio stays indoors, Gemini is in
and out like a yo-yo. The ever-open door will worry Scorpio
who likes to make home a personal fortress. They can divide
the home and leave it at that. Otherwise Gemini is going to
feel shut in by adopting Scorpio ways and Scorpio will feel
that home is not their own.

To Scorpio, friends have to be selected. They look down
their noses at people and show when anyone is not welcome.
Gemini is much more openly friendly. Scorpio will have to
attract friends, because the urge to stay indoors is stronger
than the desire to go out and be sociable. Scorpio does not
welcome chatter. They can be downright unsociable or wet
blankets.

Gemini with Sagittarius

Money/Job. Sagittarius can make a lot of money. They will gain the respect of Gemini for their audacity and enterprise. Together these two can make a success of anything if they accept complementary roles. Sagittarius is as mobile as Gemini. They can make up their minds to concentrate long enough to succeed or just blow hot and cold together. It's up to them both.

Work and money may go hand in hand. Sagittarius is a great speculator and can spot a big profit a mile away. It is largely easy come, easy go with Sagittarius. Money is a prize or a means to an end. With neither is it meant to be hoarded. They can get by one way or another.

Home/Friends. Sagittarius may stay away from home longer than Gemini. They are both happy out of doors but Sagittarius often forgets to return. Children may miss a Sagittarian parent but never have doubts about Gemini. Both have an interest in reading and finding out the odd things about life and human nature. A library is a joint essential.

Friends have a special place with both. Sagittarius is more selective than is Gemini. Friends, like anything or anyone else, have to serve a purpose for Sagittarius. They are not as easy to please as Gemini. They can break off a friendship easily if it no longer serves a purpose. Nevertheless they're a likeable pair.

Gemini with Capricorn

Money/Job. Capricorns are managerial material. They like to take charge. They have order and system and will not put up with casual or slipshod methods. It is up to Gemini to keep up to date and have a weather eye open when this serious person is around. To cooperate, Gemini ideas can be executed well by Capricorn.

There is no waste of money with Capricorn. They like to make an impression in the right places and will not spare money when doing so. For less obvious things they think twice or three times before spending. They save for a rainy day.

Home/Friends. Capricorn appreciates home. It is the base from which operations commence but it is not the center of their lives. They are conscious of the appearance of their home, so they don't like it to be untidy or disorganized. Things have to be functional and in the proper place. Home-sharing with Capricorn can be a bit restrictive for the easy-going Gemini.

Capricornian friends can be a bit snooty. They have different values from those of Gemini. Capricornians can be social climbers or snobs at worst, which will show in the company they keep. They can be very practical friends to have around once they appreciate the open kindness of Gemini. Friendships don't come easily between this pair.

Gemini with Aquarius

Money/Job. A good working relationship is possible here. Both are people with ideas. Aquarius will be content to plod along at an even pace but will not get too bothered when Gemini digresses to take on another job. They can talk to each other and that's important to both.

Neither is particularly money-conscious. Gemini is more practical as a rule. Aquarius can save but is not a hoarder. They can share money happily and not be too bothered as long as they have sufficient for their needs.

Home/Friends. Home life with Aquarius can be peaceful. They can shut themselves off from the Geminian activity. Like Gemini, they need to have plenty of reading material around them. They can appreciate, if not invent, the modern gadgetry of the Geminian home. Like Gemini they spend a lot of time outdoors, socializing. Home comes in its proper place and may be comfortable or rather bare. Aquarius seldom complains.

Aquarian friends are easy to get along with. They have a

breadth of interest that intrigues Gemini. They make no heavy demand on Gemini. Indeed the two get along amazingly well, though Geminian changes of interest can leave Aquarius a bit breathless. They each accept people at face value till they know them better.

Gemini with Pisces

Money/Job. Working together can be a bit of a muddle. Gemini provides the practical methods while Pisces may be full of great ideas that never get off the ground. Both like to be busy, so they can get in each other's way. They need a third party to keep them in line and being productive.

Both have a use for money, but it's not the most important fact of their lives. Gemini may be more practical about making money. Both can spend it, Pisces probably on someone else who is hard up. This can upset more down-to-earth Gemini.

Home/Friends. Pisces will make as many friends as Gemini. They will probably be of a different nature, even more talkative and emotional. Pisceans seem to attract the down-and-outs, the insecure and the affectionate. Some of them, even friendly Gemini will find it difficult to accept.

Home for the Piscean can be a meeting place, or a place of peace and quiet. They may seem lost or aimless, but they know what they want. Pets are an essential feature of the Piscean home. If you don't like cats or dogs you are better staying away. Everything gets attended to in due course in their homes but there will be no set time for anything, other than the pets' meals.

Love Mates

Gemini Woman—Aries Man. This get-together is like spontaneous combustion. Things will happen at once or not at all. Aries likes to get on with his life. He will find Gemini is provocative and gets him going. She likes his instant ways. She fans his fire and he really comes to life.

This is not a long-term smoldering association. Both will live for the moment. When the enthusiasm has gone there will be no regrets. They both enjoy each other while together. When they part there are no hard feelings.

Aries can learn a lot about love from Gemini. She is eager to please and admires him for his courage and the way he charges up to carry her off in his arms. He gets a boost to his ego whenever they meet or need each other. She is not in the least possessive. She lets him go his own way without demur. She likewise does not wish to be tied to one man. She's a natural flirt and her roving eye will have seen another while he has been telling his tale.

There is nothing deceitful in this relationship. It is a natural fun affair. If they decide to make it permanent they both know it can last, because neither will pressure the other. He can be master in his own house and she won't get on her high horse. She is far too sensible for such things.

She makes him feel young. Both are young at heart and can make life sing for each other. He will ignore her when she is too talkative. She has a way of explaining things that leaves him a bit lost if he cares to take her too seriously. They have to keep together on a light note. It suits them ideally.

Gemini Woman—Taurus Man. This is not plain sailing. He will find her attractive in a superficial sort of way. She is friendly and he likes the way she makes herself known to him.

She prides herself on being able to get men to take notice of her feminine charms, yet she does not want to be tied down. To him she is intelligent, full of life. If he reckons she is flirting he can have a good time with the best of them. If he begins to get more serious, he will find she cannot take his kind of sincere loving. She is not as physical as he is. A brief affair with this strong, sensual man is about as much as she can take.

The Taurus man will mean his love sincerely and can be possessive once he's set his sights on her. She hates this sort of thing. She does not wish to be possessed by any man nor does she want to possess him. Her love life has to be as free as her nature. He will suffocate her if he is possessive.

They are best having a light, casual relationship, if he can manage that. Otherwise the togetherness will soon fade and they'll both regret it. When she begins to irritate him with her liveliness or chatter, he will see where he stands. Yet he'll find it hard to just walk away. He will realize there is something innocent about this young lady, and he likes this. She will see him as a kindly man with a lot of feeling. He wants to look after her but she will generally want freedom more than security.

It's possibly a non-starter right from the beginning. But life has to be attempted. Gemini is always ready for something and someone different.

Gemini Woman—Gemini Man.
They can spot each other in a crowd. He will sense she is as carefree as is he. They are not seeking a relationship that is restrictive.

They find each other lively, suggestive, interesting, without either seeking immediate physical contact. They will be happy to fence with each other. Love-play means a lot to each. They are each aware that their stamina has limitations. They will get bored if anything goes on for too long.

Together they make an understanding duo. It is as if one expected the other's next move. They will play intelligent guessing games to arouse each other's interest. Once the first flush of intimacy is past, they make efforts to retain interest in each other by dreaming up other ways of making each other happy. Together they are never lost for ideas. Some will be a scream, others may fall flat.

They each like to be in company. This stops them from getting bored with each other. They are not jealous by nature. In a way, absence makes the heart grow fonder when they are truly attached to each other. Love is so much more enthusiastic when they get together again.

They have a light-hearted way of comparing notes. They can laugh at their own failings. Even when they are feeling down in the dumps they can tease each other into seeing the funny side of life.

Their mutual love of children has them interested in a family. If they are sure they will be happy for ever together they will be thinking of their children, home and nursery. They will not force each other. Personal freedom means too much. They're happy to be together.

Gemini Woman—Cancer Man. She may be surprised at the gentle way he makes his approach. He is obviously a sensitive man who recognizes her feminine charm. He knows that women like, as a rule, to be courted. He has old-fashioned ideas about the way to treat his woman. He will not offend her once he is sure she is for him. His attitude will be quite disarming to the casual Gemini.

Together they can enjoy a joke. Cancer man has a wry sense of humor that will match Gemini. Both are intelligent, quick off the mark, have a ready response to suggestions. The courtship can be sparkling as they tease each other or as he tries to please her by playing on her emotions. She will find she will develop her emotional nature a lot in his company. He values emotions because they are strong in his nature.

He is entertaining. He can have her in stitches when he demonstrates or describes a situation. She intrigues him by the way she tells a tale. She is never lost for a word nor he for an emotional response.

His love of home and family will soon be apparent. She can relate easily to this side of his nature. They both put great store by children. He will make her feel he wants to look after her, give her security, show her sympathy when she needs it. This may or may not appeal to Gemini. She will want all these things provided she has freedom to move around.

He is not a stick-in-the-mud, but he can be easily offended.

He can become moody. She will say things that hurt him. He can be crabby. They have to give and take if they are to stay together. It's not easy.

Gemini Woman—Leo Man.

He means to make an immediate impression on this vivacious Gemini woman. He has a lot of charm, is larger than life and not a bit shy. She has no need to find out about his assets. He will tell her about his talents and expect her to approve. She will probably feel delighted or flattered.

Leo's interest can be fleeting or more sincere. She can handle both. Together they can flirt and have a really great time. He knows how to treat her, for he is a past master of love. This is something he enjoys. Both have no immediate intention of settling down. They each value their independence far too much to be thinking of sharing all their worldly goods.

He likes to get around. This suits her. He is a passionate man. She sets him alight with her teasing, feminine ways. She soon sees he has pride and will not push him too far. She can respond freely to his ardor or cool him down at arm's length when she wants a breath of fresh air.

She does not contradict him or stop him directly from being himself. He will feel he is the boss and this is what he wants. She is happy that he should be for she admires a strong, positive man. Provided he does not take her for granted, they will get along fine. As long as she acts like a lady in company and is not too casual or flighty, he will remain interested.

He likes to be admired, so if she wants to retain his love she will soon figure this out. He will give to her freely just as long as he feels sure of his place in her heart. If he lives up to this she is happy. If he does not, she will slip away. They are both quite practical people at heart and won't be fooled.

Gemini Woman—Virgo Man.

One thing they have in common: they are not going to rush into marriage. Both are intelligent, so they have a lot to talk about. Their first get-together will be a fencing match. Each will be fishing for information about the other.

They have a lot in common. Both hate to be cornered; they

like room to do their own thing. Both have, nevertheless, a need of company. They get easily involved and are naturally inquisitive. They'll soon recognize this and their mutual sense of humor will allow them to become intimate more quickly.

He is a rather gentle man. If she is too bright and breezy he will be put off. Yet he is earthy and sensual, so he needs to love a woman physically to feel satisfied. She is not a physical type. If she tries to keep their relationship at talking level, he is not going to hang around.

There can be a "take it or leave it" situation. Neither is going to stick their neck out if they are unsure, so there can be a lot of love play and no action.

He may be gentle, quiet or apparently timid. She must not take this as read. He is a man and will want to be boss. If she is truly interested, she has the wit to recognize that he is very much a man at heart and will not offend his sensitivity.

They can live on their nerves and have a lively time together. Each is happy in company though they may not always admit it. Their mutual understanding of children is perfect. They are both really children at heart. They will not try to pressure each other, so have a lot to live for . . . if they can agree.

Gemini Woman—Libra Man. This man is cool and charming. He knows how to treat a woman. She will see that he is intelligent and on the same level as herself. She strikes him as an attractive girl who is not trying to trap him.

They have a lot in common. Neither is looking for a heavy, physical relationship. There is much more to life, they both agree, than body contact. They feel that life should be free without too much thought for tomorrow.

He will be perfectly charming. She may feel he's too good to be true. He will respond readily to her teasing without getting out of hand. This mental stimulation is all he needs to make him feel happy in her company.

Fortunately, she is not jealous. He attracts other women like a flypaper. He appreciates admiration and returns it quite honestly, so he is never without friends. He has difficulty in keeping up with her. She does not set a lot of store by close relationships. While they both think alike, he is aware that she can do without the one-to-one ties that he feels are so important. He is always looking for the exact counterpart to himself, so is not easily pleased. She seems to take everything as it comes and is not so fussy.

He is envious of her, in a way, but feels she may be too free and easy. To her, he will become a bore if he does not relax and be more casual.

They have such a lot in common they will both want to maintain some sort of relationship. The casual togetherness they both can take may suit them best, but they can live together without pressure and love it.

Gemini Woman—Scorpio Man.
This is not an easy set-up right from the start. He likes women and can usually get his own way with them. She is light and easy to get along with. She has an engaging manner in conversation. She's a tease, but avoids his follow up.

He will become impatient if she avoids his advances. He wants to make body contact and will not be satisfied until he gets what he wants. She is in no hurry to come to grips. She will fence and try to keep the relationship cooler.

She sees in him a strong man. This is fine, up to a point. But she does not want to be dominated by anyone. Having a man to care for her or to make the decisions is fine. Someone who is going to pin her down and restrict her movements is another kettle of fish.

If they get intimate he will become possessive. She is in no way possessive. She is happy to let any friend of hers live his own life provided he returns the compliment. The Scorpio man resents anyone interfering with what he considers his property. He is a jealous lover. The fact that she does not think this way will make him think she is too superficial for his attention.

They are likely to part quite quickly. He can part feeling resentful, and she with a sigh of relief. Passions can run high for a short period. She cannot take his strong emotional passion and will feel absolutely drained by his constant attention.

He may be a tough and strong man but does not share her

love of fresh air and the freedom of a social life. There is too much expected of her. She can not accept this link. He too is not satisfied.

Gemini Woman—Sagittarius Man.
This man can take her as she is. She will arouse his interest by her teasing ways. He may feel he can teach her a thing or two. He'll try to impress her intellectually and then by his exploits, though not necessarily with women.

She will admire him for being a man of the world. She will feel sure he won't cramp her style, while he may allow her to develop farther than she ever has. They are a challenge to each other. They will feel they have to give it a try.

He is aware of his individuality. Marriage is a non-starter for him, or so he feels. He has no particular interest in home life and can't stand the sight of crying babies or wet diapers. She has the good sense not to mention such things if she is set on getting tied to him.

She will not let him feel he is being trapped because she shares his feelings to a large extent. They have a terrific mental togetherness. She is as inquisitive as he is and knows a lot of things. They can talk for hours on end and maintain interest. Their friends, too, are interesting and witty. They do not easily take offense at each other's remarks when they are both feeling off color. What's gone is water under the bridge, so they bear no grudges.

They will be happy together if they keep on the move. This does not altogether suit Gemini. She will want a home and children, so she will try to get him to agree to this. He is an honest man and is not a fool. If he is sure she is the woman he wants he will give up some of his freedom to provide the home she needs. They can have a great time together.

Gemini Woman—Capricorn Man.
This will be a tense relationship. He likes things to be under his control. He expects things to be orderly, in their place, and he has high material standards. He is, she may think at first, a snob. That's not a good start.

He is considerate. He will see her as a girl, in need of a

fatherly hand to keep her in control or encourage her along the way. He will feel responsible for her. She likes this to a certain extent, because he will take responsibility off her shoulders and she feels she can flatter him or tease him and get away with it.

He, nevertheless, likes a woman who appreciates him as a physical man. He likes physical contact, despite his cool, even cold, manner. There is a lot of energy and desire under the surface. He just does not like to make a fool of himself in front of a woman or in public, so he is cautious.

When they get to know each other better, she will find he is quite a go-getter. He has ambitions and will take her with him on his upward journey if she will play her proper part in his scheme of things. He will be a good father to her children.

He is not a jealous man but he does expect a true partner to respect him. He will give her as much rope as he thinks is sensible. If she can entertain his influential friends and bring his children up as respectable citizens, he will find little fault in her.

She may settle for this. She is, herself, quite a hard-headed woman and knows life can be difficult for someone who wants to freelance it all the time. It may be a struggle but they can make the grade.

Gemini Woman—Aquarius Man.

She really goes for this man. He has quiet strength, yet is not a domineering type. He sees in her an intelligent woman who can match him, almost, in knowledge. They do not get emotionally involved at first sight. She keeps him at arm's length, which he likes. He has no intention of getting too close to any woman who is out to grab him.

They can have a great feeling of togetherness by just being with each other and discussing all manner of things. He can relax with her as he can with no other woman. When he gets a bit boring or takes her out of her mental depth, she will tease him. He likes this. It makes him feel young. He loses years when he's in her company. She has the sense, also, to know when to stop messing about. So with him she is not "bird-brained" or over-childish.

Provided she leaves him to his meditation or quiet thoughts, he will never complain. She will run his home for him efficiently. Their children will be intelligent, well read and good citizens without being anyone's fools.

They both appreciate the need to keep their distance, yet together are very loving. He has the habit of surprising her with a gift. She is always a bundle of surprises. They each love innovation. He will think up all sorts of new ideas, she will be happy to try them out. They will never be short of interest in their togetherness. Neither of them is possessive, which is why they come together in the first place. They are both open and possibly naive. She knows there is no need to be "smart" with him. To her he is like an open book. He is father and lover all rolled into one. What more could a woman want?

Gemini Woman—Pisces Man. She may find this loving man is a bit much. He may talk as much as she. He seems to have his finger in a lot of pies. He is so emotional it can frighten her off. She sees he attracts a lot of women to him though he is seldom alone with just one.

She will be curious about this sensitive man. They arrive at the same conclusions, but the route he takes is different from hers. He obviously feels for all manner of things. He has a great love of pets and small animals. This she can take, but she will not be soppy over such things. He is hard to bring down to earth. She must love a man who is not a softy and who can give as good as he gets.

Both will get involved with people. He can become totally immersed in the relationship of the day or just have emotional affairs that would drain Gemini. This emotional flightiness she cannot take. It does not ring true to her at all.

With a longer acquaintanceship she may find he is truly loving and as gentle as he seemed at first. But he may try to spread his love too far and end up with nothing. He realizes this and is frequently moody. His emotional ups and downs, even tantrums, will leave her cold once she has seen the first performance. He can put on an act all too easily. She is an open and honest girl and will speak her mind. Apart from being a tease, she cannot stand deceit.

What's more, she wants someone to look after her in a realistic, practical way if at all. She expects emotionalism only from her own sex. Love is soon drained from Gemini, for she has to respond.

Gemini Man—Aries Woman.
She has a mind of her own. He will not get round her just because she is a woman. She is either out to be boss or to find a man of strong character whom she can respect.

Gemini is not a forceful type. He wants life to pass without too much of a hassle. He will see this woman has a lot of fire. She will arouse his passions while he seems to inflame her emotionally. That is fine for short spells. Neither can sustain intense emotion for very long. If they are as realistic as they both can be, they will make the most of short spasms of mutual enthusiasm and have frequent rests.

This sounds more like an affair, or a series of affairs, than a lasting relationship. Yet it can suffice once they get their mutual priorities right. Neither will consume or wear out the other if they play it by ear.

Should Aries try to be boss, she may get a surprise. Gemini may not be pushy but he knows the male role in life. He can freeze her out as easily as he first enthused about her charms. She will take a dim view of this. They will both move on to the next encounter in search of their appropriate match. There will be no hard feelings. They can quite happily remain friends and can renew their attachment whenever their paths cross in the future.

They both call a spade a spade. They can be honest with each other and their mutual respect will grow. But there is plenty of room for either getting impatient with the other, or each getting on a high horse. Life together will certainly never be dull. If that's what they want, they have found it.

Gemini Man—Taurus Woman.
She understands physical men. He sees her as an attractive woman who can rouse the beast in him. It is an appeal that is difficult to resist. This could be a short affair or can develop into a union with possibilities. It will never be straightforward or completely relaxed.

She finds men attractive for their bodies or the comfort they can give her. Physical beauty in a man really turns her on. She can cope with this. It is the sensuality in her nature that attracts him to her. He has no intention of showing any lack of stamina, so he will use his wits to sustain her interest once he's reached his physical limits. She will go along with him if she is really interested, because she finds he livens her up and brings a new interest into her life.

He is appreciative of the attention she pays him. They can share a happy interest in the young. They both have their feet on the ground and know the world does not owe them a living. This allows them to accept each other's shortcomings.

Once she has made up her mind about him, she can be possessive. She will feel like clipping his wings if he gets around a lot in company. Even though she may know he saves his strength for her, she may never be quite sure. He should know better than to tease her on such a matter, but he is an impish man and their sense of humor may not exactly mix. This sense of humor is something that can either hold the link together under stress, or be the last straw that breaks it.

Both are simple souls at heart. They can live happily together if each is prepared to allow the other to be an individual. They are both honest and know it.

Gemini Man—Gemini Woman. These two can really get together or totally ignore each other. They may feel they know each other too well and couldn't stand the strain of being together. Equally they may feel it will save a lot of hassle, leaving them plenty of scope to follow their own paths while enjoying each other's company.

They are both simple yet complicated people. They have their feet on the ground and know how to look after Number One. Yet they must be friendly and get involved with people, for interchange of ideas is their food of life. They hate to be alone. But this does not mean they want to be dependent on anyone. Only a Gemini would understand this! So they can get along in their own sweet way together.

There is always a danger that they will double their joint worries rather than halve them. They are both inclined to live on their nerves when they are upset. At times life will be doubly exciting to them and at other times they will make it doubly aggravating.

Their physical attraction to each other is fully understood. They each know their limitations and will not abuse each other. The scope for enjoying a social and intelligent life together is great. The home will be important to them but so too will be the company they seek or keep, either together or singly. A gathering of all their friends will fill a hall at any time. This coolness will stop either from developing any sort of jealousy towards the other. Life is, to both of them, too short for that.

As long as they don't get bored with each other they can make a go of it. Common sense can avoid that pitfall.

Gemini Man—Cancer Woman. The Cancer woman
is sweet, feminine and appealing. He loves his home and children so he will see a happy prospect here. She can feel that he is a lovable man who can possibly be guided along the lines she likes.

At first encounter she may seem a bit lost or helpless, needing a man to show her the way. He knows his way about and is only too pleased to talk about her problems and protect her . . . for a little while, anyway. Her femininity appeals to him. She is responsive and soft. When they make love it is a new world opening up for him.

She is not a softy, deep down. She is very resilient and knows what she wants. A man has got to provide her with security above all. If he is weak or unmanly that is no good to her. If he can give her security, she will consider his advances, for she will want a home and family. He too likes home life and gets a kick out of being with children. They have this in common.

Yet he does not propose making the family and the home the be-all and end-all of married life, if it comes to that. He is a freelance and has to be out in the fresh air, on the move. He may feel her love is "smother love." That is the signal to get moving as far as he's concerned.

She cannot really accept his fleeting love. He may be a nice man, but she will think he has no ambition. To her, the man in her life has to have ambition. She will support him all the way if he's going places and providing. The future of her off-spring means more to her than anything.

Gemini Man—Leo Woman.
She is out for a good time. Theirs is a mutual attraction. The flame of their love will flare into life. He seems to her an interesting man who is self-confident. Her men have to be full of confidence or she will take over. If he takes her simply for a plaything she will have to put him straight.

The initial stages of their relationship will sort out a lot of problems. She expects to be treated like a queen. If he fails, there's nothing more to be said. There could be a flirtation, but even here he will have to show her some respect. He is quick to spot her weaknesses and can put on a show with the best. He gets around and knows what's going on and where to take her. It's all a glorious game between these two when they feel free from possible entanglement.

When she is in search of a long-term mate, Leo is much more circumspect. He has to keep her in style. He has to allow her freedom. He must have some position, have his own business or, at least, be self-employed. More than that he has to be a man who can be boss. When she finds a weakling she is inclined to be vindictive or autocratic. That's when the rough side of her will show.

Seeing her in her full dignity can intimidate Mr. Gemini. This is not his idea of an ideal partnership. He's just as likely to take to his heels. Anyway he won't stay where he's not wanted. That's not cowardice, just plain old common sense.

They can make a go of it. She can be magnanimous if he gives her the material things she needs. He can be proud to take her around among his friends.

Gemini Man—Virgo Woman.
She may seem timid at first. She could be a virgin at heart. Yet she has an impish sense of humor. They can strike a common chord instantly.

He has no need to tease this woman. She will beat him to the draw. They have a lot of fun just teasing each other and keeping their distance. Each enjoys company, each can chat away merrily, and neither really wants to get down to brass tacks too soon. They both like to keep the pot boiling and retain the involvement.

The relationship may get no further. They could be happy with a sort of brother-sister relationship on the surface.

She is an earthy woman, though, and can get easily hurt if he does not get beyond the talking and intellectual stage in their romance. She likes physical contact, no matter what she may seem to project. But she will want to be sure of his good intentions.

She is always considerate of her health. A woman, to her, must bear children. If she cannot get the right mate she will stay a virgin all her life. Such are her standards. He must accept this. He will realize she is eager to make physical contact but for a purpose, so he cannot trifle with her affections.

To him she is a bit of a mystery when they get more intimate. He can respect her for this and either leave her in peace or be her true lover. He will not take advantage of her modesty. Their children will be a credit to them, the product of two lively and intelligent parents. Neither will bear a grudge, and each can have fond memories of the other.

Gemini Man—Libra Woman.
She has calm, grace, appearance and intelligence. He may think she's ideal. She tries to be the ideal for all men. Gemini sees what he wants to see and that's quite enough in the beginning.

Her beauty is not just skin deep, at least not to Gemini. She is as logical and down-to-earth as he is. A Libra woman may be the center of attraction, but she is no softy. That is part of the veneer which she uses to attract or disperse the opposite sex.

She is sociable. Both sexes seek her company. She seems to be a maiden yet is a mature woman in some mysterious way. Gemini likes his women to be young. He feels more comfortable when they are not too set in their ways. She seems able to understand all his moves and moods without making him feel at all embarrassed or out of place.

She copes with life calmly, makes him feel comfortable without giving him the direct "come-on." She has to be courted, he soon will realize. This is not beyond his talents. He can sweet-talk with the best of them. She appreciates this. It will keep him at a distance for a while anyway and avoid the physical body contact about which she is not so keen. They are agreed on this. They both know there is more to their ideal mate than sensual and sexual togetherness.

They will take their physical contact in small doses and be glad they can satisfy each other. Neither will make too heavy a demand on the other.

Together they like to socialize. They can be the ideal host and hostess or the life and soul of any party. It is a comfortable relationship worth consolidating.

Gemini Man—Scorpio Woman. This intense woman will intrigue Mr. Gemini. His lively conversation may have no affect, or she may be interested in him for some reason he cannot fathom. His curiosity is aroused by anything that he cannot sum up logically.

It will probably be a short relationship. These two do not get on at all easily together. If they are just interested in a flirtation or a night out on the town, they can enjoy each other's company.

She looks for a man of substance. He must have physical strength and staying power to match her deep emotions. She sets a lot of store by her sex drive. She is aware that men are attracted to her because she is magnetic. She draws them to her and can handle any man she gets close to. Physical love is a must with Scorpio women. This is not the first priority of Gemini, though he will make the effort. That is fine for a passing romance but he cannot maintain the effort on the level she desires.

They can part good friends. She is a nice, friendly, sociable woman on the surface, and that's probably as far as she allows Gemini to go.

If he gets deeply involved with her he is going to be dominated in more ways than he imagines. He will find it hard to be the boss when she's around. She will lose respect for him if he cannot match her high standards. She is a very jealous lady and will not like his socializing or sliding off on the quiet. He hates interference in his affairs. If either is in any way deceitful, the sparks will fly.

It is most unlikely these two will ever get round to settling down together. That's just as well.

Gemini Man—Sagittarius Woman. This woman likes men. She feels she's among the boys and can be their equal in debate and story telling, or so she thinks. She has a natural attraction for Gemini, who is drawn by her openness and frank manner. They pull no punches when they're together. They have a lot of things to talk about. They seem to have been places . . . or are going tomorrow. The present is all-important but they each have the urge to move on.

Both feel they will allow the other as much rope as is necessary. Gemini will find it hard to think of her as a home-maker for his children, but she's full of surprises. She has a soft spot for animals and that appeals to Mr. Gemini. His logic will tell him there is a wish for children also.

Courtship can take a long time. She seems able to make instant decisions about some things but will not commit herself to the altar in a hurry. Gemini may hang around and wait, or he may decide on the spur of the moment and that is settled. Both are like this, so they can accept the situation.

Her love is warm. She is passionate, like him, in small doses. They both enjoy this. Each has an opinion. She will make sure she gets her viewpoint across and he can take it or leave it. Neither is going to attempt to force the other to change a viewpoint. They both, in fact, can change an opinion over and over, so they see little point in belaboring something that may alter in the fullness of time. A lot of their harmony comes from their both talking at the same time and neither heeding the other, but neither will get upset about that.

Gemini Man—Capricorn Woman. They may take a long time to get acquainted. She is naturally cautious and may think he is a bit forward. To him she may seem older than her years, as she can talk sensibly with him.

She takes stock of all men as she does everything else. There has to be some practical potential in her men. They are not much good to her if they have no ambition. She probably has enough for two but will not make that too obvious till she is older.

She likes strong, physical men. Their appearance means a lot. If they look as if they have the staying power, she will be interested.

Naturally, the proof of the pudding is in the eating. She will not accept anything or anyone, especially a man, at face value. Mr. Gemini will have to prove he's of the right material and is going places in this big bad world.

He is not without ambition, but he will want to get to the top in his own way. It will not be as direct as Capricorn would like. He is a man of fits and starts. He will not want a woman continually harassing him from behind. He likes to look good when he's out but does not set that much store on trying to kowtow to people with influence. He is not a social climber and she is.

There are a variety of things outside the sexual act on which they will differ. It is too much to expect this relationship to prosper on peaceful lines. There is always the possibility of a lasting friendship, since Gemini is the last man in the world to cast aside a friend. But little else will happen.

Gemini Man—Aquarius Woman.
They have a lot going for them. Her eyes are inviting. She is really cool. He likes this woman instinctively. She finds him stimulating. His cheeky ways amuse her and she likes the way he talks.

She is always interested in types. She takes all men as they come, since she knows there is no hope of changing them. So she is at ease with Gemini, knowing she has him taped. He is eager to find out more about her. She does not have a lot to say about herself, but is a fund of knowledge.

He finds her physically attractive and she feels the same way. She is no egghead when it comes to loving, though she may be able to discuss all sorts of intellectual matters. She is a sincere lover who can calm him down and yet enthuse him. He will feel quite at home with her. They are both straightforward, simple types when they get down to brass tacks, yet each is inquisitive and wants to look to the future or get to know more about people.

They have a mutual interest in all sorts of human involvement which can lead them to better understanding of themselves.

They are never cold to each other, though they can both freeze unwelcome guests with a steely look. She can be benign when he is childish. He will accept that she is rather straitlaced when she's serious.

Neither of them are likely to get over-emotional. They feel things deeply but make little show. Both know this while others, less observant, miss the point.

Their love for each other can be deep and abiding but they won't make a fuss about it.

Gemini Man—Pisces Woman.

The Gemini masculinity will want to cuddle her. Her emotions will possibly turn him off. She can be a bit too much for him to take at once. He knows he can bubble with enthusiasm but she leaves him standing when she's being emotional.

A relationship is possible because they are both lively and inquisitive. He may be happy to look after her and be protective, but the experience will be wearing. She is very moody. Some of this he can accept, women being what they are, but he will not have tears continually on tap.

She may find him too logical and hard, as she will see it, but she can survive. She is extremely resilient and bounces back like a rubber ball. He likes this about her, for he has his own ups and downs.

They make assessments differently, though they may arrive at the same conclusion. They have a caring thought for little things, the deprived or pets. Here they are on common ground. That's not enough. They both are inclined to get involved and together can easily get lost in the maze. He can be direct when he cares to take the lead, but he may feel he's taken on more than he bargained for here.

They will both side-step and dodge the main issue. They are intelligent enough to find ways round problems. Together they can wriggle through life in this way. They can let outside influences control their lives. This is eventually going to rile Gemini who likes freedom and fresh air. A lot has to be done in this relationship through mutual love and a vast amount of understanding. It's no easy job.

IV. Cancer

The Cancer Character

Cancer reflects the tides of the ocean. Both men and women of the sign have their emotional highs and lows with unfailing regularity. They are creatures of feeling, sensitive to everything that goes on around them. The symbol of the Crab fits them perfectly.

At heart they are progressive. They have ambitions and hate to stay too long in one place. Like the crab they are at home either on land or immersed in water. Because they are sensitive, they have to progress cautiously. This gives the impression of their being afraid to try anything or of walking sideways.

They are, in their best aspect, very kind, soft and understanding. Even the male Cancerian has this tenderness in his nature, so is often considered a "softy." They seek to protect those who come to them for help and comfort. They are only too well aware of the necessity of security and find it hard to turn an appeal away.

Because of this quality in their nature, they are always prepared for ill luck or an adverse turn in the tide of their affairs. They bank on nothing except their own ability to prepare for a rainy day, so are in a way quite independent people. Security and reserves are a priority. They have great reservoirs of sympathy and love for those who care to ask. Their sensitivity does not allow them to make a thing of this, so they will not advertise the fact that they can help. They feel that those who understand life as they do will come when the need is there. Consequently they attract sensitive people to themselves like flies to a flypaper.

They have emotional ups and downs like a yo-yo. At one period in the month they go out of their way to talk to people around them. They have a terrific sense of humor. They do outrageous things and see the funny side of the most impossible situations. They are nature's dramatists. They frequently are professional actors and actresses or involved with theatrical matters. They have terrific powers of persuasion because of their sense of drama or the ridiculous.

It could be said that one thing dominates their lives . . . security. This can be interpreted in four ways: money, stomach, home and children. All are practical and understandable aspects of daily life. Cancer is aware of the everyday facts of life and is no dreamer of hopes that cannot be realized. They are exceptionally good business people. Their feelers prejudge the market. They are prudent with their money. They take no serious risks and they mean to make a profit if they offer a service.

They have home and family always in the forefront of their thoughts. Their children will never want. They will be encouraged to come home to Mom and Dad whenever they're in need, later in their adult life. Family ties are stronger than any other link. Cancer will make a home from a pile of orange boxes anywhere on earth.

Because of their moodiness Cancerians are often misunderstood. They are extremely touchy at some period of the Moon's cycle. As the Moon is the sign ruler, it gives some indication of their ups and downs. Neighbors will find they are downright inhospitable at times. They will ignore passers-by who were enthralled yesterday by their verbosity. The most well-meaning appeal for support will be considered and scrutinized before a dime is contributed. Only the family will merit any consideration at all and even they have to be careful what they say or where they wipe their feet on coming indoors.

When the Cancerian is in this sort of mood, both men and women seem to go back into their shells. The drama becomes heavy and full of foreboding. There seems to be little possibility of anything but rain and clouds. They are best left to their own thoughts right now. They worry about all sorts of things that really don't merit such concern. It will build up inside them and they frequently have stomach problems. It must have been a Cancerian who initiated stomach ulcers.

They will unexpectedly vent their resentment on an unsuspecting individual, if they go out of the home. They feel secure indoors, so are better cooking or tidying up the home. They have sharp tongues. Being sensitive themselves, they seem to take great pleasure in snapping at others with their pincers, generally in a verbal way. They will wonder why they make few permanent friends, so they often feel sorry for themselves. Tears that were sympathetic yesterday turn to tears of self-pity overnight.

They are naturally ambitious. Security is part of this pattern. One must have a firm and reliable base from which to go out to make a fortune. Their desire to succeed makes them grasping and very materialistic. They give nothing away and expect more in return if a bargain is made. They change from being a shrewd operator to a twister, playing one off against another. They have studied weaknesses of human nature in their efforts to be secure. So they will take advantage of any weakness of a colleague or a competitor.

They do not come openly to battle or to mischievous contact with friend or foe. They keep out of sight. They are crafty.

How Cancer Gets Along with Others

Cancer with Aries

Money/Job. Problems will inevitably arise over money. Aries makes money and will spend it. Money burns a hole in the Aries pocket. This is a constant source of worry to Cancer. They probably never come to terms on this.

At work they are both ambitious. Cancer may seem to take a back seat but will want to get ahead. Methods of succeeding differ greatly. Cancer can work from the inside while Aries has to go direct to the fountainhead. Cancer picks up all bits of inside information and tittle-tattle, and will patiently wait for an opportunity. Both are good workers and know it.

Home/Friends. Home is the most sensitive part of the Cancerian scene. They will have a comfortable home and this has to be accepted. Aries likes to be free and easy indoors. The pretty china collection and other memorabilia round the Cancer home makes Aries feel ill at ease.

Aries is always direct. A "crabby" experience with Cancer can put Aries off for good and all. Life is too short for Aries to bother with someone who cannot take a joke, or accept them as they are. Both have an adequate word for anything. These two will often show their feelings for each other if they ever bother to be friends. Lots of steam can be expected when they both blow up!

Cancer with Taurus

Money/Job. Taurus is a conservative type. They understand the value of money. It is a means to an end and must be made to work. Both will save but even Taurus may get a bit concerned at the amount being put away in the stocking by Cancer. They can work it out with a bit of give and take.

Taurus may accept that Cancer has a better sense of business than they. Both signs are industrious. Taurus can take the strain but must not be exploited by Cancer or there will be an explosion. Taurus is straightforward. They expect honesty from their staff or boss.

Home/Friends. The Taurean at home will cause no bother provided they are allowed to relax. Good food is welcome. Perhaps Taurus has to be a bit more careful where things are put, if room can be found for their simple souvenirs.

Taurus friends are usually well-behaved and easy to please. They are patient and have simple tastes. Their loyalty is beyond reproach. They will never accept a friendship without contributing their full and fair share. They try to please and value sincerity. They are sentimental and hanker for the past quite a lot. They will find Cancerians can fit in with their ways quite well.

Cancer with Gemini

Money/Job. Gemini has feet on the ground and is not a fool where money is concerned. They know, in their own special way, how to use the stuff. They do not collect or hoard, so they will try to get the Cancerian to be a bit more adventurous with funds.

Gemini is not going to stay at any job that is not interesting. There has to be a bit of enjoyment in what they do. If Cancer is astute they will see in Gemini a good intermediary or agent for their business projects. Each sign needs to follow their own bent or work will be fruitless.

Home/Friends. Gemini likes to have freedom and room to let the children be boisterous. They may be able to come to terms with Cancer who could provide a children's play room, secure and fully equipped. Children will probably be the co-ordinating point in the combined Cancer-Gemini home.

Gemini friends are varied. They may be a source of worry to Cancer in a bad mood. Gemini can let all manner of things bounce off, so they may be able to put up with Cancerian tantrums if the tantrums are not too trying on the nerves. New interest can be brought into Cancer's life by the variety of Gemini. This is no bad thing for Cancer. They will have more opportunity to study human nature.

Cancer with Cancer

Money/Job. As far as money is concerned they will vie with each other to put it away in a safe place. They will be competitive, each seeking to outwit the other in interest rates or return in some other way. No quarter will be given and none asked.

Working together can be a bit of a trial. On the other hand they will know each other's methods. They will rather have one of their sort in charge than trust anyone else. They will also keep their fellow Cancerian workmate on tiptoe for promotion or wage increases. Running a business together could be either a flop or a success, depending on how they decided to make progress.

Home/Friends. The home will get its full recognition from both. Neither is in any doubt about the sanctity of the home. They will have to take turns at cooking or dusting. Either that or agree to the duties they are each to perform. It could become a museum.

Friends will be closely vetted before being accepted, especially if they are to be guests or to stay any length of time. Even family connections and relatives may be scrutinized before acceptance. There will certainly be a record kept and all intimate details known. Once accepted, friends will feel welcome and wanted and settle down comfortably.

Cancer with Leo

Money/Job. Leo has a strong belief that money should be spent. It has to be seen, not hidden away in some secret vault. Leo will have no stocking under the mattress. Valuables are essential but are there for exhibition. They like to have money and like to spend it or have it spent on them.

At work Leo is a good worker if there are good prospects. They are much better at managing others at work or working on their own at a chosen occupation. Cancer will need to keep a low profile with Leo around and can be the power behind the throne.

Home/Friends. The Leo home is tasteful and probably large. They like room to show off their love of nice things. Cancer is also selective about the decor, but the atmosphere in the Cancer home can feel, to the Leo, a bit restrictive. They can both relax and are each a bit selective about who is welcome inside the door.

Leo friends are larger than life. Some are interested purely in the effect they create. Others are genuine, open people who wish no one harm. They can be generous to a fault. They neither suspect nor think ill of anyone. They bear no grudges though they can be a bit sensitive about appearance and pride. Some give and take is necessary for Cancer and Leo to agree fully.

Cancer with Virgo

Money/Job. Virgo believes that money has to be earned. They value money because it is hard-earned. It serves a purpose and is no problem as long as they are fit enough to earn the daily crust. They can be generous to those in need or live with very little in their purse.

It is essential that Virgo be employed or in a job. They can be lost souls without something constructive to occupy mind and hand. They can be exploited because of this. Cancer will be quick to spot this. Virgo is not a fool and will quietly resent such exploitation, until they slip away to another job and another boss. Tact is needed between these two.

Home/Friends. The Virgo home is busy. It can be untidy, though something somewhere will have to be just so. Virgo makes work where none really exists, just to be on the go. They enjoy cooking, so they will want to take turns in the kitchen. They will probably be happy to do the chores. It keeps them busy.

The gentle Virgo makes a sensitive friend. If the conversation can get away from health, food and stomach long enough, they have a wide range of interest. They enjoy watching others act. They are terrific mimics. Together with Cancer they can have a whale of a time, but they too have their moods.

Cancer with Libra

Money/Job. Libra has good business sense. They are analytical and will not take on more than they can manage. Money is to be used and seen to be used. They use their funds intelligently. They will let others do the donkey work so that their resources increase. They are experts at balancing the books or seeing that the books are balanced. This fits well with Cancer's business sense.

At work the Libran is a bit selective. They will give their all if it is, to them, worthwhile. A job is not the be-all and end-all of their lives. A partnership suits them. They can then feel more secure. At times they are indecisive and dithering.

Home/Friends. Home has to be nice as well as comfortable for Libra. Decor is important. They are seldom completely happy with the home. They like to keep up with the fashions. Old-fashioned things unnerve them. They are not collectors.

They are very sociable and will make anyone feel at home with them.

Libra has a polite way of vetting friends. They do not put up with anyone, but will try to make all their friends conform in some way to their standards. They are quite sensitive to criticism though they are far too polite to show it at the time. Many things do not fit easily into place between Cancer and Libra. Perhaps they each sense the other's weaknesses.

Cancer with Scorpio

Money/Job. Like Cancer, Scorpio has a special interest in money. They are sticklers for balancing the books and having order in their finances. They are good at looking after other people's money. If Cancer can trust a banker, Scorpio is there ready-made. Scorpios can make good use of money and are not so bothered about security. They will make money if they need it.

Scorpio is never afraid of hard work. It has to be appreciated or there will be harsh words. They cannot stand interference, so are better fitted to be boss or to work on their own. They can be hard task-masters but expect nothing more than they themselves are prepared to contribute to a job.

Home/Friends. The Scorpio home is secure. It is also efficient and spotlessly clean. It may be a bit cold for some but is genuinely welcoming to those who are invited in. Children are always welcome, and so are teenagers, who find Scorpio attentive and understanding. It's a no-nonsense place which contains a lot of love. Cancer can appreciate this.

Scorpio friends are reliable and trustworthy. Once they accept you they will be true to the end. Emotion plays a great part in their life and in their attitude to others. They hate deceit and will quickly scent anything or anyone a bit off the straight and narrow. They are by no means prudish: just straight to the point.

Cancer with Sagittarius

Money/Job. These two will never see eye to eye on money. Sagittarius will make a lot of money and get rid of it just as quickly. They are seldom poor but if they are they know they won't stay that way long. They like making and spending their own money. Banks can be, to them, an abomination. The broker makes better use of any spare cash.

Sagittarius will be a good worker, honest and conscientious, just as long as it suits his or her purpose. They are happy to work in any part of the globe. They will not disagree for long with a colleague. If Sagittarius finds a workmate is too sensitive he'll just ignore him. No offense is meant. Responsibility ties the Sagittarian down, but they are quite efficient.

Home/Friends. Home life is of little interest to Sagittarius. They take it as they find it. They collect memories and that's enough. They don't collect things. Home has open doors and you take your chances when you visit. It's friendly but don't expect to be mollycoddled. Children are not essential.

Friends are bright and breezy or may be bookworms. At least they bring in a breath of fresh air or possibly the smell of animals. They are invariably intelligent if not always well-traveled. Their conversation will be stimulating. They are happy-go-lucky.

Cancer with Capricorn

Money/Job. The Capricornian may be happy to let Cancer look after the money. They are ambitious and socially aware. They know that a prudent financier is a necessary support if they are to succeed. They will spend in the grand manner when there is some tangible return. They are possibly not as astute as Cancer and will admit this where money is concerned.

Work means much more to Capricorn. It is through work or

because others work that a career is built up. They will apply themselves to the job in hand. They mean to get on in the world and know that work can lead to this end. They are natural management material. They know how to look after people under them and get the best from the boss.

Home/Friends. The Capricorn home will benefit from the Cancer touch. Capricorn is conscious of order and appearance. They like old-fashioned things around them. They value dependable things. Tradition counts for a lot. They keep a clean and orderly, functional home.

Capricorn friends like to be sociable. They are not naturally prudish but have a sound sense of values and of appearance. They can respond to the Cancerian outrageousness or the tearful sense of drama. They like the theater. They like to be seen in the right places. They will not let you down in company.

Cancer with Aquarius

Money/Job. The Aquarian is not very interested in money. If money can be put to a good cause or gets an organization working, they are happy. The are not hoarders. Money is a necessary evil. They are free with money to those they love, and that could be an individual or a cause. This does not fit with Cancer's need for security very well.

Work is done thoroughly by the Aquarian. It is a necessary part of life's pattern, so it should be handled properly. They make good employers, because they will not interfere with individuals when working well. As employees they expect fair treatment for themselves and all their colleagues. They are idealists.

Home/Friends. The Aquarian is not greatly bothered about the home. They're quite happy for someone else to do the arranging, and Cancer is glad to oblige. All Aquarians need for themselves is a reference library or a reading room. Children are tolerated with affection but no excess emotional fuss.

They like to find things in a regular place. They get bothered when they have to search for things.

Friends of the Aquarian are numerous. They have a way with all manner of people who accept them as a central point of reference. Cancer may not understand this. They do not get involved, so make few lasting ties that will restrict them. They are loyal. They will give the shirt off their backs and think nothing of it. They hate to be crowded.

Cancer with Pisces

Money/Job. Pisces collects and can hoard. This doesn't work with Cancer's approach to money. But they usually find a use for their money before it gets too cold. They can make and spend freely according to their mood. Like their emotions, resources will fluctuate a lot. They always seem to surface, often because someone gets them out of a hole.

At work they like plenty of variety. They don't particularly want responsibility. They will happily do their own thing if it allows them to be creative and imaginative. But as a rule they like company when they work. They get on well with all their colleagues. They don't like to offend.

Home/Friends. Pisces at home is not well organized. They make home cosy but it may not be as spic and span as are many others. They are inclined to fuss around. They have a variety of things just to be sure that they can cater for all tastes. They do not stick to a routine. Meals happen when they're wanted.

Friends of Pisces have to take them as they find them. Pisces is gentle and will not offend. They have many interests, mainly in people and their doings. They can be inquisitive, but in a nice way. They gossip but are not malicious. They are extremely imaginative. They have a rare sense of exaggeration which fits in with the Cancerian drama. They can be a scream together.

Love Mates

Cancer Woman—Aries Man. He is not a man to be put off. She sees he has potential but is a definite risk. He has no thought for tomorrow and does not like to be kept waiting around.

If they first meet when she's in a good mood they will get on like a house on fire. He loves her weird sense of humor and her way of exaggerating things. Their next meeting could find her totally different and he'll wonder if he's made the right date.

She can't afford to muck about with this man. He'll be off to find someone who is more predictable. He will find out, if he stays long enough, that he is getting involved with her family as well. That is a definite discouragement.

She likes the way he pays for things, at first. Then she'll try to get him to hang on to his money. That again is a rebuff for Mr. Aries. He is the boss and will not like a woman telling him to be careful. He has no intention of being careful. He lives from day to day and that means taking risks.

They have a mutual affection for children, but she is far too attentive to the little ones for Aries. He encourages his children to be tough and brave like himself. He dislikes people who creep up on you. She has a way of getting him when he's least expecting it and that does his ego no good at all. He knows she wishes to look after him and is glad in some ways but hates being smothered in affection as much as he can't understand why she gets so moody and won't talk.

They both want to get on in the world. They have ambitions but their methods are different.

Cancer Woman—Taurus Man. His woman has to be full-blooded. He finds Cancer is very much a woman and has the emotional attraction that makes this obvious. He likes the way she will fuss over him, make him comfortable and stop him from wasting his money on buying worthless presents.

He values his money and knows what it can mean to be without. However, he makes use of his money in his own way and does not like to be refused or dissuaded when he's being generous in the way he knows best. He will get upset if she harps about saving his money.

Women are a physical attraction to Taurus. At first she can satisfy his every need. Her emotional vigor can soothe his tension. Deep down she is not a very physical woman but, being a very feminine woman, she knows how to look after her man. Her emotion makes up for any shortage of physical desire.

They are both rather sentimental. When she is moody he will sympathize with her. He has patience and can stand having his head snapped off, provided his stomach is filled. She may repent being rough with him and be genuinely sorry for hurting his deep feelings. But she will realize that she must not repeat this too often or he will look for a more comfortable easy chair where he will not be disturbed.

If he makes plenty of money she will be happy. If he lacks ambition she will be unhappy. She has the ability to encourage him to take a higher post, and he knows she means well, but he will object to being nagged. They can have a lot going for them if they both exercise their natural patience and allow each other to be natural.

Cancer Woman—Gemini Man.
This man is a bit hard to pin down. Cancer, looking for a home and security, may feel she's off the track here. His interest in the young will make her feel more at ease.

He is quite a gentle man. He may talk a lot and together they can have a wow of a time, when she's in a good mood. He won't like it when she is crabby or sulks. He'll try to liven her up with a bit of light banter but can get turned off if she takes it too seriously.

He will listen to her when she brings up the subject of money. He doesn't care a lot about saving for a rainy day so may just agree to keep the peace. He will not like it when she goes on about costs and prices. He wants a home as much as she does but will worry about paying for it after he is in residence.

She is going to find he likes to be on the move. She also doesn't mind changing houses or apartments as long as there is an improvement and she can have her say in getting it organized. He won't argue on that score.

She makes emotional demands on him that he finds hard to meet. He is not a tenacious man. He lives on easy street when he can and tries not to get too exhausted. She may not make physical demands on him but can go on emotionally and drain him. He sees things in a logical light and cannot understand why she gets so uptight, almost hysterical at times. He will learn not to worry too much about this as she quickly gets back to being practical.

They can tolerate each other but are never likely to make a great success together: A casual romance maybe.

Cancer Woman—Cancer Man.
These two know each other almost too well. Emotional depth is matched. They each know when to employ tears and when to dry up. They should make a working match, if they apply their natural common sense to the situation.

He is more considerate of her than are most men. He knows she is insecure and suffers all sorts of fears that he will try to eradicate for her. He is a gentle man in the truest sense, and none the worse for that. They must try to avoid getting under each other's feet in the kitchen or the nursery if they raise children together. A schedule of duties could solve that situation.

He will seek her advice on business, so she will be more to him than a love partner. The union between them has to provide more than a romantic and physical contact. He knows how to make her feel wanted without her needing to prompt him. They naturally will do a lot of things together that other more romantic couples would consider commonplace. They are a very commonsense pair. Once agreed as mates, they will do things together and miss nothing.

He is no less a man in her eyes for being a good shopper or

cook. She will expect him to understand her side of the bargain as she will understand his business life. They will be looking forward, right from the start, to a joint business as well as a home.

They enjoy similar interests. They do not need a lot of friends to keep them company, but they can be sociable when the occasion demands. Much of their happiness will come from their emotional rapport. They can be devoted to each other since they will feel that no one else can possibly understand how they feel.

Cancer Woman—Leo Man. He will want to look after this most emotional woman. She seems to adore him and he feels every inch a man. She will melt in his manly arms and quiver with ecstasy when they are together.

He likes to be flattered, especially by women, but he must not take this too much for granted if she is a young, attractive woman. He will find she has things in mind for him. She may be soft and cuddly but she's no pushover. He will be encouraged to spend his money wisely, even when he is buying for her. This can set him back on his heels. Women, in his eyes, always seem to be glad when he is generous.

She means this well. She will be thinking about the possibility of a nice home where he could better use his cash. He means to keep her in style so she should have no fears about that: but she will. She has an inbuilt system of insecurity that even he cannot put straight. He will find it hard to curb his exhibitionism or his passions naturally. Her ways will, at times, put a damper on his enthusiasm and then they will both get moody. She can sulk and so can he, but for different reasons. His pride cannot stand too many knocks.

She will want to look after him as a mother. He does not want that sort of loving. He likes to show his women off, to his advantage, no doubt . . . but also to theirs. She is not an exhibitionist, though she can put on a terrific act when she's in the mood. Her home and family will be her pride and joy, if they ever get around to that.

It may strike him that he is not going to be the apple of her eye once they have a family. That won't do.

Cancer Woman—Virgo Man. He is a considerate
man. He feels she needs protection. He must take her as he
finds her and this does not worry him too much. He is a sensitive man himself and knows what it can be like to feel insecure. He will try to help her practically without making a
fuss. She appreciates his tenderness, realizing he will not take
advantage of her. They are both modest when in the mood.

She will surprise him when she's feeling on top of the world.
The quiet girl shows she has another side to her nature. He is
attracted to a woman who can make up for his quietness, but
in small doses.

They both have a conservative streak in their natures. He is
prudent. Like her, he sets store on material values. When he
is sure he's on the right track he is happy to talk about families
and the little cottage with roses round the door. He has imagination but tries to keep his feet on the ground, to avoid disappointment. He is easily hurt. This she will have to remember
when she's in a bad mood. He cannot get a hurt out of his
system as easily as she. Her tears wash away suffering but he
does not cry so easily. He takes it inwardly.

She can bring out his emotions and relieve his pent-up feelings. When he relaxes he is a marvelous lover. He is physical
without overdoing it. They can be an ideal match for each other,
neither wanting to go to extremes of physical contact or emotion, when they are together and in love. They are considerate
of each other.

A great deal can come from this union. They have it in them
to make allowances and live contentedly.

Cancer Woman—Libra Man. He is a man to turn
any woman's head. She finds him attractive, gentle, courteous.
He knows how to treat a lady. She may think he can make her
feel secure but her feelings will tell her otherwise. She always
trusts her feelings. They never fail her.

He finds her attractive, sympathetic, emotional and all
woman. She may be feeling in need of assurance when he first
meets her. He will boost her morale. That may be as far as he's
willing to go. He is not one to get too deeply involved at an
early stage.

She will find out that he is as insecure as is she. He has difficulty making decisions. He hates to be cornered, and obviously does not want too intimate a relationship if it means responsibility. He will not try to possess her or to master her. He will go along with her in stages without committing himself too far ahead. He is here today and possibly somewhere else tomorrow. This is not what she is looking for. Good looks are fine, but she wants to feel secure for the future with the man of her dreams.

She can put him to the test when she has an emotional outburst. He just cannot take this. He will try to calm her down but is not prepared to put up with extreme situations that shatter his emotional balance.

She may come to think he is not a marrying man and is possibly too soft for her needs. They can quite happily have an affair and be good friends for the rest of their lives, but that's about as far as she can go if she wants to have a reasonably comfortable union.

They can quite happily agree to differ on major issues, and have a lot of fun together.

Cancer Woman—Scorpio Man. He knows she needs
to be cared for. She does not have to go into an act to let him know she wants a strong man to look after her. He can take her emotions. They stir him up inside and he knows where he stands with her.

She will relax in his strong, masterful arms. She is not going to complain about anything. She'll make sure she can satisfy his needs and he can be hungry for her love. She is a great untapped reservoir of emotional love which she has saved for this day. He knows how to tap it without draining her dry.

He knows instinctively that she loves children. When he takes her round to his place she will make her domestic abilities obvious. He likes to be looked after by his woman. She is only too glad to oblige. They both love the home atmosphere. He will take to her family and she to his without a quibble.

He is boss right from the start, but he respects her as a woman. She can get around him to get her own way in some things. She is not a submissive weakling and he will not cross her without good reason. She is an excellent manager and this, to him, is another feather in her cap. He does not want to do everything though he is happy to look after the main worries and be responsible for their mutual failing if he thinks that justice has to be done.

They can both be moody. She will not put on an act when he's quiet unless she is sure she can raise his spirits. He will take her as she comes and correct her if she seems to be getting out of hand. A look will usually be enough to make her stop nagging or getting all upset about trifles. Together they're great.

Cancer Woman—Sagittarius Man. This man is hard to pin down. She may very quickly give up trying. But she is tenacious and does not give in too easily. She will try every feminine trick in the book to make him pay attention to her. He cannot fail to react, for she is very much a woman.

He will try to impress her with his personal exploits. He's a great storyteller. She quickly latches on and can enlarge on his stories. This may surprise him, amuse him, or intrigue him. He is possibly going to get out of his depth with this emotional woman, and he would hate to drown.

He is inclined to be a loner. He gets on much more easily with men. He may be a rough diamond or just a man's man, so he feels a bit uneasy when he is with domestic women. He fears being trapped. Yet he would like to give her some protection, for she seems so vulnerable. He does not want to stay too long looking after her. She may try to get him to stay by looking after his needs. He is afraid to be mothered. He wants to roam, though he means her no disrespect. He's likely to run like mad if she starts talking about home and children. They are like lead weights when the wanderlust is on him.

On the whole he's not much of a ladies' man and she can be a bit too much for him to take. He may have a faint suspicion that she is more interested in having him as a lover and husband. That could be the last straw or it may convince him that they can have a very nice casual relationship that he can take up when he's back again in these parts. They may settle for that.

Cancer Woman—Capricorn Man. This man has all the qualifications she's looking for. She will not make it so obvious, of course. But she will set her cap for him if he's a bit slow in making the move.

He is old-fashioned. That suits her fine. He can take his time. He will not sweep her off her feet. He pays her the compliment of treating her with the consideration due, she rightly feels, to a lady.

He lets her know he is a physical man but is not going to make too much of an issue of the fact. She needs a strong physical man to soak up her emotional outpourings. He has a lot of strength, quiet strength that he will keep for her alone.

They are equally ambitious. This could be the clinching factor between them. She will help and promote and support him all the way if he is determined to make a success of his life. He will get for her what she desires in more ways than one.

When they have a home, which is a priority to them both, the family has to follow. He is not going to be jealous of the affection she will then pour on their children. He will be happy enough to keep them all in security the rest of their days.

They will make plans together, these two. Neither is afraid of the future when they are together. They complement each other perfectly through fair weather or foul. They can discuss both sides of a question without blowing a fuse. They can share and share alike, working to their mutual goal.

They know that love is a many-splendored thing that develops naturally with the years.

Cancer Woman—Aquarius Man. These two will fence a bit. Curiosity may get them together. He is attracted by her femininity. She is friendly and he likes to be liked. He responds to her outrageous sense of humor. He is a student of human nature, as is she, and delights in seeing anything or anyone who is a bit different.

On the surface he seems to her to be a strong, silent man. He should be reliable and could give her the security she seeks. He does not flap. He gets on with everyone and does not fuss. He seems a benign sort of a man.

She will find that he has great hopes for the world and is not particularly interested in families. He also spends quite a lot of his time encouraging others to put the world to rights. She believes that charity begins right here at home. She may wonder if he's fooling her, for he's such a nice man.

He may not show it, but the thought of being comfortable at home with a horde of children around him drives him up the wall. He can be an uncle or some such relative but has no plans for domesticity.

He may be cool, but is not a cold man at heart. He will not lead her up the garden path. Neither will he be able to take her emotional outbursts and fluctuating moods. He likes life to go quietly and smoothly unless he feels inclined to overturn things. She will think, at times, that he is a cold fish who has more time for friends than for intimates. At heart he does not want to get too intimate with anyone. It will cramp his style. He likes his freedom and independence. Money he can take or leave. Security is in himself. It's a no-go situation.

Cancer Woman—Pisces Man. This is an emotional confrontation. He is as excitable and dramatic as she. They can turn each other on at the twinkling of an eye. It could get a bit much and they are likely to drain each other, but they each have a great reservoir of love and affection.

He will try to please her. He feels her insecurity. He will admire the way she tries to handle this. He realizes she is no weakling, so he can let her have her way about things. She responds to his emotional needs. She will take on the role of mother quite happily, for him and for the children they will both love passionately. But he will have to do what is right by her, for he is the man and she is the woman. She can bring out the manliness in him that he never pushes to make obvious.

He has a way of getting along with people, so he does not need to be arrogant to get on in the world. She understands this and will let him look after her in the way he chooses. If he, however, tries to wiggle out of his responsibilities, she will give him an appropriate reminder. Both are easily hurt. Both can get rid of this hurt easily. They can be fed up together or on Cloud Nine in ecstasy. He can show her what romantic ecstasy can be. It appeals to her sense of drama. They do not stay in the doldrums long enough to get depressed, so they can have a high old time together.

Both love home. He can take children or leave them. He will not interfere in her plans. She can manage the domestic side and he'll not quibble. If need be he is quite capable of doing all things. He's a nice guy.

Cancer Man—Aries Woman.

This woman has a mind of her own. She will expect her man to be a go-getter. She wants a straightforward relationship with no strings or conditions. She is honest and will expect her opposite number to be equally direct.

He is a sensitive man. She attracts him by her strong personality. He may feel they could go places together with all this energy between them. He is ambitious and cannot easily turn down a good offer.

She will like his sense of humor. She can be either completely charming herself or blunt and crude. As long as he has a positive desire to get along and accepts her as she is, they'll do well together.

She is not a domesticated woman, so he will not have a mate who is going to warm his slippers. Their love will be instant and highly emotional, but is not likely to last for a long time. They have different ways of assessing things. He is naturally cautious. She is adventurous and feels herself a match for any man. She will not be cosseted or protected. He finds this difficult to accept.

She has plenty of self-confidence, or so it seems on the surface, and he has his doubts about keeping the pace she sets. He wants someone to share his emotional life and she seems to blow hot and cold as the wind changes. She may not like the way he broods when he's rebuffed and cannot understand why he should be such a softy.

They can have a great time when emotion and ardor combine

in instant love. They cannot keep up this sort of emotional pace for long stretches. An affair or the occasional get-together will please them both.

Cancer Man—Taurus Woman.
They have a soft spot for each other. She is sentimental, he is compassionate. They will feel close as soon as they meet. It may be the look in their eyes. Both have an appealing way with them, especially when downcast.

He sees in her a strong reliable woman with his best interests at heart. She is all woman, physically attractive. She sees a man who understands what it is to feel insecure and seems likely to do something about it. There is no basic problem here. He will feel he can rely on her; she seems to have good sense. She will value him and what he has to offer her. They are natural "home-birds" and know this right away.

They each have their feet on the ground. She may wonder why he has to get so emotional to make this point but is patient with him when he feels insecure. He makes it quite clear he has ambitions and will need her for support. This compliment she really appreciates.

She is stable in her moods. He can get upset about the slightest things and sulk. She is not talkative but will be patient and try to help him with a caress or a cuddle. Sometimes he will rebuff her and she will be hurt. She does not show hurt as readily as he does. He can make a song-and-dance about anything, good or bad. It is amusing up to a point but gets a bit wearing by repetition. She can become as moody as he, only for longer periods, if he does not give her due attention.

They are both a bit romantic at heart. They need some escapism to get them off the ground. The theater attracts them, for they can sit together and hold hands just like old-fashioned lovers have always done.

Cancer Man—Gemini Woman.
She is a flirt. He likes changes and understands the emotional ups and downs of life. She sees in him a man with a strong sense of humor who can be quite a laugh, or like her, a tease.

He has definite ideas about the woman of his dreams. If she

is interested she will not show her hand too soon, but play him along. She is fond of children but not particularly keen about settling down at home too early. She may feel she can manage to cope with everything he asks and still have a lively time.

He will be full of admiration for her ingenuity. He thinks her brave and adventurous, but not too forward. She has a gentle, persuasive way with her that he finds hard to resist. She may be like a child to him, and he'll want to look after her. Like a child, though, she will be mischievous and may not heed his admonitions about running up bills or having a good time while the baby-sitter takes charge. He does not like baby-sitters in his house.

She is far too astute to upset him badly. She will generally be able to persuade him to see her point of view but it must make sense or he will not be mollified. They both have a strong practical streak in their natures. She will supply the logic while he will feel strongly whether things are right or wrong.

They both like a good gossip. The day's events are a source of merriment, tragedy, mimicry and emotional liveliness. They can make love in their conversations.

Neither will make heavy demands on the other. Physical love has its limitations with them both. They each hate to sit in silence, so they can be good mates.

Cancer Man—Cancer Woman. They have lift-off right away. It depends on their moods at the time whether they have a whale of a time together or go off in different directions. They can click immediately or be too much to bear.

He knows that she needs a strong, reassuring man to look after her. He also knows she is resilient and not at all as fragile as she makes out. She feels sure he can make the grade for her if he cares to make the effort. That will show her whether he has the right sort of ambition that can get them to the top, where she wants to be.

They have things all worked out long before they are making their second date. Each will play it by ear, knowing that the other is also checking the ratings. They are not going to be caught out at this stage and will respect each other for being true to type.

Their loving is soft and gentle. He knows how to treat a responsive and cuddly woman. She will give as much love in return. She is not mean with her caresses. Neither is heavily physical. They are romantic and considerate of each other. They are patient and make allowances, for they can both be shy.

Loving is much more to them than the physical act. They will want to be settled if they take to each other. They will be planning a home and nursery together in no time at all. But they are cautious and must make the necessary arrangements. This mutual interest in detail is something they both dearly love. The togetherness they experience can be something out of this world. The ordinary routine of life is full of wonder for both. Together they can go places.

Cancer Man—Leo Woman. This relationship has its problems. She is proud though friendly. She will be looking for a man who can give her a good time and also have substance. Money is a lot but not enough.

He sees in her a very attractive, spontaneous woman who seems to be sure of herself. In his book she may give him security but he knows he must play the leading role, so he is not too sure.

There will be immediate problems if he is not too keen about spending his money on her or her entertainment. She is not a big spender on anyone other than herself but expects her man to foot the bill and be glad about it. If he is someone of social importance she can go along with his ways for as long as it suits her. He will be glad to show her off to his friends and to his family.

If they get round to sharing an apartment they can come up against further differences. He expects every place of his to be a home and she considers her abode to be a reception or entertainment place. She is choosy about having people in when they are trying hard to get to know each other, and can make him feel foolish in front of his friends.

He's a very sensitive man. He wants to make a mark for himself but he expects his mate to play second fiddle. She is not going to buy that one. She wants to hog the scene and makes no bones about it. He will be surprised at her lack of feeling, though she never gives it a thought and queens it quite happily.

This is not the sort of woman he has bargained for. She may be attractive, passionate and good company but that will not be enough. She's not a homemaker.

Cancer Man—Virgo Woman.
She has a quiet innocence. She has a twinkle in her eye and goes out of her way, he feels, to tease him. He is quick to pick up the gentle touches of the women he meets. Virgo will get him on edge to carry on their relationship.

She knows instinctively he is rather a shy man, just like herself. Her lively mind makes her ingenious if she wants to attract a man. She feels reasonably safe with him. She sees he is not arrogant, that he is eager to please and that he can be gentle. He will listen to her, indeed encourage her to talk about herself. She likes to listen to him. He talks a lot of good, old-fashioned common sense. They will grow closer as time passes.

Both are romantic, though they may not advertise the fact. He, in his lighter moments, is a bundle of wit and fun. She can mimic him and they grow affectionate together on the most everyday of terms.

She is also practical. She loves a cuddle. The physical embrace means a lot to her, but she will not make demands on any man. This man, she finds out, understands her needs and will supply them with love and a lot of emotional feeling. Barriers of modesty break down when they are together, but neither one will go too far. A lovely relationship could break under such pressure.

So they will be modest and moderate with each other, giving and taking only what they each need of the other. They achieve security together without fuss. Each is happy to fuss over the other when the occasion demands. They don't ask a lot and are quite capable of getting what they want. They should be happy.

Cancer Man—Libra Woman.
She is, to him, a charming lady who has an answer for everyone and a way of pleasing

them, too. He may wonder how she can remain so calm when things are hectic. She is not cold, but neither is she over-emotional. Yet she is so much a woman.

She will spot in him a sensitive man who has plans. She hates to be still too long and likes a man with a bit of get-up-and-go. She will follow and support such a man.

She is an analyst. She has to weigh everything up calmly before making up her mind. He intuitively wants to know what makes people tick, where their weak spots are. He is conscious of his own need for security, so he will try to find out if others have the same doubts or fears. Her composure makes him feel more secure.

She is polished, an ideal hostess and seems capable of handling any situation elegantly and with no fuss. Deep down he has an emotional need. He may wonder whether she feels as deeply as he does. She seldom does, so his intuition does not let him down if he is cautious with her. He will be as gentle in making love as she could wish. She does not like heavy physical contact but she can take his emotional ways. He finds she will do all she can to please him so he will not take liberties with her. She is delicate and he sensitive, each with a mind of their own.

She cannot abide being out of fashion. He likes the good old-fashioned things. He collects and she will throw out. They both like artistic things, but for different reasons. Love is accepted in the same fashion.

They will last together for any length of time only with a struggle. Possibly they will make good friends.

Cancer Man—Scorpio Woman. He knows right away she has him down cold. They could be meant for each other, perhaps. He will have to show his dominance or at least merit her respect. She will not tolerate men who are weak, shift-less or mean. He will feel at once that she has strength. With her he could be secure. They are both conscious of the future so they are not going to blow all their chances on a passing crush.

They are deeply emotional. He may not realize this fully till he knows her better. She has a great sense of humor and likes the way he expresses himself. She knows he is not a showoff but hides his feelings when he dramatizes life. She will not reveal her true feelings to anyone until she is quite sure of their relationship, so they can be patiently playing with each other's emotions for a while.

Neither is in a hurry. Neither wants to get hurt. Neither is a weakling but both are reserved. They each have values. They each have deep compassion. They each know what it means to care and get little in return. So they will not abuse each other, nor will they forget a hurt or kindness. She forgets very little. She does not beat about the bush but she will not willingly hurt another's feelings unless that person has hurt her before. She does not forget easily and he knows he must treat her right or it's no go.

If he is the right man for her, she will not try to make him feel less than master in his own house. She is the mature woman and knows exactly where she stands with men. She will not be with him five minutes if he is not up to her standards. Once that is agreed he has a true lover for life. Security is assured.

Cancer Man—Sagittarius Woman. She may be interesting but rather outspoken. She probably makes the first move. She seems to like being with the "boys" and chats away with them on their own level.

Cancer has immediate doubts about this woman ever running a home. He may decide then that she is a waste of his time, or still be attracted by what she has to say.

She is independent, intelligent and probably well-traveled. She does not hang around long in one area but likes the wide open spaces, fresh air and animals, expecially the wild variety. Central heating gives her the colly-wobbles. She's no home-bird.

She's a great name-dropper. This is something that can attract him. Oddly enough, he finds that she is quite old-fashioned. She is a great believer in precedent and has principles, her principles. They may not fit in with his but he can give her credit for speaking her mind and not depending on anyone other than herself. In some ways he may envy her this freedom.

Her lack of security is, to her, a form of security he'd never thought of before.

He could learn something from this lively and knowledgeable lass, something he's unlikely to get elsewhere. They can be passing lovers, but neither would expect it to last. Each can gain in experience from being with the other, even for a short while. She will promise to look him up or give him a ring when she's next around. Tomorrow she will probably be miles away.

Their togetherness will be educational rather than inspiring. They are not living in the same sort of world, so why get involved?

Cancer Man—Capricorn Woman.

He'll think she has her head screwed on right. She is attractive, physical and mature. She looks confident. He can feel she is attracted to him and this makes him bold.

She is very much a woman, though she tries to look older than her years. She likes older men and he seems to be sensible and gentle. She wants a man who is going places without being arrogant about it. He looks to her like a man with common sense and a will to get what he wants quietly and efficiently. She knows all about being efficient.

Without a lot of fuss they will both get themselves organized. Neither is in a tearing hurry, so they will get to know each other properly, just to avoid making mistakes they might both regret later.

Once can supply the needs of the other. She needs to feel his emotional passion. She has a lot of emotion inside but does not make it apparent except with the man she can truly trust. She is always concerned about her appearance or public image . . . not just the way she's dressed, but what people think of her. He will not let her down for he soon realizes she is a very warm-hearted woman deep down.

They have a common understanding that life has to be lived in a practical way. Romance takes its proper place in their scheme of things. Each has ambitions. She will make it her business to see that he gets on in the world. She has to be careful not to depress him by asking too much. But neither of them will agree to make a go of it if they are unsure of the road they are traveling. They're well suited for each other.

Cancer Man—Aquarius Woman.
He is not too sure about this woman. She seems to have no favorites. She is not a shrinking violet, or overly feminine, yet does not make a fuss and gets on with everyone.

She will surprise him with her conversation. She is a natural communicator and does not beat about the bush. She can be quite outspoken without being in the least offensive. She is not insensitive to his feelings and will take him as he is. He is surprised at their first meeting and will be continually surprised no matter how long they are together.

They are by no means an ideal couple. He is a home-loving man and she has no strong desire to be at home. She is more interested in people in general and the way they tick than in individuals.

In some ways she may seem cold. She is not at all cold. She just does not want to get involved. It slows her down. She has a lot to find out in her life and connot afford to spend time on trivialities, like fixing emotional hang-ups, families, or hangers-on. She has a great belief in independence. She will not force herself on anyone who does not want her around. She is happy to accept a man who takes her as she comes and she will give him all the love he needs. She respects freedom and will help anyone when they ask.

She gets all mixed up when emotions are heavy. This is something with which she cannot cope, so she's likely to show a clean pair of heels if things get too sticky or confined. She is, above all, honest, and possibly a bit naive until the end of her days.

Cancer Man—Pisces Woman.
These two make an ideal pair. Emotion and romance suit them perfectly. He has the manly, practical touch and she is the eternal mysterious woman.

They have a lot in common, all of it sensitive, emotional and feeling. They will read each other's thoughts. How can they disagree when they live in each other's pockets?

He will gain confidence because she needs to be looked after. At least that's the impression he may get. Her emotions are more volatile than his. He fully understands this and will be ready to reassure her when she's at a low. It makes him feel good.

She is even more tender and loving than he. She's no fool. This brings out the master in him and makes sure he will be even more ambitious. She has a bit less interest in the home than does he. They paint their dreams together. She's a great dreamer. The cottage with roses round the door will mature thanks to his efforts, and she will encourage him with her love.

She is fussy. She loves to run after him and tend to his wants. She will not nag him, but will attract his attention if she so desires by feeling a bit under the weather. When he's in ill health there is no better nurse. She delights in giving service.

She is inclined to spread her love around a bit. She's not a bad woman. She just likes to look after all who are having a rough deal, or have had a bereavement, or can't understand why the world treats them so.

He thinks that charity begins at home. He'll find she has charity for him and more.

V. Leo 🦁

The Leo Character

Leo the lion is king of the animal world. This is a proud sign and justly so. Neither man nor woman Leo will accept second best.

They are warm hearted, magnanimous, larger than life people who see no harm in anyone till it is proven. They move serenely through life, giving an appearance of superior beings obviously meant to be served.

They are conscious of their own personal role. They do not seek advice nor help, feeling they should know best. They help other less fortunate people as a matter of course. They ask nothing from their fellow human beings, other than respect or recognition of their authority. Authority often comes to them quite naturally. They are seldom looked upon with disrespect, though they may be envied.

Leos have a way of getting what they want without a struggle. They are not natural workers in society, fitting more easily into the role of boss or manager. They are well organized. Because of this talent they often give a lot of their time to organizing others. Their decisions are not usually rejected. Leos see things clearly and have no favorites when at their best. They do not take advantage of those who fall under their spell or their strength.

Left to their own devices, they are hard workers. They would rather be self-employed or the boss than have to serve someone else. But they will show due respect to anyone who has honest principles. They practice what they preach. They are naive in their relationships with others, expecting all to be as open as themselves. They are lovable people because of this simplicity of their nature.

As a rule they do not say a lot. They leave the talking to others and when they do have something to put across they do it in style. They mean what they say and do not repeat themselves.

Leos are sunny people. They want to live life to the full. They take an enthusiastic joy in doing things for the fun of it. Sports, especially where risk is attached, suit them perfectly. They are natural speculators with their own talents, physical and mental, as well as with money. They love a bet and are happy on the race track, usually as the owners of horses. They don't mind losing as long as the race is fair and the odds are right.

In love they are just as open and generous. They will treat their partner with open warmth. They do not stint their affection.

Children take their proper place with Leo. They are given the best of everything and expected to be models for their fellows. Provided they do not get in the way, children are given love and encouraged to stand on their own feet, like Mother and Father Leo.

Leos attract the attention of envious people. As a result they take a dim view of those who challenge their authority. The Lion can be quite conceited if given too much leeway. They sometimes think themselves above the law and end up in confined circumstances. This really hurts their pride. They will not talk about such a period in their lives. Because they like the good things of life, their sins often occur where riches, gold, or money are involved. Leo at worst should not be trusted with money or valuables. They fail to meet their bills, embezzle and generally live beyond their means. Despite the show they make when out in company, they could be well in the red at the bank.

They crave popularity, considering themselves to be the tops. They hate to be ignored and will go out of their way to attract attention to themselves. As a consequence they seem to others to be empty-headed and lose respect even more. Leo does not seem to recognize this, and is inclined to go from bad to worse.

Pride will stop them from admitting they are wrong. If exposed they will bear a grudge against anyone who has crossed them. They are stubborn and do not give up.

Words do not come easily. Leos are often inarticulate and

resent those who can express themselves. To compensate for this personal shortcoming, they will show off, like a peacock spreading his great tail. They cannot tolerate anyone being better than they are, and are bad losers. Instead of being the King or Queen of the castle, they will fawn on people in any position of influence in the hope of getting a favor. They find it very hard to accept their weaknesses, so they are inclined to go from bad to worse. Instead of standing alone on their own two feet they look for the support of people of low principles and so try to control the weak through force.

They will become autocratic and dictatorial if they cannot get their own way by fair means. They set more store on superficial appearance than on the truth. They will not face up to their responsibilities and let people down through broken pledges.

They will turn to the wrong people for advice because they cannot fact the truth. Anyone who will flatter them is their friend when they are sorry for themselves. What love they have is self-centered. They gradually isolate themselves from their fellows.

How Leo Gets Along with Others

Leo with Aries

Money/Job. Each has straighforward ideas about making and using money. It is not meant to be stored away for the next generation. Both signs make immediate use of money. They are quite fortunate, as a rule. They will each take chances to make their money grow. When without the stuff they will set to and make more.

Working together causes neither any problem. They are both individuals in their own right and respect each other. If there's any argument about who is boss they can resolve it realistically. Both are happy to work on their own rather than be supervised. They are generally reliable.

Home/Friends. Aries make good friends of Leo. They both have a joy of living. They are naturally lively and bear no ill will, so will get along with Leo fine. Aries is not very sensitive. This suits Leo. They can be frank and take no offense. They each like to go their own way and will not crowd each other.

The Aries at home is easy to live with. They ask little of others and can take the home as they find it. If it is not to their liking they will do something about it rather than bitch. Home is a lively and interesting place when Aries is around. Most things have a use. Aries does not like to have too much clutter. They love things that shine, like brasses.

Leo with Taurus

Money/Job. Taurus is determined to do a good job. There is mutual respect for this shared quality of character. Taurus will be quite happy for Leo to be the boss. It will save them the worry of administration and paper work. Taurus, nonetheless, will not be exploited. They have a lot of potential together.

Money is meant to work with Taurus. They are more thrifty than Leo, but both signs are conservative inasmuch as they have set ways of making and using money. Neither is going to make the other change their ways. There is usually a mutual respect. They do things thoroughly when they do them at all, So each can have a lot or nothing.

Home/Friends. Taurus needs a comfortable home to rest weary limbs. Good old solid furniture, a reliable bed and plenty of food in the larder. They are proud of their homes, and hospitable. They are not keen on going out once they are settled, so some care is always taken in making home just right for them.

As a friend Taurus is dependable. Both male and female make good neighbors and reliable house-mates. They do not expect to take out more than they put in. They are loyal to a fault, slow to anger, considerate and ready and willing to help in trouble. They do not scrounge and can be a bit moody or quiet.

Leo with Gemini

Money/Job. Gemini does not hang on to money. They are practical people and know how to make money when necessary. They take life as it comes and can be caught short. But it does not generally get them down. They will use their intelligence to raise more funds. They are never really at a loss for money. As Leos only like money for what it can buy, they understand this.

At work the Geminis are busy. They hate a boring, monotonous enviroment. They are inventive and find ways of doing things more quickly and usually better than others. They have to have room to move around. Ideally they are salesmen or representatives. This gives them plenty of scope.

Home/Friends. The Geminian home is always busy. Doors are more open than closed. They like to have plenty to read and take a delight in family games and pastimes. They are not too fussy about food. A snack will do if they are in a hurry. They are nice people in their own homes or in others. They fit in easily. A Leo's home is his castle, and must be opulent. This can lead to conflicts.

Friendship means a lot to Gemini. They try not to upset those they call friend. Leos may not be able to deal with all these friends. They have a lovely sense of humor, naive and almost childlike. Their manner is light. They can keep the conversation going in the heaviest of company. They do not willingly let anyone down but they can be a bit feckless. Even so they are usually good time keepers.

Leo with Cancer

Money/Job. Cancer will never understand what Leo does with money. The two signs are totally different in their attitude. Cancer insists on saving, even when there is no need. At worst they are miserly. This is something Leo cannot abide. Cancer could be handy to Leo as a money lender, for the Lion will pay exorbitant interest to get what is wanted.

At work they can get on together, provided one does not interfere with the other. Cancer will accept Leo as boss, probably because Leo will pay good wages. Leo will not want to serve under Cancer who is always scrimping. A Cancer colleague will be too sensitive for Leo, and possibly too sly as well.

Home/Friends. Cancer is a natural being at home. This is the Cancerian citadel. They make home the center of life, which can seem fussy to some or a haven of peace to others. They like to have lots of ornaments or memorabilia around them. A clutter is probable. They are hospitable to those they invite.

Cancerian friends are sensitive people. They do not relate too easily because they are misunderstood, being emotionally variable. Leos don't notice this until it's too late. They make caring neighbors and close friends and enjoy a long talk.

They are more interested in having family around than outsiders, whom others would call friends.

Leo with Leo

Money/Job. They should recognize each other. This may cause a struggle for supremacy or an agreement to be pals at work. Both feel they should be boss. Both are reliable and hard working, especially if they can get on without anyone looking over their shoulder. It can work out or may be a complete failure. Pride will decide the outcome.

They can try to outdo each other at spending their money, yet they are quite realistic in their more sober moments. They can amass quite a lot of capital which can be put to good use, at least that part that they don't spend on pleasure and high living.

Home/Friends. Leos in the home can be the ideal host and hostess or lions in a cage. They make home what they want. They expect visitors when they are invited. They do not like to be caught unawares, with washing on the line or beds unmade. One will keep the other alive to domestic responsibilities. They may share.

Leo friends should be nice people. They expect to be treated properly and will return the compliment. They are usually reliable and will not let an equal down. They can be a bit snobbish when tired. They mix on their own terms and do not suffer a fool gladly.

Leo with Virgo

Money/Job. Virgo is a conservative type. Money is a tool, to be used wisely and not too adventurously. They can be penny wise and pound foolish. They do not set much store on worldly goods but appreciate the practical necessities that money brings. They think they have to work for their money.

Work is the Virgoan strength. They are often workaholics. Leo will quite naturally be accepted by Virgo as the boss. There is no argument. This suits Leo. They can make a good couple so long as these social and practical roles are accepted by both. It only remains for each to allow the other to get on in their own way with their own job.

Home/Friends. Virgo likes home to be comfortable and usually orderly. It must be serviceable, though little knick-knacks do increase with the years. Pets are welcomed. Virgos do not like a lot of show in the home. Color schemes will be quiet, but tasteful. They look after the kitchen, and believe in good food.

Variety is the spice of life with Virgo. Though they make no fuss about it, they are versatile people. Their friends have a variety of talents and interests. The brashness of Leo can make Virgo feel a bit rejected, so they may not come out into their full glory as they should. Modesty can stifle genuine Virgo.

Leo with Libra

Money/Job. Libra can spend money with the best. They like to keep in fashion and will do it in tasteful style. They try to please whomever they want to impress or whom they love. Money is one practical tool for this job. They also value money but only as a means of barter. They do not hoard.

Libra can be particular about the work they do. They like things to be in their proper place. They can be fussy or particular. They will work with brain rather than brawn. They are happy with a colleague and don't like going it alone. They are usually agreeable and will play second fiddle to Leo.

Home/Friends. Libra is nice and sociable. They have a lot of friends. They find it hard, therefore, to concentrate on one, but somehow they manage at least for a short time. They set out deliberately to keep the peace. Any disagreements will be sorted out in due course, sensibly and without display or emotion.

Home is a place of beauty to the Libran. The decor and furnishings will be just as they should be. It is a comfortable place, but not to the taste of everyone. Libra likes comfort: comfort in style. They are not too keen on children running around and this may suit Leo. A nursery will be provided. Librans are excellent hosts and hostesses.

Leo with Scorpio

Money/Job. These two are likely to clash head on over money. They both value it and make use of it in their individual ways. It is a means of exercising power to Scorpio. They are always interested in managing money, especially other people's money. They can be conservative or progressive with financial resources according to their long-term needs.

At work Scorpio is a determined operator. Both sexes have a reason for working. They will do menial jobs or be the boss whenever it suit their purpose. They will not put up with injustice or interference from anyone once they are fully involved. They are loyal and don't forget anyone who abuses their efforts.

Home/Friends. Scorpio like comfort and quiet at home. They hate to be away from their own fireside, so are happier at entertaining, playing host or hostess, than accepting an invitation from friends. They like the young around them but keep them in their place. No one takes liberties in the Scorpio home, yet they will feel welcome.

As a friend few are more loyal than Scorpio at their best. They make no fuss but will be ever alert to get anyone they like out of a scrape. They usually have limited interests, so gather round themselves only those with like feelings. They hate vanity.

Leo with Sagittarius

Money/Job. The Archer is as free as Leo with money. They have a rare talent for making money by speculation. If anything they are more expert than Leo at this. They like to gamble. Money is a means to an end with Sagittarius. They will earn or win what is needed when funds are low.

Sagittarius is a conscientious worker. Both man and woman believe in doing a full day's work for a fair day's pay. They may stay at a job they like all their lives, or they may seek the wide open spaces and work willingly in any part of the world. They will not challenge Leo if the boss' place is up for grabs.

Home/Friends. Home to Sagittarius is a place to change wet clothes and have a snack. They are not home birds at all. They appreciate parents but were never meant to settle down too long in one place. They like to have a study to which they can go when they are seeking peace and quiet.

Sagittarians are very friendly people. They seldom make enemies, thought they frequently upset people by the way they say things, being honest and realistic they call a spade a spade. They are dual characters. One side is adventurous and likes the wide open spaces. The other is quietly studious. They are often here today and gone tomorrow. They don't like to be tied down.

Leo with Capricorn

Money/Job. They will disagree on money matters. Capricorn has old-fashioned ideas about money. They are as much concerned as Leo about keeping up appearances but will not waste money in the process. They are sticklers for getting value for money. They have the patience to watch money grow through careful management and will never put it at risk.

Capricorn is an expert manager or executive. If they go above this level, as they may for they are very ambitious, they can come unstuck. So they will concede the boss' job to Leo if Leo does it properly. They will be critical of all with whom they work, Leo included. They are conscientious and expect others to be the same.

Home/Friends. After business, home is the Capricorn's greatest need. They appreciate the security and comfort of a solid home. They like old fashioned things around them. They are sociable and like to show off, in a dignified way, what they have achieved. Home can be snobbish. Like Leo they do not suffer fools gladly. They are choosy about the company they keep. They can get under the Leo skin, for they assess things differently. These two signs can rub each other the wrong way.

Leo with Aquarius

Money/Job. The Aquarian considers money with equanimity. It has its uses but is not, personally, a vital necessity. As a social factor it is essential. They will save or spend as they feel fit without making a great thing about it. They are quite happy to let Leo spend theirs in their own way.

They both like to be loners at work. Aquarius can be boss, and a very good boss, allowing workers to get on with their jobs. They are not bothered one way or the other. They often end up in charge from popular demand. They are democrats, often more interested in the working conditions of colleagues than in their own.

Home/Friends. Home is accepted by Aquarius without a lot of fuss. It may be well organised or in chaos. When it is untidy, it will be sorted out in due course. They are often methodical at the office and untidy at home. They like to have reference books and literature handy.

Aquarius is the most friendly of people. They will treat everyone the same. This will offend Leo. They do not hang on to friends and can freeze any intruder out. They hate to be tied down. A true friend is all they ask. They can do without hangers-on. It is difficult to be intimate with Aquarius, but they are the truest of friends, though a bit too cool for Leo sometimes.

Leo with Pisces

Money/Job. Pisces is not very careful with money. They have it, and it's gone without trace. They are not selfish with their money. They are just as likely to give their last dime to a beggar and then beg from a neighbor. They are not proud in the material sense.

At work they are no challenge to Leo for the top job. They are quite happy to do as they are told and they will do this conscientiously. They work better if they are allowed to use imagination and don't get into a rut. They usually get on well with colleagues and management alike.

Home/Friends. The Pisces at home can be orderly or untidy. They take each day as it comes and that is how they will always live. They may like a very quiet home or have a lively home where everyone is talking. They will never allow their home to be boring.

They are sensitive friends who have a lot of talent. Leo may easily underestimate this friend's potential, for Pisces often underrate their worth. Artistic and imaginative, they can bring a different dimension into the Leo life if it is allowed. They are imtimate people and this does not always go down with Leo. They are not show-offs, but are great actors and actresses. Theaterland brings both signs together.

Love Mates

Leo Woman—Aries Man. They make a fine couple. She likes the cut of Aries' jib and he sees her as a proud beauty. They will go places, each encouraging the other.

Aries man expects to be boss. He has no time for a woman who is without fire and ambition. He will win the Leo affections if it's the last thing he does, and he's no quitter. She is attracted by his vigor. He does not let the grass grow under his feet. He calls a spade a spade and lives for today.

She will make heavy demands on his courage and his strength. She must be sure she has the right quality. He is happy to take up the challenge. That, to him, is what life is all about. They do not get in each other's way. He is not devious. He has eyes for no one else. He will see she gets what she wants just as long as he is interested.

They are a passionate couple. They will cut out all unnecessary details when they are sure of each other. Pleasure interests are mutual. He does things at top speed and takes risks. That is just what she would expect of her man. They make love as if there was no tomorrow. Indeed they seldom think about tomorrow.

Social life suits them. They can take it or leave it when they are together. If people are not impressed, they will simply take their company elsewhere. The world owes them nothing and they are quite happy with each other.

Mutual trust and honesty is the hallmark of this relationship. They can conquer the world together yet don't care a fig for the impression they make on others. The world's their oyster.

Leo Woman—Taurus Man. This man is not going to be rushed. He sees and likes her at once. She has, in his eyes, class. There is a challenge, and he cannot refuse a challenge.

She sees him as a solid, reliable man, perhaps a bit slow but with possibilities. She puts a value on most things, her men included. He should be a good investment if nothing else. He is strong. She admires strength in a man. She likes body contact with the man of her choice, so is rather choosy about that. He is eager to have her in his arms where he can show her his strength. They will not long remain at arm's length.

He has a sense of values also. He wants to show his woman off to her best advantage. He'll take a lot of stopping once he's made up his mind. She wants to be shown off and needs no encouragement, provided he goes to the right places. He's no fool and will know where they can both make the best impression.

Neither of them do things by halves. If they disagree they can sort it out right away. She will hurt his feelings, possibly. If he thinks that it is worth the suffering they will go on and improve the relationship. It's all a matter of value for money in a way, though neither would consider their togetherness to be a purely material thing.

Pride can hold them together. Pride or stubborness can separate them. They are not to trifle with each others' affections if they mean to make a life-long liaison. Each will resent interference from outside the relationship, so they will do what they want to do, come what may.

Leo Woman—Gemini Man.
She may look down her nose at this lightweight, but he has a way with him. He likes a good time and is not afraid to spend his money on her.

He tickles her fancy. She can manage him and have a lot of fun. She does not have to take his advances too seriously, so they both are happy and relaxed. Should he fall short of her requirements she can and will tell him. He takes no offense. He's a friendly man and is used to being criticized for his light-hearted acceptance of life. If he gets fed up with her demands, should they reach that scale, he'll just move on.

She will soon realize this. She can make up her mind to have him as a free-lance lover or take a serious interest in getting him to toe her line. It is unlikely she will ever succeed in achieving the latter. They'll probably both roll up laughing about it all.

There is a mental attraction. She is an original woman with

her own ideas about a number of things. He has a quick brain and can spot a phony a mile off. Social interests can make up a lot of their lives together. They can leave each other to enjoy mixed company without being jealous. This makes the following get-together that much more exciting.

He stirs her up and does not make heavy demands on her. They are affectionate, like youngsters. He makes her feel young and desirable. He knows how to attract her attention and hold her interest. He will not restrict her, for at heart he knows she's the tops. They can have a great time.

Leo Woman—Cancer Man.
This relationship will be a bit prickly. He is not a free and easy man. He knows his limitations and these could be financial! She does not want a man who counts his coppers.

He is over-demonstrative at times and then won't say a word. She cannot understand . . . nor will she tolerate such behavior in her company. She expects to be treated personally and with constant respect at least.

At times his humor gets her going. He is a bit different from her usual company, but he does got emotional. She likes to enjoy her loving direct and straightforward and can't understand why he has to be in the mood. She is always in the mood when the right man is available, even though she has to do her own selecting. She gets her priorities right and is not too choosy if she is in need of a caress. He just does not fit into her scene when he's emotional.

He does things the old-fashioned way. She does not mind that if it means he shows her respect. But she hates hole-and-corner romance and will walk out on him if he is not direct. He takes far too long to get round to the vital question. By the time he does she'll give him a short "no."

He seems to lack confidence. She is not around to be surety for anyone, especially a man. He must stand on his own feet if he is to be her man. She is boss in her own kitchen and he seems to know more about the domestic scene than he does about courtship.

They may make an emotional relationship when she is in

need of company or wants to share a problem. Long term togetherness is just not on. They are poles apart and will know it from the start.

Leo Woman—Leo Man.
The two great cats are stalking each other here. They know what to expect and will each know whether they can supply it or have the inclination. Pride can throw them apart rather than together. They do not tolerate anything below their own high standards. They can be evenly matched and then the sparks can fly.

There are no punches drawn when they are in a happy co-operative mood together. They are perfectly frank with each other and have their defenses down. This they both love. They hate to be secretive or defensive. Life will be one long pleasure round if they get their own way.

Making love is one of the great joys of their lives. They are perfectionists at making each other feel good. They each want to hold and to give. It's a great feeling. Neither is possessive in a negative way, and will not hold back that which they feel should be shared. But they each resent outside interference in their love life. They are happy to be alone with each other's company when it suits them. They are not anti-social, just agreeing with each other and showing their mutual respect and love for the other.

When they feel like it they are happy in company. They trust each other. They like to be seen together and make it plain that they are going steady. That is clear enough notice for anyone with ideas to keep off the grass.

They are, neither of them, averse to casual relationships when they are not committed to each other long term. They enjoy life too much to have any hang-ups on that score.

Leo Woman—Virgo Man.
He will find he has work to do to please this woman. She sets her sights high. She may not be a snob but she does expect her man to show he is the boss. He can be overawed by this woman's aura and composure. He is more likely to worship her than seek her partnership.

There's not much of a chance they will hit it off for very long.

A short interlude in each of their lives, perhaps. He knows his limitations and is inclined to underestimate himself. She'd rather have a braggart than someone who is humble. He will not make a show. He is inclined to get behind or disappear altogether when she makes a public appearance. She likes the bright lights and he is afraid he'll get dazzled. She'll dazzle him all right, but will not feel it's been worth her trouble.

He is a practical, conservative man. She may be conservative inasmuch as she wants to retain her position, but she is not the lady to save her pennies. He will not be able to keep his in his purse or pocket if she takes him out. While he expects to succeed by work and service she expects to be served and will bend the knee to no one, with the possible exception of Maker or President.

He is rather afraid to take a chance. That really is about the last straw with Leo. She can see he has a certain type of courage, but it is not the sort that gets her going. She may find it hard to be polite to him when she's in the mood, though she will like the way he fusses over her.

These two may have a passing romance or affair but are not likely to make a long term go of it.

Leo Woman—Libra Man. He has a lot of polish. He will flatter this glamorous woman and won't fail to make an impression. She will like his manner. They make a fine pair in company. He says just the right things and she has all the charisma that's needed.

Libra man is not as dependable as he appears on the surface. He can charm all the ladies but has to be careful how far he goes with some. He gets out of his depth too easily, so he has to keep a tight rein on his promises and his emotions. She is probably a bit too overpowering in her passion for him. He will manage in occasional spells but cannot sustain her speed.

He knows his limitations. He will keep the relationship going for his whole life if it is necessary or convenient. But he will not commit himself to her if he feels she is going to dictate. On the surface he will try to please and may seem to be giving in to her every demand. He never does concede everything, so she may be kidding herself if she thinks he's her lap dog, but she occasionally will settle for this sort of attention when she has nothing better to do.

He has ambitions. He likes his comfort. He is, like her, not overenthusiastic about earning his living by hard work. They have a lot in common which they can intelligently put together to make life easy for them both. If they both don't push it or stand on their dignity they can have a loving and happy time together.

There is scope for a light-hearted occasional relationship here, or a long lasting link that gives both a lot of joy and peace.

Leo Woman—Scorpio Man. Here we have a trial of
wills. Both these two are proud. They will each wish to dominate the other. No quarter asked and none will be given, for they have very basic ideas about male-female ties.

He is immediately attracted because she is proud. He does not respect a woman who scrapes and bows. He will either try to conquer her or may dislike her. His judgments are never half-way. If he does not like the cut of her jib he'll just ignore her. That will really get her upset. Should he decide to make her his mate, he will fight to the death to make her his alone. She does not like outsiders to interfere in her life. He will really show her what that means. His love is total and jealous. He will not let her get far from his sight till he's quite sure she is faithful. He does not mind having a good time: he can stand the strain, physical, emotional and material. But they must have that good time together, exclusively.

He is a possessive man. She hates being a chattel. She will not be any man's chattel or kept woman. He will have to accept this or he has a bitter and resentful woman on his hands.

He is a man of deep emotions. She is a woman of passion. She will burn herself out before his strength fails. He can dampen her ardor when he's moody.

They can have stand-up fights without losing mutual respect. They have to trust each other completely or it's no go. He is not a social type, so he may balk at showing her off to his influential friends. It's very much up to them. No one else will decide.

Leo Woman—Sagittarius Man. They make a happy-go-lucky couple. Both have a great desire to live and be free. Neither will cramp the other's style. He is not at all sure about getting linked for life but will make the most of their time together, be it short or long.

His courage intrigues her. She likes to listen to his tales of the adventures he's had. She believes all he says, for she appreciates that he is a gifted story teller but he can't invent it all.

They have a lot of interests in common. He is a man's man and is not too bothered whether she wants his company or not. That's a challenge to Leo who will prove she is worth his attention or die in the attempt. She won't throw herself at him but will at least try to teach him a lesson. His lack of courtesy or consideration she can take, but only from Sagittarius. Deep down she knows he likes her and appreciates the female form but he hides his feelings by talking.

They are a passionate pair. He does not have her staying power but is worth every moment of their togetherness. He will get closely involved if she will allow him room to breath. She values her own liberty too much to deny him that. She knows he is honest and will trust him.

He doesn't enjoy her social ways. He'd just as soon be studying or taking a trip into the wilds as attending a social function. But he can take his chances. He's a speculator and is not in the least jealous. They have a lot in common and can make a go of it.

Leo Woman—Capricorn Man. They are not too sure about each other. That could be the attraction. One may just be inquisitive enough to want to find out the missing link.

He's a conservative man with ambitions. One could be to make this attractive woman his mate. She does not like being anyone's ambition. She wants a lover who pays her due attention, undivided attention. He is fascinated at the way she conducts herself. He can see her as the ideal hostess for his influential friends. He's likely to be a social climber or at least a man who means to advance in the world.

She may be modestly impressed by him. She can see he is

a man of some influence, though he does not flash his money around. She will put him to the financial test. If he can make her comfortable and happy in the manner to which she feels she's entitled, she will consider his advances. He is patient.

She is not a patient woman where love is concerned. She makes her own conquests and he may be taken over. He is strong and physical. He likes to keep that side of his nature under wraps, but in private he does not hide his ambitions or desires. He can be a worthy champion if he can convince her that he is a man of substance.

They both have a liking for social life. He will be happy to let her take the limelight at the appropriate time . . . and to foot the bills. But he does not waste time or money on something or someone who does not help him towards his goals.

They both should know what they want. They are people with feet on the ground. It's up to them.

Leo Woman—Aquarius Man. This cool man can infuriate her. He makes no more fuss of her than he does of any other woman. In fact, he's not apparently bothered about any. She will feel obliged to put him to the test.

He's a friendly man. She sees at once that they have a lot to offer each other. He takes her as she is and does not try to force her in any way. He will happily pay her compliments but is not sloppy or out to impress. She will wonder if he has any ambition.

They enjoy social life together. He, like her, does not get involved with people. They will be intimate with each other only. He pays her the compliment of his undivided attention when they are lovers and pledged to each other. She will feel guilty when or if she is tempted to break her pledge because she enjoys living. He will be hurt if he knows but is a tolerant man and accepts the failing of human nature.

He has great ideas for the world. She can encourage him in this respect. She can see the long-term purpose of life through his eyes. Deep down she is an idealist. They can create new hopes together. He makes her aware that there is more to life than the simple carnal pleasures. This makes her admire him all the more, for he asks so little of her and will freely give her so much.

There is no one else who can make her aware of her creative potential. He has it in him to broaden her whole life, give her a goal and a purpose by his side. She can truly love this man.

Leo Woman—Pisces Man. He may seem a bit soggy to her. He is not pushing. He seems content to be trodden on. She will ignore him completely unless something unusual happens.

He can be an unusual man. He does not seek to impress anyone by his strength, courage or showmanship, but he knows what makes people tick. He's a bit of a magician.

He is a most emotional man. She finds his attention either flattering or a bit too much. He makes her see the funny side of life. He takes all things as they come and can act any part. She is intrigued by his imagination.

As lovers they can hit it off if they are in the right mood, or just not get together at all. He is a man of changing moods. When he's on a high he can charm her and win her heart, for a while anyway. When he's low she will get impatient with him. He is unreliable in this respect, so she is not going to put up with his emotions on a long-term basis. But she will accept his caring love when they are both in the mood.

He is a fuss-pot. It is difficult to make him concentrate on anything for very long. He is never going to concentrate on her until she is ill and that's not on her schedule if she can help it. He spends a lot of time on people who are no-hopers. This is not her idea of living. She is independent and has a lot of pride. He seems to have no pride at all.

It's very unlikely they will have a lifetime together. Love is wonderful, so who can be sure?

Leo Man—Aries Woman. She will have to accept him as the boss. It is not a thing she will advertise, but in her heart she is not troubled. He is a man of appearances and substance in her eyes. To him she is a firebrand who really turns him on as a passionate man.

They are meant for each other and are never likely to forget it. They are jealous of each other without being destructive. They are individuals with minds of their own but willing and happy to go hand-in-hand through life together.

He is a truly generous, loving man in the grand tradition. As long as she is true he will never let her down. She will never meekly accept his rule but there is no one else in her life while he's around. They are both attractive to the opposite sex and know it. This attracts them to each other more strongly.

Neither will interfere with the other in their aims and ambitions. Where possible they will cooperate. But they are both individuals and must do some things in their own way and style. On this they agree. No one will come between them. When the need arises they can gang up and take on any competition.

Their love-making is ardent. They know exactly when each needs the other. They do not need to play for time or make a heavy thing of love. It is, to them the most spontaneous and intimate thing in their lives. No one else can possibly understand how much this matters to them.

They are passionate. Life is immediate and for living in the present. Tomorrow may never come, so they make the most of today. They are not selfish, just very much alive.

Leo Man—Taurus Woman. There is a strong sexual attraction between these two. She is a vigorous woman looking for a man of substance. He will convince her of his manhood.

They do not immediately fit each other's style. He likes her because she's a woman and there is no doubt about that. But she may be a bit complacent or slow off the mark. She doesn't quite have the polish he expects of his women. She is just as likely to tell him take a hike if he shows this, so he has to be careful if he's really interested.

She pulls no punches. If she is interested in him she will listen patiently while he tells her all about himself. She will coo and flatter him. She is quick enough to see his failings. This woman knows what she wants in a man but is not going to miss an opportunity through being too choosy.

He will be choosy if he's acting normally. He likes to be seen with well–set-up and regal women. He expects to have the pick of the bunch at any time. He's not a hole-and-corner lover.

They each have their pride. If this get-together is to mean anything they will come to terms. Neither will weaken. He will take the male role and she the female. That does not mean that one is considered better than the other, just that they can accept each other as lovers with a strong desire that has to be satisfied.

She expects body contact and he knows this. He may expect more, which she will give when she is content that he cares. She is a sentimental and soft woman and does not like to refuse a worthy man.

Leo Man—Gemini Woman. She gets him going. She is a tease. He will chase her but she is fleet of foot and not easily caught. She keeps that little distance from his reach till she is sure he has got the message.

He'll probably think she will make an ideal partner for a mild flirtation. That is the impression she gives. She is not as superficial as he thinks. She has a mind of her own and knows what she wants, but she is very much a female and believes in window dressing. He has to get to know her better if he is to have her heart, so she will keep him on a string. That's something he won't admit, not even to himself.

She is a nice woman. She is intelligent. She will talk as an equal with him on a number of subjects. He will become impressed by her knowledge and quick wit. Every so often there will be a mercurial flash between the two of them and he's aware that she is still teasing or putting him to the test.

His crown can slip a bit if he does not play her game. But he also has his cards to play. She has a strong attraction to him. He is something, even though he obviously puts on an act to impress her. She can see that he is a nice man, a sincere man with a loving heart. She will not tease too long just in case he decides to give up the chase.

They can take each other as they are. Neither wants to restrict the other's freedom. They have a mutual desire to live life fully without getting tied down to routine. They have the situation weighed up and can either flirt the rest of their lives as true friends or tie the knot. No regrets from either.

Leo Man—Cancer Woman.

She can have him worried for a while. She is so much a feminine woman that he wants to protect her. She sees him as the man who has everything. She has to persuade him to share his strength with her. It's all a matter of procedure and tactics.

She attracts him by her lively behavior. Her sense of humor is unusual, to say the least. She will attract attention, even when he cannot pull the spotlight. Now *that* must be an achievement in his book. He's seeing her at her magnetic best when she's like this. She knows when she holds his attention and will not let him go too easily. She hangs on to any catch she wants to bag.

He will find she is a bit too emotional or changeable for his liking. He is honest in his love. He plays it straight down the line with the woman in his life at any moment. There is no question about his intentions and he hates to be misunderstood. He is choosy about his women. They must not make public exhibitions of themselves and take the limelight when he's around.

She has too many moods for his liking. Today she is full of life; tomorrow she will be doubtful, in tears and totally insecure. A little of that appeals to his manliness and he will reassure her. But he expects once to be enough. He does not want to repeat the lesson.

He is generous and will give her a good time. She cannot resist the temptation to mention money and security. This will get under his skin like nothing else. After that there's little hope of togetherness.

Leo Man—Leo Woman.

They know each other very well. The two great cats know how to stalk each other, and what to expect. Each will know immediately what the other wants, and whether they can supply it. Their high standards may throw them apart when others might think they should get together. Neither will settle for anything less than the best; when they are well matched, they will work very well together.

These cats play with their claws extended. When they are in a bad mood, this can be devastating to the person on the receiving end. When they are in a good mood, they drop their defenses and are perfectly frank with each other. Each will see this as a good thing; both hate to be secretive or defensive. Since Leos are kings of the jungle, they hate to defer to anyone's sense of propriety. They will be very happy if they always get their own way.

When they are well-matched, no couple can be happier. They love making the other feel good. Neither is possessive in a negative way, and they will share all they have with each other. Outsiders are not so fortunate. They resent interference. They are quite happy by themselves. They don't dislike other people; they just feel no one else can show them the same kind of love and respect. At other times they are glad to be out in company, being seen as together. They like others to see they are attached.

They won't insist on a long-term commitment if the other doesn't want one. They can enjoy life one moment at a time.

Leo Man—Virgo Woman. He may pass her by without a glance. He may feel she's a bit of a mystery. His interest, once aroused, has to be satisfied. He must know all his subjects and she has something he cannot quite fathom.

She can play him along. She is a coquette. She knows that men seek to overpower her, so she appears to be a frail, virginal maiden. If she is truly this oh-so-pure woman, she will tell him so, modestly of course. If she is the earthy maiden who knows all about her body, she can lead him a dance.

Leo will not know what she is hiding from him until he gets to know her better, so he will not try too hard to belittle her or make her look up to him too much. He may indeed, lower his standards, at least in his eyes! She does not set her standards by the same mark as does he. She knows what is good for her and can get it. She will just as easily put him off the trail as she got him on it.

He can learn a great deal from this Virgo woman. She is loyal. She will not demean herself. She will respect him if he is true but will not lick his boots. He will realize she has a lot of feminine talent and versatility to offer. She is mentally alive, ingenious, and has a dry, earthy sense of humor. She likes life and can live it happily with her feet on the ground. She has no plans to take over his social limelight but she will help him quietly to maintain and strengthen his image. She is not jealous and does not want him to envy anyone or anything on her behalf.

She has pride. If he can accept her simple code he can live with her. She can be fun, otherwise.

Leo Man—Libra Woman.

She will set out to catch his eye. She does that to all of the men. He sees a polished, intelligent, sociable woman who never seems to change, never seems to flap or lose her temper.

She will flatter him. He may try to flatter her. He need not bother. She's forgotten more about controlling people, especially men, than he will ever know. She seems, to him, to have all the feminine attributes. He attracts her because of his self-confidence and the way he does not get intimately involved with anyone in public. He is attractive in a very masculine way. She may encourage him to hunt her, for she will see that this man is not going to be put off once he has decided on his queen.

There can be a lot of love-play between these two before they make any firm decision. She does not reach any decision quickly. She must have many things to weigh up or this would not be the case. He'll find that she is a perfectionist. She is not too impressed by body contact, though she knows it is all part of the mating game. She will keep him at arm's length for some time, unless he gets impatient.

He will not want to dominate her into submission. She obviously tries so very hard to please him and yet will elegantly hold him at bay. When they are sure of each other's devotion, she is a most affectionate and loving woman. She does not need to show passion. She can raise his enough for them both. She will fan his fire, but never crudely.

He will realize he has a genuine lady here and would be a fool to let her get away too soon. They both need the other sex. They happily can agree.

Leo Man—Scorpio Woman.

He recognizes a woman of character and strength. She will accept his advances. She will say nothing to stop him when he advertises his assets. She's heard it all before, so many times.

He finds her magnetic, simply as a woman. She knows this without him realizing the fact. She is a woman who loves deeply and will have it no other way. She can have a good time with him as a fling or decide he is the one and only. If she is to have him as her lover and life-mate, then he'd better not cast his eye in any other direction.

He will quickly realize that he can stir up a hornets' nest with her. Her smouldering passion is as strong, if not stronger, than his. He will enjoy their togetherness. He will see that he cannot dominate her sexually. She is a mature woman and knows all the tricks. She does not call them tricks; they are her nature. She may be impressed by his pride, for she too has pride. She will not be impressed if he boasts. She believes in action from a man. He has to convince her of his substance. Performance is what counts.

She is quite happy to have a social life, but she can take it or leave it. She will never let him down no matter how catty or envious the opposition may be. They will have a fantastic love life. All they both need from the other is honesty. They do not know the meaning of half-measures, so they can accept each other right from the start. They will click or will fall apart, it's that simple. Mutual respect can grow into strong mutual desire. Neither will find it easy to break this bond once it is forged.

Leo Man—Sagittarius Woman.

The attraction is instant. They each have spirit and know it. They know right away they can have a good time together.

Neither is seeking a lasting relationship at first. They each want their freedom, though he may want to dictate the terms to some extent. Sagittarius is his match here. She lets him know she is not for sale if he's looking for a domestic mate.

They are ideal for an affair or romantic encounters when they both feel inclined. She is happy in his company as she is in the company of any man with a sense of adventure. She is happy to take him on as an equal at outdoor sports. This will open his eyes. She makes no particular attempt to beguile him in maidenly ways. She gives as good as she gets. She will do her own thing her own way, and expects his appreciation. He will see that he cannot tell her the usual tale and get away with it.

She also has a tale to tell. She may have been around the world more than he has and have a lot to say on the matter. She pays little attention to what he says. Neither is going to heed the other's advice if any is given. They have to be themselves and that's flat.

She does not make any fuss about getting on in the world. The world does not owe her a living, so she is not bothered about hitting the social headlines with or without him. That's his business.

She will return his passion. They make good lovers and enjoy this being together. But he is not going to get her willingly into apron or even royal robes. He has to make her feel wanted and independent.

Leo Man—Capricorn Woman.
She wants to advance. She will see him as a man with potential. There can be mutual admiration with a certain tension right from the start.

She is practical. She wants her man to be a physical man and a man of the world, all rolled in one. She has high aspirations which she will want realized by her partner. She will make her own contribution, for she is no lightweight. She is prepared to do her full share in any worthwhile union and can suffer willingly to get what she wants. She is no martyr, but she can accept the hardships of life along with the best.

He does not intend to suffer in life if he can help it. This is a new angle and one that has him a bit worried. He wants to be a shining light and will agree with her about getting to the top. Neither is content with half measures. They want to be admired and looked up to.

He will like her as a woman, because she is conscious of her position. She has, like him, a lot of pride. She is as choosy as is he. They have a lively admiration for each other.

Her practicality he will find hard to accept. She can be hard and, he may fear, a bit tightfisted. She likes to appear in public and be regal, but not in the manner he likes. She has designs about everything. He is naive in comparison. She may be calculating and an excellent manager, but he never feels completely free in her company.

They can make social and friendly links. A life-long tie seems unlikely.

Leo Man—Aquarius Woman.

This is the meeting of opposites. It's a challenge and a recognition. She is cool where he is passionate or spirited. She will not bat an eye when he recites his virtues. She'll wait till he can prove it.

There is a continual appraisal between these two. Neither will get away with anything. He knows she is his match and she has a respect for him that is not apparent to the casual observer.

He is possessive, or wants to show his strength and power. She will take that as given and not be in the least perturbed. She has no intention of being possessed or dominated by anyone. Her independence is to be admired. He is the first to grant her the respect that is her due.

She fans his fire by remaining detached. He knows she is as honest as he. She will not go from the straight path of their shared love once she is agreed, but she will not be pinned down to a queenly role or be his handmaiden. She is a monarch in her own right, though she would give it a different name. She is a democrat and does not like him when he throws his weight around.

She will freeze him in his tracks if he takes liberties. She will be as ardent in her love as any other woman when she feels so inclined. She will always consider him her best friend if he wants to love her or stay with her. That is the highest award she will give to anyone, man or woman. She bears no ill will and will not be jealous or covet what is his.

He has to take her as she is. Nothing is going to make her a hypocrite. They make their own choices.

Leo Man—Pisces Woman.

This lively, loving woman can be a bundle of fun. She's all woman and knows it. He will probably want to be in charge. She will not object. She makes no attempt to stand on her dignity. She willingly agrees to be bossed around as long as she is treated like a woman.

She has very loving ways and will flatter him without knowing it. She admires men with strength and purpose. It saves her having to make all the decisions. She knows all the feminine angles and ploys and is quite happy to let the men be the men.

She is most emotional. She is up and down like an emotional yo-yo. He likes this for a while because it is different, but he can take only so much and will not be able to get on with his life if he has to change course to suit her moods. He will be firm with her, and it may work for a time; but she is just not capable of controlling emotions all the time and seems to go from crisis to crisis. That is too much for the realistic Leo.

He could not possibly leave her in the lurch, though he may be tempted. He knows he can come back to her when he's in need of emotional refreshment. She will want to share his ardor from time to time though it saps her when she takes on too much. She does not want to damp down his ardor, nor he to drown in her emotions.

They will make their own arrangements and see each other when they need mutual comfort. They are good for each other in small doses but too much of a good thing wears love thin.

They are both genuine and know this.

VI. Virgo

The Virgo Character

Virgos have a use for everything. They are THE practical people of the zodiac. They keep their feet on the ground while their eyes take in everything around.

They have little time to spare and like to be busy with constructive things. Unproductive time is, to them, pure waste. Their main role in life seems to be getting things to work. They are never workshy themselves and can't stand people who won't work. Give them anything that is jammed up and they'll put it right. This applies to people as well, so they are noted for their healing abilities, and are often nurses, health advisers or doctors.

Health interests makes the Virgoan a good-food enthusiast at times. They are interested in diet and food content. They have a great understanding of purity, wholesomeness and value for money. They will never exaggerate the qualities of anything until they have made their own analysis. They take care of themselves and in consequence are able to advise or encourage others on sensible remedies or methods. They have no patience with careless people or slipshod methods.

Virgo may pass unnoticed in a crowd. They are never "pushy." They will be present, nevertheless. They do not like to be involved with other intelligent people. Because they are modest they will take a quiet back seat and only insist on their version when they cannot contain themselves any longer. They like to talk but, as a rule, do not waste words. Actions speak louder than words, in Virgo's book. Advice they give will be good, well-tried and based on practical common sense. They are often the strong, wise people behind the scenes who know all the answers but who never get public acclaim or credit for their contribution. They do not like to be in the spotlight but they do like to be acknowledged for their special know-how and individual skills.

Virgo is the jack of all trades or the maid of all work. They are most versatile. Their professions range from the highest to the lowest. They only specialize in perfection, doing whatever they set out to do in the best way possible. They are often proud of never missing a day's work or a performance. They will never give up till they feel they have any undertaking completely buttoned up. They are their own greatest critics.

They have a lively, earthy sense of humor. They are terrific mimics, and frequently earn their living in this way. They are conservative but not, as a rule, prudish. They consider love as a practical means to an end and give themselves wholeheartedly in love. The young find Virgos understand them. The perpetual Maiden has a young mind and a special place for children. Both male and female Virgos love children and the love is freely returned. Virgo parents bring out the natural potential of the young. Children in their care feel free yet obedient.

Virgos are often misunderstood. This is probably their own fault. They can be particular in the extreme, though they would never admit it, and find fault with everything they see or touch. They do not even accept their own efforts without criticism and on the surface will underrate themselves. They are quick to check the individual, however, who finds fault with their work or habits.

It is their personal sensitivity which damages them most of all. They like to be in company or to get involved but their criticism or carping will stop people from being their friends. So they are often lonely, overlooked or "left on the shelf." Their humble acceptance of a minor role gets them ignored and they draw more and more into themselves. They then can become lonely old maids or bachelors.

They will busy themselves with whatever can occupy their minds and refuse to give up. This makes them timewasting and interfering. They can lose their sense of personal initiative or invention and get into a rut. They will not come up with ideas and behind the scenes will criticize all those who are above them.

Love seems to escape them, once they have had a misunderstanding with a potential partner. They are afraid to let go and lose the lively luster of their youth.

They become hypochondriacs quite easily. They will try all manner of patent medicines and pills. Their imagination runs away with them when it come to ailments. They look up medical books to "give" themselves some complaint that will be different from that of their equally ailing friends.

Dieting becomes a habit with them and will do them more harm than good. They become cold and unsociable and take a lot of understanding. They really need a cuddle to reassure them but just reject those who can truly give them love.

They go off on their own and will become more disillusioned or bitter as the years pass. They often live long, so they can punish themselves more and more. They will know this, no doubt, but somehow seem to take a delight in martyrdom, untidyness and demeaning occupations. They are their own worst enemies.

How Virgo Gets Along with Others

Virgo with Aries

Money/Job. Aries does not believe in holding onto money. The prudence of Virgo can cause friction. A nice item bought at a good price will bring them together, but their individual methods of handling money will never quite be in agreement.

Aries is not lazy. These two can work well together since they both have feet on the ground. Aries is likely to be the boss or take the initiative while Virgo follows happily as long as the job is worthwhile and productive. They keep each other on their toes.

Home/Friends. Aries brings a lot of life into the home. They are honest and will be happy to let Virgo keep order and system in the home. Aries will ignore Virgo fussiness to avoid arguments. They like home to be somewhere to live and not just a place to sleep or be a show piece for visitors. Agreement is probable, despite the occasional disagreements.

Aries make good friends. They do not take offense too easily. Virgo will appreciate their honesty. Both signs are intelligent and one can put that little bit extra into conversation that the other has overlooked. Aries will not get involved in health or dietary affairs. They will agree to differ on many things.

Virgo with Taurus

Money/Job. Taurus values money. That's fine by Virgo. They each know how to save and to spend. Neither is going to disagree with the other to any great extent. Taurus will have big ideas about getting and using money but they are both prepared to earn their daily bread.

Each has a determination to work. Taurus gets more easily into a routine but Virgo will soon follow if the routine is productive. Neither is very keen to be the boss. Taurus will usually take the role because they don't like to be messed about too much and Virgo can be a bit finicky.

Home/Friends. Home is where you put your feet up, in the Taurus book. Virgo will do all the fussing around and this will suit Taurus. They both like good food and comfort, though Virgo may be a bit on the choosy side. However, they won't fall out. Both can cook.

Taurean friends are easy to get along with. They are not too talkative and enjoy hospitality. They may be difficult to move from their own fireside but are pleasant folk when they get used to company. They have an earthy sense of humor. They are reliable in a crisis and will not panic. They can be trusted and have their feet on the ground.

Virgo with Gemini

Money/Job. Gemini is a practical, worldly-wise person with money. They seldom miss a chance to make a quick profit. Virgo is alert to opportunity and will respect the ingenuity of Gemini. They can make a lot together. Gemini may need watching when it comes to spending the stuff. Virgo is the better banker.

Each has a lot of versatility. They can cope with anything that comes along. Gemini is more inclined to change jobs, but usually to improve their chances. They can get under each others' feet if working together. Virgo will probably work out a sensible schedule. Neither is keen on being boss.

Home/Friends. Geminian friends are intelligent and probably talkative. This suits Virgo who is always ready to put in his or her oar. Gemini is gentle enough not to stop Virgo from participating. The two signs have something in common and make a go of most things.

Home will be a lively place. It may be tidy or untidy but is unlikely to be dull. There will be a lot of gadgets and time-saving equipment around if Gemini has anything to do with it. Jobs will be left undone but this will not affect the general efficiency of the home.

Virgo with Cancer

Money/Job. Cancer is prudent. Even conservative Virgo will find Cancer hangs on to money too tightly. They may have difficulty in agreeing how best to make use of money but will agree when it comes to putting it away in a safe place. Cancer can make too much of an issue over money.

Both signs are good workers. Virgo will be able to get on with the job in hand knowing that Cancer will not pass the buck. Cancer can be a bit bossy. They will each be critical of the other. They can keep each other in line or get on each other's nerves.

Home/Friends. The Cancerian home is the most important feature of life. Virgo may not accept this as easily as Cancer may think. Cancerians like to run any home, and this can cause domestic strife. Virgo will go along and keep the peace but is bound to have something to say in the course of the day. Together they can make home charming and peaceful or the opposite.

Cancerian friends can be a bit sensitive. They are never really at ease out in the world. They need to have security and outside the home are a bit choosy regarding friends. They are emotional and have their ups and downs. Both Virgo and Cancer are misunderstood because they are touchy. Nevertheless they should be able to see this in each other.

Virgo with Leo

Money/Job. Leo is not going to hang on to money any longer than possible. They will earn or win money and will spend it in the grand manner. Virgo will have a job containing them. The two signs are most different in the way they spend. Best that Virgo be the treasurer if that can be arranged.

Leos will work hard and honestly. They are not too keen about doing chores, so they make better bosses than employees. Other than that they'd rather work for themselves. Virgo will be happy that Leo takes on the boss' role. Leo will plan and Virgo will operate. There will be no disagreement about who does what so long as they are both honest and conscientious.

Home/Friends. Leos like home to reflect their position in life. They want it to be just so when anyone calls. Virgo has a functional home where there is a place and job for everything. Each has taste but in different styles. They can make home a comfortable place and look after their guests.

Leo friends can be very big-hearted and generous. They will possibly overawe Virgo for a while. But Virgo will expect them to live up to their claims and expectations. Virgo can bring Leo down to earth in a quiet way without offending their pride. They can take each other as they are without falling out.

Virgo with Virgo

Money/Job. They will each have their individual quirks but will generally agree on saving and the amount that can be spent. They will keep an eye on each other, so they are not likely to go over the top either way. They are both excellent bookkeepers and like to get value for money.

There will be no quarter given at work. Each will strive to outdo the other. They will watch points jealously. Some unnecessary time can be spent watching the other if they are not conscientious. They will probably be happiest if each does a particular job so that neither one is either boss nor employee.

Home/Friends. Home can be a busy place. Many jobs may be left unfinished, though this will cause no great problem.

They will each have their pet fad and can attend to that to their heart's content, so long as the other does not poke a nose in too far. The kitchen will be well stocked with first-class food, but nothing is going to be wasted.

Friends come in all sorts. Both have interests that attract a variety of acquaintances. They are not too keen to make lifelong friends but like to have intelligent and understanding people around. They will be quiet and considerate to neighbors, who neither will disturb.

Virgo with Libra

Money/Job. Librans can be very practical about money. They like the quality things of life and are prepared to pay for them. They will therefore need to have sufficient cash handy to satisfy their changing demands. They like to keep up with fashion, and that costs money. They will save but only for some item they want in the near future. They may find Virgo too fussy about money.

Librans are conscientious workers. They don't like physical work but have plenty of intelligence and are not wasteful. They are easy to get along with. They can save Virgo much unnecessary labor by the use of their knowledge. They will probably be more happy as boss or overseer than doing all the donkey work.

Home/Friends. The Libran at home is as pleasant as in any other situation. They like to be up to date. Old fashioned things turn them off. They like light and delicate things around them and they like their comfort, so they want to relax and entertain at home. Virgo will be glad to keep everything in order.

Librans usually have a number of friends. They are naturally sociable and will make a point of getting on with anyone if they have to. They can usually get anyone round to their way of thinking, so they can keep the peace or make everyone feel wanted. Intelligent conversation and discussion comes easily.

Virgo with Scorpio

Money/Job. Scorpio can be very tight with money. They are excellent bankers and know how to apply a squeeze. They are well-disciplined but not mean. They can be trusted with the money of others, so they are the natural keeper of the money-box keys. When they have something really worth buying in mind they will go out and get it, then save again.

At work the Scorpio is thorough and perservering. They will not admit that any task is too much for them. This will suit Virgo, who also has a lot of pride in work. Scorpio does not take orders easily, so, of the two, is the natural boss. They are systematic, and this will suit Virgo, who often likes to be shown what is to be done.

Home/Friends. The Scorpio home has to be comfortable without being cluttered. They are very clean people. The kitchen may have to be shared. They like to cook and enjoy good food and drink.

Friends of Scorpio can be a very select band. Scorpio will only take to those who have substance. They do not like to associate with people who talk but do not perform. Their friendship is very special. They will not fail if asked for help. They make no fuss. Virgo will appreciate their company in quiet periods when silence is golden.

Virgo with Sagittarius

Money/Job. The Sagittarian is not very interested in money. They will make much and get rid of it just as fast as they get it. They are great speculators and can make money because of their good judgment in the market. They manipulate in order to make a living or just to show how easy it is to get money. This will drive Virgo crazy.

At work the Sagittarian is conscientious. They will accept routine for a time as long as that routine is fruitful. But they like to be on the move, seeing the world, so they may have a number of trades to their name. A steady job which holds their interest and allows them room to do their own thing is good for them.

Home/Friends. Sagittarians are not natural home-lovers. They accept it as part of life, but not really for them. They are happy in any place that gives them cover for the night. They like animals around them wherever they are. There can be quite a variety where they settle for long enough.

Sagittarians make good friends if Virgo is prepared to listen to their tales. Sagittarius likes to hold the floor at times but is never a bore. They hate to be taken for granted. Their friendship will last through the years but they may not see Virgo very often, which means they won't wear out their welcome. The two signs can take each other in small doses.

Virgo with Capricorn

Money/Job. The Capricornian likes the look and feel of money. They are careful and know how to use it well. They have an eye for quality or durability in whatever they buy, so they do not spend where they can save. Both signs are practical and appreciate that money is a necessary part of their lives.

At work Capricorn is conscientious and responsible. They are the natural managers and executives, so they will be glad to supervise such a willing and efficient worker as Virgo. The two signs will get on well together, each in their proper role. It will be a productive cooperation.

Home/Friends. The Capricornian home is tidy and well organized. It may be a bit cold when others have the central heating going full blast, but it is not an unfriendly place. They love to have old-fashioned things around them, heavy furniture and family heirlooms. They take a pride in having influential people visit them, so their home has to be up to scratch.

As friends Capricorn will not take advantage. They care about people and are genuine friends and neighbors. They can be a bit bossy or selective in the company they keep, so they may be seen as snobs. They like to get into good company, but are down-to-earth people at heart and like to be sociable.

Virgo with Aquarius

Money/Job. The Aquarian will not bother Virgo over money. Aquarians do not take a lot of interest in making a personal fortune. They are good advisers to other people because of their disinterest. They will manage funds well and there is no fear of them going off with the kitty. Money is a means to an end and no more in their book.

The Aquarian is a steady worker. They would prefer to work with brain rather than brawn. They are good at organizing and are more likely, of the two signs, to be boss or overseer. They are agreeable people and usually easy to get along with. They can fit into a routine if it suits them.

Home/Friends. Home for the Aquarian will be comfortable or spartan. It depends just where their interest lies. They will not stop anyone else making home to their standards, just so long as the Aquarian has a quiet room where he or she can research, read or study. Their homes are often modernized. They are a law unto themselves at home, as everywhere else.

Friends are the most important thing in life to the Aquarian. They are true and loyal. They can be quite affectionate and allow others to live their own lives as they wish. They give freely without seeking to get involved.

Virgo with Pisces

Money/Job. There could be a difference of opinion about earning or using money. Pisces can be easy-going with money. They are often dreamers, and seem to think cash grows on trees. Virgo will have to take charge of any joint funds or they can just disappear.

At work Pisces will be generous. They get enthusiastic about doing things that please them. About jobs with routine they are not at all turned on. They will leave a job if they don't like it, without counting the cost. They like to use their sympathy or imagination at work.

Home/Friends. The Piscean home is likely to be in chaos most of the time. Only they will be able to find what is wanted. They can also be neat and have artistic appreciation. Virgo will never be quite sure what to expect in the home when Pisces is around. They are not ones for regular meals. The kitchen may be full or bare.

As friends Pisces are loving and affectionate. They get very intimate with everyone and always seem to know what is going on in the neighborhood. They are likeable people and get away with all sorts of things others would not try. They seem to be innocent or down-trodden, so they are often given friendship to cheer them up.

Love Mates

Virgo Woman—Aries Man. This can be an edgy relationship. Aries is positive, sure of himself and cannot take criticism. Virgo takes a critical view of all things, men included.

She will admire his positive manner as a truly manly quality, and be glad that he looks after her. When he gets a bit too positive she will want him to stop. This he will not do until he decides. In fact he is likely to go to extremes just because he is criticized. Aries does not take a happy view of feminine criticism.

He may be straightforward. He is honest and cannot understand why she doesn't see things as clearly as he does. To him a spade is a spade. She notes the finer points and he goes to the heart of the problem. He will think she pussyfoots around too much. He will accept this because she is a woman, but only so much. He is a busy, impatient man. Life is too short for frills and niceties. He likes to make an immediate good impression and that's that.

She is honest in her own way. It just happens that her way is not his.

Each is sensitive to criticism, in fact. She too can be upset by his abrupt way with her. She expects to be treated at least civilly, since she will not challenge his authority. He is an excellent provider, should they agree to live together, and will make a fine father for her children. He is full of nice surprises. He will show her a life she would never expect to see. But she wants a quiet life. She likes to be loved warmly and consistently. He is passionate one minute and out of sight the next.

Virgo Woman—Taurus Man. He is a man with feelings and understanding. There is no doubt that he values security. He has his feet on the ground. She likes all these qualities in a man.

He will be firm yet gentle with her. He takes his time and

makes no attempt to rush her off her feet. She likes to get to know her men at her own pace and is appreciative of his consideration. She will feel she can trust him to be considerate and treat her like a lady.

He likes to touch. He, like her, is a sensual person. They make judgments on the same basis. They will agree about things without needing to say a word, because they have an instinctive harmony.

She will fuss about and look after all his physical needs, apparently enjoying it. He likes to be served, appreciates comfort and will be glad of her attention. He will provide quite happily while she does the womanly things and saves him the bother of looking after details. She knows that the shortest road to a real man's heart is via his stomach. She will see that he is well-fed and wined, if need be, according to his wishes.

They are both rather quiet types. They can do without people. They will be happy in each other's company. Home life or private life will be satisfying. Their togetherness means a great deal emotionally to them both.

When it comes to the crunch they can each look after the practicalities of life. If need be she will work to keep him her man. He will always look after her, showing his love in a practical way. They match.

Virgo Woman—Gemini Man. They are mutually attracted. He is a lightweight and does not try to impress her with his passion. They will have a great time getting to know each other. They are both mentally alive and enjoy teasing each other. Their sense of humor is similar. They each know what they are after and make it a joke. Life becomes interesting and lively when Gemini is around.

He likes this woman who has her feet on the ground. She makes no heavy demands on him. He does not want to be too heavily committed to anyone, so he can be casual just as long as he wants. He takes his time to get to know her intimately, though he feels he is in tune with her right from the start. Courtship preliminaries are important to both.

They will do a lot of talking and sharing in practical ways, as well as in making love. He always has something different to say or describe whenever they get together. Neither of them likes to get in a rut. He keeps her amused and sometimes irritated because of his lively changeability. She will wonder whether he will settle long enough to make a home for her. He will make her feel better about that when they get involved with children together. He loves children and so does she.

He will realize that this woman is not a flirt, even though she may tease. She can provide him with an anchor that is strong enough for him. He will be faithful but does not like to be weighed down. He likes to have a night out with the boys. She fully accepts this and will not make heavy demands on him. If he gets out of hand, she'll nag him!

Virgo Woman—Cancer Man.

He is a cautious man. He will make a fuss over her in a gentle, caring manner. She likes this but is not quite sure. She likes her men to show strength in a more positive way. He has the sensitive touch and manner of someone who is feeling his way, rather than asserting himself.

He finds her comfortable, attractive, and intelligent, and likes the combination. He may not show off but he has ambitions. These he will not tell to anyone, so he has to be sure before he will open up his heart to her.

She will be struck by his sense of humor on occasions. He changes moods with the wind. She never quite knows what to expect, so his presence livens her up in expectation. She, too, can be moody. She is a worrier and when he's in the dumps they will make a miserable pair. When he's feeling good they will hit the emotional high spots.

He has old fashioned ways. He treats her like a lady. That makes her feel good. They are both domesticated and really love home life. He may get under her feet if they set up a home together, and this could be a bone of contention. She likes men who know their place and are, first of all, the breadwinners. He is well able to make his way in the world of money and this is something that satisfies her practical mind.

Loving is a most emotional experience. He can make her relax, feel romantic and forget all the daily worries. His sense of drama will give her a new outlook on things. She will be entranced by the way he paints a picture for her. She has a great imagination that needs such stimulation. They can have fun.

Virgo Woman—Leo Man. He is out to impress her.
She will listen and show that she admires him. It pleases him, because he likes to be admired. She has a quiet dignity and yet is provocative. She makes him feel he is the only man in the world. There is no better way to catch the Leo man.

He likes to choose his women. He has his own standards and will pass on if he feels he is not appreciated. At the same time he hates to be ignored. She is quiet and may not rise to his bait immediately, and will tease him in this way. She may be a bit overawed by his style or just feel he's laying it on a bit thick. To her there has to be something firm and reliable to back up the show. He will impress her in practical ways if he thinks she is for him.

He is a generous man. He loves to love and be loved. With the right woman he will be loyal and ever-loving. With others he can be out for a good time. They will come to their own conclusions on that score. She is a sensual, earthy woman and likes a cuddle as much as anyone. She will not pass up a casual involvement if they both want one. If they decide to make the togetherness a permanent relationship she will be the dutiful partner. They have a problem here. He is a good-time man at heart and she is quiet, conservative and not really a show off. He may want her to be happy in the background and not steal his thunder, but he's more likely to want a partner who will share his limelight.

They have to do some considering before coming to the altar, if they ever do get there. It's not an impossibility, but unlikely.

Virgo Woman—Virgo Man. This is a possible union
of two quiet conservative people. They will not make heavy demands on each other. They are both considerate and will probably be happy to jog along through life at an easy pace.

They can fail to raise that extra bit of spark that makes love so vital to life. They can also know each other well enough, right from the start, to waste no time on preliminaries and have a great time together.

They are practical people. It is the practical types who get a terrific kick from romance. It catches them unawares. This can happen without their understanding what has hit them. The future will depend, when they get down to cases, on their ability to come to grips with realities. They are not people to build up hopes or dreams. They will go for something that is possible, though they may still retain dreams.

Respect for each other is natural. Neither takes the other for granted. They will feel secure enough and not wish to cause any problems for each other. They both worry. Loving can take some of that worry away for a time at least.

A relationship has to be productive if it is going to last. That is understandable to both. If they choose to be casual, they each know how to please the other. They may be modest, but in private are strongly sensual people who value and love body contact. Private life means such a lot to them both.

Should they decide to make a long term relationship, they have the interest and patience to make it most fruitful. They know about love and devotion.

Virgo Woman—Libra Man.
This man pays attention to the woman in his sights. He can lay on the charm and mean it. He will see in Virgo a woman with discrimination and possibilities.

He is a polished operator. He will leave nothing to chance if he's out to get her. She will find his attention very difficult to ignore. Virgo knows what attention means. She, too, is concerned with getting things just right: fitting pegs in the right holes. They have a lot in common.

He is an intelligent man. He has a way of putting things that she will find hard to resist. He seems to know what he wants, she will think. He is not a man who likes to struggle to get what he wants. Courtesy usually breaks down barriers for him. He does not wish to soil his hands.

Practical Virgo may see him in a different light when the polish has worn off. She is sensual. She likes physical love, though she will not shout it from the housetops. A man must be strong to suit her. She may think that Libra is lovely on the outside but has little inside to last her pace or measure up to her emotional needs. Virgo is no fool and looks for productivity in all she does. She wants more than a shop window. It is the goods that count.

He respects her intelligence. He likes comfort and is not inclined to fuss too much. Things have to be just so for him. He will see that she can attend to his needs but he may not be prepared to share her love of physical, natural living. They can accept each other quite happily, neither wishing to dominate the other. They're happier with a casual relationship.

Virgo Woman—Scorpio Man.

She will be quite happy that this masterful man wants her as she is. She will lose a lot of her shyness when he takes over. If he is too forceful or crude, she will retreat gracefully and get out of his sight. He is too much of an emotional man to be teased. He needs no encouragement to come on to her.

First impressions mean a lot in this relationship. They are both sensitive, possibly psychic, so each will instinctively know what the other is thinking and planning. If it's to their liking they will not beat about the bush.

He needs a sensual, physical woman to satisfy his passion. Virgo may seem quiet but he will sense she has depth and feeling and will want to please him. She does not need to be demonstrative. It is quite obvious to him.

She will want to look after him. He may boss her around if he wants. There is some mutual satisfaction in this. He will protect her jealously if he decides she is his woman. It does her good to feel that she is desired with such passion. She has every intention of being the perfect woman when she feels he is truly hers.

They are both intimate people. They have little need for social life. Enjoyment of the simple things of life together is all they need. She will provide the comfort he will require, cook and serve for him, provided he is true to her, shows he loves her and cares for her as a man should do.

There is a strong sexual attraction between them which can lead to casual love-making. They will choose.

Virgo Woman—Sagittarius Man. This variable man can have her worried. He likes his freedom yet has his quiet moments. He likes to be sociable at times, but can go off and spend hours with books.

She is intelligent and can accept most things. He is, to her way of thinking, much too unpredictable. This can be a fascination, for she is curious about all manner of things. He seems to be a man of the world, and that also intrigues her. He is a realist and she is practical. They can see eye-to-eye on many things. Neither will stand for being hoodwinked. This can keep them from getting too involved with each other. They have lots of things going when they are together but each is aware that it all could be for a short time only. Tomorrow he'll be off somewhere miles away and she will miss him.

They are likely to agree on a casual relationship. He does not want to be saddled with a home and family while she does not want to do both his job and her own in his absence. They both like company but have to choose for themselves. She will quietly withdraw if she is not comfortable in company. He will upset whoever causes him offense and drive them away. They have different ways of handling things. Together for too long at a stretch they'd play havoc with each other's nerves. They can have a good time together if they don't take life too seriously.

He has all the enthusiasm and exuberance to bring her out of her modest shell. She has the maidenly understanding to make him feel wanted as a man when he's available. They will not get under each other's feet or in each other's hair if they play it cool.

Virgo Woman—Capricorn Man. He is a strong, capable man. He could be her ideal. He latches on to her immediately. She may be a bit saucy in order to attract his attention. She probably thinks he's a bit slow in getting off the mark and will encourage him.

He is old-fashioned in some ways. He will treat her with respect and find she appreciates this. He is not a man to rush blindly into any relationship. He is noted for his caution. She is quiet and conservative, so she will appreciate there is method in his madness. They will take their time getting to know each other and enjoy the experience all the more.

Both have physical desires. Neither is going to make that too obvious at first. There has to be a proper courtship as both will want to be sure of the other. They are naturally suited for each other and will probably be looking for a lasting relationship. If they have a casual affair in mind they will not beat about the bush too long.

Capricorn is an ambitious man. He is looking to the future, to the mother of his children and the social position he and his family will occupy. This is way ahead of Virgo, who will be doing her best to make him feel comfortable. She will follow his lead happily. She knows that life will improve with him. He will lift her as he gets on in the world and she'll be glad for him. She is not asking too much but she wants to see something for her efforts. He will provide and she knows it. To her, he is a good man in every respect.

This is likely to be a relationship that lasts all through life. They will not regret what they do and will prosper privately and socially.

Virgo Woman—Aquarius Man.
She will see him as a cool customer who seems to have no particular interest in anyone. It may arouse her curiosity. He can be attracted by her vivacity or her quietness. She may seem a bit of a mystery. They are on uneven ground in this relationship.

He is a logical, pleasant and friendly man. She is a physical woman who is modest and attractive. Neither is going to force the pace. They may get absolutely nowhere. On the other hand they may be mutually intrigued; then the situation is changed.

He does not like brash women. He appreciates her gentle and modest ways. She likes him because he seems to be cool. He treats everyone the same without causing any ill feeling. He will spend his time with either sex, being sociable.

He is a straightforward man. He is loyal and a friend to have if one is in difficulties. He does not like to get involved. He will be glad to help but expects to keep his independence at all costs. Marriage can be, for him, an unwelcome situation if it restricts his freedom. He is interested in people rather than in individuals. This is the part that Virgo finds most hard to understand and accept. She gets involved because she wants to help. He helps and avoids involvement. They will misunderstand each other all too easily.

He is not a jealous man. She may wish that he was at times, when she sees him chatting away with other women. He does not get upset when she gets involved with other men.

They have a lot to learn about each other. Their love will have to be trusting. He is passionate when aroused, so they can have a lot of fun. It could work.

Virgo Woman—Pisces Man. This is a challenge. Each sees hope in the other. They know they have something the other needs. They can draw back or get into a clinch. He is an emotional man. Where she will hold back her feelings he just lets them go. He can bring out her hidden depths. She can help him control himself and avoid getting carried away.

He has a great deal of love in him which he may make no attempt to curb. This can be worrying to Virgo who keeps her feelings in check. When she sees that he is being natural, she can relax with him. But she will make sure that he does not get too emotional when she's around. He loves this practical woman who can manage things so capably, yet with genuine feeling which he can sense. He knows she is as soft as he is, deep down.

He has difficulty keeping to a straight track. He is easily persuaded to change his mind. She may think he is easily led. He follows his feelings and occasionally gets confused. He is misunderstood and wonders why. She has that common sense he apparently lacks, so will bring him back on course when he strays.

They can have a great emotional life. They blend perfectly keeping each other in check. Together they get a great deal out of life by doing things for other people. They don't mind, either of them, sacrificing a bit of their love for those who seem to get none at all. They seem to have love to spare when they agree.

It is a togetherness that is difficult to fully appreciate. There is terrific possibility whether they are casual lovers or they live together a lifetime. They give and take. That's what it's all about.

Virgo Man—Aries Woman.

She means to have her own way. She may think he's a slow mover and try to push him around. If he is what she thinks he is he will let her take the upper hand.

He sees a lively and individualistic woman with a lot of energy. He is attracted at once by her fire. He has no long-term desires but she will rouse the animal in him. He's a physical man and knows passion. He may not show it.

They are an unusual pair. A lot of tension can build up if they don't succeed in getting the physical feelings out of their system. She has a feeling he wants to make body contact and wishes he was more aggressive about it. She will taunt him to make him come to life. He will rise to the bait if he is inclined. This must be a short-term affair. He will not stand being dominated by a woman for any length of time. For a brief spell of mutual physical pleasure he is ready and willing. He can get rid of his modesty when the need arises.

They are not meant to spend a lifetime together. There would be too much aggravation. She would have to spend so much of her time getting him to the boil, it would not be worth her time and energy. She is not interested in lengthy passion. She is quick off the mark, and responds instantly to encouragement.

Having agreed that a long term relationship would suit her, she will need to be dominated. Virgo shows no sign of wishing to take her over. He just admires her get-up-and-go. That is not enough. She must make the most of life while she can. Time does not stand still. He is far too gentlemanly for her.

Virgo Man—Taurus Woman.

They have rapport. They will enjoy each other's company, come what may. He is eager to have her as a friend. He'll be looking forward to a closer link.

She is a strong woman and likes a strong man. He must appreciate that she is soft and lovable. She sees that he is modest and feels there is something worthwhile beneath the surface. They both like body contact and are aware of this instinctively. They can be patient with each other. The love they feel will grow as they wait.

They are not a talkative pair when in love. Feelings and actions speak louder than words. They will talk when they have made love. Then she will tell him of her feelings, knowing that he will listen and understand. They share a common sort of wisdom. They will not be shy in each other's company. They each like privacy and feel really comfortable when they are intimate.

He's a man of regular habits, but he can change. She is not likely to change her mind once it is made up. They will feel secure with each other. He can be critical but knows what it is to be hurt, so he will be gentle with her. They are a sentimental couple and do things the old-fashioned way, taking their time and trying not to offend or hurt each other.

Home life is appreciated. This gives them the privacy they both cherish. They will socialize when the spirit moves them but are happier with each other. That is one routine they will not want to change.

Theirs is the sort of love that grows. Both will grow in love and devotion with the years.

Virgo Man—Gemini Woman. She is a light-footed woman who covers a lot of ground. They have immediate intellectual rapport. They think along the same lines and waste no time in finding out about each other. She will not let him get away with anything. She has a way of getting what she wants because she can persuade men by looks, actions and words.

He is a practical man but is also lively and intelligent. He can keep up with her and show her a trick or two. They will respect each other for this.

She has her feet firmly on the ground. He senses she needs a man who does more than talk, one who will take charge. His physical attraction does something to her. He has something more than expertise and book learning. He is a capable man who knows about a lot of things. His modest demeanor is no true guide to his inner depths.

They should have a very interesting relationship. Neither is going to make up their mind for a little while. They will have a lot of fun finding out about each other, for they are both inquisitive and ever-ready to learn as well as to teach.

She is a flirt, given the chance. He, too, can provoke the opposite sex, so they are on equal footing and know it. They could be quite happy meeting casually when they feel like it. They will feel comfortable together. If they decide to go straight and raise a family they are again in tune. Both love children. They know that children keep them young. He will want to prove his manhood if he loves her truly.

There is a lot of potential between these two. They can tease or satisfy each other, just as they wish.

Virgo Man—Cancer Woman.
She changes with the tide. Her emotions are obvious. He may be attracted by her gaiety and sense of drama at first meeting. She likes him because he has a wry sense of humor that tickles her fancy.

She is looking for a dependable man who can give her security. He may not stand out at first, but she knows about men, despite her apparent shyness when she's feeling moody. She will feel he is sensible and gentle and that's quite a step towards her ideal. She will like him to be fairly pliable, for she can be demanding. She has plans for her man when she catches him. Mr. Virgo will have to be ambitious as well as capable and kind, if he is to fill her bill.

He takes stock and sees a comfortable woman who will make him a home and look after his children. He may not, at first, notice her ambitions, but they will not deter him if he's attracted. He will get on in the world. She will have to be patient and that's OK by her, just so long as she knows she'll get her wish.

They are both domestic people. She will make this the center core of her life. The affection she showers on him now will be later transferred to their children. He is probably aware of this instinctively and will accept the change. He can love with all his heart and not make heavy demands on the one he truly loves.

They are both practical people. He will find she has a keen interest in his financial affairs. He must come to understand that she needs to be secure or her love is strained. He will be wise enough to set her mind at rest on that score. It can work.

Virgo Man—Leo Woman.
She needs a lot of attention. In no way is she going to settle for a mediocre man. She will naturally attract someone who is also a show-off or who thinks can master her. She wants to be boss, which can lead to problems.

Yet she has charm. She draws men because of her apparent passion and strength. She will be the center of attraction if it kills her. None of the other women around her will dare to trespass on her ground once she's laid claim.

If she takes a fancy to Mr. Virgo he has a lot to live up to. He is not as docile as some may think, so he will cope just as long as he feels necessary. He likes to be with such a strong personality and can make her happy in his own way. He will not steal her thunder but will happily promote her and take a back seat. She has a soft spot for him. He is not a weakling, despite his modesty. He is made of substantial stuff and is also intelligent. There is a lot wrapped up in this male package.

He is not going to hang around with her too long if he's looking for a permanent mate. He will have a good time with her because she likes this, is a good sport and is genuinely loving. They share a lot of sincere feeling for each other. But she is looking for someone different and he knows it. They will be good friends and occasional lovers if it suits them both.

He will carry on looking for his true soul-mate and she for hers. They each have their pride and this must be matched by their long-term partner. Neither is going to settle for other than the right mate. They both have better things to do with their lives.

Virgo Man—Virgo Woman.
They will want to compare notes. Natural curiosity will get them together. Something clicks and they'll have to find out why.

Perhaps they will give up as soon as they cotton on. They each like to have a change and do not intend getting in a rut. But they may feel comfortable knowing each other's faults and fancies. It can be a most interesting situation. They will not be able to agree on some things. There will always be plenty to differ or argue about. They are good for each other at the intellectual level. They look for a practical end to their joint efforts. They know fairly well what are the sensitive spots they should avoid. Each is very touchy and easily hurt.

There is an unhelpful side to this relationship which may or may not show. While they will make merry when things go well, they will both suffer when things go ill. They will have to agree to make an effort to cheer each other up or seek happy company when that situation arises. As they are both sensible they should be able to work or talk themselves out of their depressions.

Neither needs any lessons in making love. They will know what turns each other on and where to draw the lines. In private they are much more open than they appear to be in public. They are always concerned about appearances when in company. Their private lives together will be a mutual revelation to which they will both look forward. It is this quiet privacy that so attracts Virgo. They are both physical people, and will enjoy their embraces all the more when they are confident of each other's love. That is their business and so it will stay.

Virgo Man—Libra Woman. She is always attractive.
He is a man of discernment and discretion. She gives no one the direct "come on" but has a way of getting the best from men around her. He will feel a challenge to his manhood and will try to prove himself.

She is cool and charming. She obviously has intelligence and can get along with anyone. Nothing seems to ruffle her, yet she does all sorts of things to keep the party going. She does not settle long and does not want to make an attachment in a hurry.

He can be delicate. He has a soft touch and knows it. He can match her intelligence and likes the way she handles herself. He will be physically attracted and find that she too can play at that game, but she is not too keen on body contact. She likes to know what is being offered by her men and what is expected of her in return. She's no shrinking violet, but neither is she goint to commit herself till she's quite sure what she wants. She can sit on the fence for a long time, and Mr. Virgo may have to be patient. If he feels it's worth his while he will wait. If he feels otherwise, he will look elsewhere. But he will always have a pleasant memory of a lovely lady playing it cool.

They have a lot of interests that can bring them together. Both are gifted in getting thing in their proper places. They have the artistic touch. They are both particular in their ways so take everything as they find it. They analyze life in general.

Once they have scrutinized each other they will remember the nice things they have uncovered and be good friends, possibly occasional lovers, for life.

Virgo Man—Scorpio Woman.

She has a magnetic appeal. His physical nature will spring to life when he meets her. She knows of her powers of attraction and will remain outwardly cool.

She sizes up every man she meets. This man will, to her, have potential. He is quiet and that, to her, is a sign of quality. She hates to be stuck with superficial men. Give her the strong silent type. They are the only ones who ever really get her right.

Male company is good for her. She makes her choice and is quite happy to shop around till she finds Mr. Right, but there are different horses for different courses. She will be straight as a die with the man she takes for her permanent mate. Other interludes can be filled by a man who has something to offer and is a man of strength.

Virgo man has physique to offer. He has devotion. He respects her for her beauty and composure. He will be proud to be her escort, love or champion. He will realize that she will not let him go if they agree to go steady. She is a jealous woman. Any other woman who comes near her man will be sent off with tail between legs. He is not suited for this strong stuff . . . at least not for life. He will not usually stray, but he might if he felt too restricted.

They can come to terms on this if they are happy about other things. She is too wise to dominate him. She can get her own way by being a woman and letting him think he's boss. She is not deceitful, she just knows what she's after. He, too, knows what he wants. She may fit his bill nicely. They are honest and sensitive people who are prepared to give a lot.

Virgo Man—Sagittarius Woman. She is here today and gone tomorrow. She likes being with men and is hardly noticed as a woman. This does not seem to bother her. She has a word for everything and everybody who cares to chat or takes her interest. It is obvious that she does not like to be housebound and will be happier out in the fresh air with animals or men.

She is not forward. She is not looking for a man. She just has to be different from the usual run of women and does not appear to give two hoots what anyone thinks.

She has quite a lot to say. Her opinion is freely given, even when it's not asked. She has no intention of getting involved in marriage if it is going to restrict her freedom. She is not really a good-time woman but she does like to go her own way. A man will have to be easy on her. She will give as good as she gets in any relationship, so she will expect fair treatment. She is not very interested in having children. They would tie her down. She will be happy with a man who travels and is not too concerned about home comforts. He will have to take the rough with the smooth in any home she runs.

She likes men well enough as lovers. She is not against anything but she cannot face having to spend life in front of a sink of dirty dishes. She is passionate. She does not prolong her loving and likes a sharp lively encounter rather than a long drawn-out courtship. She is honest and true. She would rather love today and be free tomorrow, leaving herself free to come back when she feels like it. Her man has to be tolerant if he loves her.

Virgo Man—Capricorn Woman. Not quite as good a combination as Capricorn man–Virgo woman, but they can do well. The Virgo man will recognize many of his own traits in a Capricorn woman. Both are careful with money, hardworking and cautious. He is interested in keeping an organization running smoothly; she has more ambition than that.

They are very similar in their approaches to life. Both look for a partner with the head and not the heart, showing reserve and restraint when they meet. Neither is likely to make the first move until they really know each other. Even then, their feelings are private. They may well decide they are a suitable match, and they'll tell each other so. There will be no passion, though; she is so afraid of rejection that she'll never release her emotions without being pushed, and he's afraid of pushing where emotions are concerned. Her emotions are her business, to him.

The Virgo man is not highly physical in his expression of emotion, though his love can be very strong. He shows its strength by his devoted service and his unflagging attempts to please. She will settle for this, though she would love someone who could see through her shell to the emotional core. They will work for stability and a good future, she pushing him to succeed for himself. Instead, he ends up using her direction to find where he should go.

They are both looking for permanence and security, and will find it in each other. Loyalty and faithfulness are their watchwords—not much passion, but a strong relationship.

Virgo Man—Aquarius Woman.

She is cool, calm and collected. She takes everything in without getting involved. He is intrigued by her manner. She is good company and they will feel at ease together. She will not fly off the handle at anything he says and he is far too careful to make mistakes at first meeting.

She is honest, straightforward and open. He will be amazed at the speed with which they get to know each other. She will see that he is a shy man and not make him feel uncomfortable. He is always inquisitive and will get a straight answer to anything he asks. This may shake him.

She is passionate. Her private life is her own, rather like his. She finds he comes to life when they are together in private. She likes this quiet and private man who has so little to say for himself. That is, to her, a point in his favor. She will give him all the love he needs. She is not shy with her man.

Intimacy has to take its proper place in her scheme of things. She is very independent. She believes in giving as good as she gets, so she will not be relying on any man for her security. She wants the freedom to choose her own path and will take her responsibilities squarely. She hates to get involved. That takes away her freedom. But she is not careless. The man who accepts her as his wife will have to accept her as she is. She may seem to be cool but she loves deeply.

She sees no point in heavy emotion which upsets her. She is, to her true love, his best friend. To be a friend is to be everything a partner can need.

She will not live in anyone's pocket but she will be a loving mate when she's committed.

Virgo Man—Pisces Woman. Emotions run high between these two. He will find it hard to contain her and she will get under his skin. She really lets her hair down when she's emotional. He will go along with her and surprise himself. He has a lot of emotion penned up inside. She has the happy knack of making him relax and let it show. It will do him good.

She will put no pressure on him. She may seem weak and defenseless at times. He has the ability to look after her. She is extremely resilient and he'll find her in a dozen different moods in as many days. This femininity will arouse the protective male in him and he will do all he can to look after her.

He will find she has her own feminine way of getting things done and is never really as down as she seems to be. She has a great ability to understand and accept life. She does not appear to fight but yet manages to get on quite well. She has a lot of gentle love which she is not afraid to spread around. If he's a jealous lover he is going to have a rough time. She is loving to many, though she is not promiscuous. He will find she does many a good turn with what she has, and does without when someone is in need of love or comfort.

Love to this woman is a universal thing. It is not, in her book, to be denied to anyone or anything. That goes for animals too. If he's thinking of having her as his life-mate, he'll have to be prepared to have stray animals in or around the house.

Together they are good for each other. He can bring her down to earth long enough to make a happy life. She will make him open up and be more affectionate.

VII. Libra ♎

The Libra Character

Men and women born under Libra are refined, likeable, and well balanced. They can see both sides of an argument and are fair in their decisions. They like the lighter side of life, and are drawn to entertaining or amusing people, and when in such company they shine. They are very responsive to the characters of other people, and become depressed and despondent in a gloomy atmosphere. To some degree, they take their mood from others, and will alter and adapt their own ways in order to fit in well.

They have an active social life, and are fond of associating with celebrities. Libra people have perfect taste, and they are very particular about such things as food and wine, and very knowledgeable about them. They like to live in beautiful and harmonious surroundings with those who are not too demanding.

They are good at expressing their feelings, and eager to please. If they live in a climate of approval and praise nothing will be too much trouble for them, but if not, they become discouraged and give up quickly. This applies to all areas of their lives, both emotional and practical.

They hate arguments, quarrels and scenes and will go to great lengths to avoid them, and to mix only with people that they know will, like them, want happiness and harmony. The Libra person is not looking for trouble and is not really a fighter. They will always try to turn away from unpleasantness, and withdraw from any situation that looks like it may become explosive.

Their home will be a very pleasant place to visit, warm and

comfortable, and with well-chosen and artistic touches. The Libra person can charm the birds off the trees; everyone feels better for seeing them, and their lightness, charm and wit can brighten even the dullest gathering.

They are also very good at bringing together people who have quarrelled or separated. It is natural to them to want to see the natural order of things restored, and they will try to patch up differences between their friends and loved ones.

They are very artistic, and often intellectual. They love beautiful clothes and are prepared to spend a great deal of money on their appearance and their surroundings. They are also profoundly affected by color; bright, happy colors cheer them up, and gloomy colors depress them.

They are affectionate, loving and outgoing, and they want others to be the same to them. They like demonstrative people who will express love and sympathy towards them. An abrasive character makes them shrink away.

They are not solitary people; they work best in partnership with others. Basically they are sharers: they like another person to share the responsibilities with, and a partner to enjoy the good times with. Success seems hollow to them if they have to celebrate it alone.

They are even tempered, and appear to be placid, but they are not really. Inwardly, they are extremely sensitive and easily hurt, and it is only due to their retiring nature that they do not show it. They are gentle and forgiving, and will always meet the other person half way, anxious to forgive and forget. They hate smouldering resentments and sulks. They have an instinctive wish to smooth things over, tidy things up, and generally to be liked and thought well of.

Unfortunately, this makes them somewhat negative at times. They are fond of a life of ease and pleasure and wish to obtain this with the minimum of hard work. They want status in the community but they don't really want to have to earn it. They often feel injured when they are not, and look for slights that are not there, and the Libra person needs to guard against these tendencies. They are not always entirely truthful, perferring to tell a white lie rather than face a confrontation, and could let down a friend in a difficult situation, if called upon to give loyalty which would put them at some risk themselves. Their friendships tend to be somewhat superficial, partly because of the people they choose as friends, and partly because they don't really want to give or receive friendship on a very deep level.

Although absolutely charming, they do tend to be rather lightweight characters, dreamers who drift through life taking the easiest and most pleasant way without too much thought given to other considerations which may be more important. They are not very interested in the future, living for the moment, and they would do well to give some thought to how one of their actions is going to affect them in a year or two, rather than just thinking of the situation as it affects them today.

The most fortunate Libras grow wiser with age, and learn from life to look before they leap, to reason rather than just take the line of least resistance. If this is done, it will be a happy life.

How Libra Gets Along with Others

Libra with Aries

Money/Job. The Libran likes working with the Aries person. Aries will always be prepared to face a confrontation, in fact they enjoy it, but Libra shrinks from one and will retreat into the shadow of the Aries person, and let them sort things out. The Libran loves beautiful and expensive things and if Aries is in charge may be prevented from having enough money to obtain them. Aries is not mean, but does not believe in wasting money, particularly if it is for what they regard as frivolous. However, the Libran likes and respects the Arien for honesty, hard work, and taking the lead, and will give a good return, provided there is not too much pressure. The Arien will appreciate the artistic contribution Libra makes, and all will be well so long as tact is employed. Hurt feelings make Libra inactive.

Home/Friends. This is a good combination, because Aries likes a nice home they can be proud of, and Libra has wonderful taste in decor and furnishings, and a real talent for entertaining. The Arien may have to restrain the Libran's spending from time to time, but basically Aries is realistic and knows it cost money to have the sort of home they want, and generally they will pay up without too much argument. A lively home, happy friends.

Libra with Taurus

Money/Job. Not much difficulty here. If Taurus is in charge, it will work well. If Libra is in charge, Taurus will be a tower of strength—but always thinking they could do it better. If they are partners, Taurus will naturally take the lead, and Libra will be happy to let them. Taurus is an achiever, ambitious and materialistic. They measure their own success by money, so they will be anxious to succeed financially. So will Libra, though for different reasons. Libra always needs money to finance the sort of lifestyle they like, so they will have a common goal. Both have artistic good taste, and Taurus is a hard worker who will motivate Libra to work hard for reward.

Home/Friends. This is a good, workable relationship. Both are luxury lovers, and both like a really nice home and are willing to pay for it. For Taurus it is partly to demonstrate their success to the world, and partly to live in comfort and style; to Libra it is the sheer pleasure of making a perfect home and happy and harmonious atmosphere. They will entertain quite a lot: Libra people love to entertain and Taurus will quite enjoy it. In any case Taurus people are always good hosts and hostesses, because they always fulfill their obligations. If there are children, they will see eye to eye about them and provide a good and stable home.

Libra with Gemini

Money/Job. Very good indeed. These two make perfect partners. They are both very quick-thinking and have a light touch in business as in everything else. The Gemini will not pressure the Libran, and the Libran will relax and work well. They have great harmony and can achieve a great deal. The Libran admires the Gemini wit and quickness of mind, and working days are happy, with quite a lot of laughter to help them along. Nevertheless, they do both want money—Libra for luxury living, Gemini for travel—and they will work hard, in short bursts, to achieve this.

Home/Friends. The Gemini is not so home-loving as the Libran. They like a nice place to live, to arrive home at and depart from on their travels, but they have so many interests and friends that they really like to use home as a hotel. However, as the Libran is so wonderful at organizing a beautiful and well-run home, and secretly dislikes any interference from a partner, preferring to choose and decide everything themselves, this suits them quite well. If there are children, they will be brought up in a busy, lively household with many friends in and out, and their own friends will always be welcome. They will have a cultured background, and parents young in mind.

Libra with Cancer

Money/Job. Neither of these people is really strong enough to motivate the other, as both the Libran and the Cancerian have a love of luxury and high living, but are disinclined to discipline themselves to the hard world of business. They would be most successful in an artistic enterprise, since they are both artistic and have excellent taste, but neither of them would really want to take the responsibility and be in charge. This would suit the Libran: they like to work in a partnership anyway, but the Cancerian is happier working under the instructions of someone else. If they can get organized, and stick at it, there could be success.

Home/Friends. This is a different matter. They can have a happy and harmonious home life together, each making the other very happy. They have the same sort of taste and both like the very best. Provided there is enough money, they will enjoy creating a home that everyone will want to visit. They like entertaining, especially the Libra. The Cancerian is more reserved, but loves looking after people, so they will make a good host and hostess. If there are children there could be difficulties, because although the Libra will get on well with the children, and be a good parent, they will not wish to enforce discipline. This means it will be left to the Cancerian, who does not want to do it either.

Libra with Leo

Money/Job. Libra is a lavish spender; Leo is really extravagant. Even Libras, luxury lovers that they are, sometimes quail before the thought of the money Leo is spending, and wonder where it is to come from. Leo will provide it. The Leo person is afraid of poverty and security is top of the list for them, so that even when they appear to be spending out of control, they have worked it all out and can and will afford it. They are hard-working and clever in business, and, provided they are in charge, will utilize to the full the artistic talents of the Libran, and turn them to gold. If the Libran is in charge, or if it is a partnership, nothing will stop the Leo from leading; Libra can trust them to do it well.

Home/Friends. Where the home is concerned, this should be a good combination, since both like a nice home (Leo in order to shine, Libra in order to create something beautiful). In the matter of friends they differ. Leo is a wonderful friend, strong and loyal. All they ask is that their friends do things their way: then all is well. They choose friends wisely and well, and in small numbers. Libra chooses to have many more superficial friendships, and no really deep ones, and will drop a friend if they become tiresome. If there are children they will want for nothing, Leo being a grand provider. Although Leo expects much from them, gentle Libra will keep the balance right, and keep the peace.

Libra with Virgo

Money/Job. Not a very good combination. Virgo is a hard taskmaster, and Libra is not anxious to work hard. If Virgo is working for Libra, they will serve tirelessly, but will not approve of Libra doing so little. Luxury-loving Libra wants to spend a lot of money: thrifty Virgo would not approve and would always be trying to stop them. The Libran uses the money to make things beautiful and harmonious around them, but the Virgoan sees this as a waste and would be resentful. This partnership would not be likely to work well, except in an artistic enterprise, when Virgo would keep quiet and bear with the excesses of Libra in order to reap the benefit of their artistic ability, which Virgo lacks.

Home/Friends. It would be very difficult for Libra and Virgo to share a home. For the Libran to have the home they would want to create would cost a lot of money and take up a lot of time; the Virgoan would not be prepared to accept this, and there would be tension as the Libran, unwilling to give up their lifestyle, either gave in unhappily or went on spending defiantly. If there are children they will be properly looked after and have all their needs attended to and be pressed to do well at school by their Virgoan parent, but will get most of their affection from the Libran. Virgo has too few friends; Libra has too many.

Libra with Libra

Money/Job. Two Libras together will provide a great deal of artistic talent and ability. Unfortunately neither of them will want to take on the job of organizing and utilizing it. They are both pleasure-loving, and not money-seeking, except that they need quite a bit to sustain their luxurious lifestyle. The best solution is for them to have a partnership. Librans always work very well in partnerships and enjoy having someone else to share triumphs and disasters with. It will not work well for one to be in charge of the other, because the one in charge will refuse to lead—and the one not in charge will refuse to follow. If it is an artistic enterprise, marvelous.

Home/Friends. Lovely. Librans make a wonderful home, beautiful, luxurious and welcoming. Two Librans together make it even better. They will entertain their friends regularly, and prefer a glittering circle, with the odd celebrity or two, to groups of deeper friends. They are not looking for depth of relationship, but for happy, entertaining occasions. They are greatly in demand at parties and make perfect guests, as they are charming, and can be depended upon to defuse difficult situations. If there are children, they will have a happy and comfortable home and loving parents, but perhaps too little discipline and guidance.

Libra with Scorpio

Money/Job. Scorpio is a very ambitious, hard worker, and will expect Libra to be the same. Libra is not interested in working hard but in pleasure and luxury, and only works at all in order to afford the lifestyle they require. If Scorpio is in charge of Libra, there will be a lot of pressure and Libra will be miserable. If Libra rules, Scorpio will work hard but be inwardly exasperated to see Libra doing so little. In a partnership Scorpio would be inclined to force the pace. Scorpio does not appreciate Libra's artistic gifts and Libra is put off by Scorpio's money-mindedness. Only if Scorpio can motivate Libra to work hard for the luxuries they like can this partnership succeed.

Home/Friends. Scorpio does not like the sort of friends that Libra makes: they find them superficial, and also think there are far too many of them. Libra gets bored by the Scorpio tendency to stick to one or two old friends, and family. Libra loves parties and going out; Scorpio likes a quiet home life and staying in. They will agree about the home, though; both like the very best of everything and Scorpio will like Libra's good taste, and be quite willing to pay for it. If they can compromise over social life, Libra will benefit from a more stable life, and

Scorpio will quite enjoy the charming people Libra collects. If there are children, Libra–Scorpio parents are a good mix.

Libra with Sagittarius

Money/Job. Quite good. Sagittarius will not pressure Libra, but they are very lively and quick-thinking and any enterprise they are involved in will hum along like a dynamo. The Libran will respond to the pace and will enjoy working with a Sagittarian, whether in partnership or employment. Their working relationship will be more like play, and because there is a happy atmosphere, they will both relax and work well, although not all the time. A lot of the time they like to play. The Sagittarian will be quick to spot the artistic potential of the Libran, and to use it, and the Sagittarian himself has very good taste and an instinct for what the customer will like. They should make a good team, and prosper.

Home/Friends. Not quite so good. Both are fast moving and have a lot of friends and like plenty of social activity, but whereas the Libran uses a great deal of time and money making a beautiful home, the Sagittarian is not very interested and not very appreciative of their efforts, though they won't complain about the expense. The Libran is quick to be hurt if no praise is forthcoming, and the Sagittarian gets tired of saying how wonderful everything is. If there are children, they will like the Sagittarian parent, whose deepest loyalty and love is theirs, and theirs alone, but they will be brought up by Libra, in a cultured home.

Libra with Capricorn

Money/Job. These two are opposites, and never more than in the field of business. The Capricorn, correct and hardworking, does not approve of artistic, luxury-loving Libra, and will be appalled at the extravagance of the lifestyle and the money it is costing. The Libra will dislike Capricorn applying pressure to make them work, and they will slow down more and more, because they simply cannot work in unsympathetic circumstances. If the Libran is in charge, he may decide to overlook the disadvantages of Capricorn because of the hard work and faithful service they give, if they are in partnership there will be strains, but if the Capricorn is in charge it will be a disaster, for crushed Libra and thwarted Capricorn alike.

Home/Friends. A disaster area. Capricorn likes a quiet, calm, orderly home, kept clean and tidy, with expenditures as low as possible. Libra likes warmth, luxury, and comfort, and entertaining a lot of visitors. They cannot both be happy. If the Capricorn is in love with Libra, and can take pleasure in the brightness and warmth of the personality so different from their own, they may accept the lifestyle. If not, they will not remain together. If there are children there will be conflict over them; on one side loving, comforting Libra; on the other, proud but stern Capricorn.

Libra with Aquarius

Money/Job. Libra and Aquarius are well suited in all fields. They share a light touch and a happy disposition. Neither of them are very businesslike, but they both take care to do a good job and although not very motivated by money, they usually do well. The Aquarian will appreciate the artistic nature of the Libran, and will be artistic themselves and painstaking in the preparation of any work. Both have good taste and a similar outlook on life in general, and they would be likely to work well together, particularly as Libra does not like working under pressure, and prefers a partnership, and even if Aquarius is officially in charge they do not seek to take over and will happily allow the Libran freedom in developing their own working pattern. In return, Libra will give value for money.

Home/Friends. An ideal combination. They are both undemanding, and like to have a lot of friends in and out of the home. Their circle will be amusing and entertaining and there will be very few serious discussions. They love giving and going to parties, and are in demand as guests. The Libran has a real talent for making a beautiful and harmonious home, and so does the Aquarian. They like each other's taste and will live happily together. If there are children, they will make few demands on them and will provide them with a happy and relaxed home.

Libra with Pisces

Money/Job. Libra loves beautiful surroundings and luxury; so does Pisces, so they will have no disagreements about money, so long as there is enough of it. They can work in harmony together in what may look to the outsider like organized chaos, since they rarely work to a fixed plan or timetable, but each evolves the best way of managing their working life to provide the money for the high lifestyle that they want. Pisces will leave Libra alone and trust to Libran judgment, and Libra, artistic too, will appreciate the talents and gifts of Pisces. Neither will take charge; they are a team.

Home/Friends. Both love a beautiful home and are willing to spend a lot of time, money and energy on getting it the way they want it. Libra is outgoing and friendly, and likes a busy social whirl. Pisces is a lot more retiring and shy, but is good at entertaining since they like to care for people, and they work in the background while the Libran sparkles in conversation. They will have a pleasant home and a pleasant life, with no major arguments—they both hate scenes. If there are children, the Libran will get along well with them. Librans understand young people and let them develop at their own speed, while the Piscean will be loving and giving. The children will be busy and happy.

Love Mates

Libra Woman—Aries Man. She is all charm. This works on him in a wonderful way. Without her, he is abrasive, aggressive, and dominating. With her he can reach his full potential, as she skillfully steers him clear of excessive rashness, and covers up his blunders smoothly.

The Aries man will always take the lead in this relationship, and never more so than in their love-life. He will lead, she will follow, and it suits them both perfectly. He is a good lover, and her response is all he could wish for. She is loving and affectionate, and shows her feeling for him, and this encourages him to show the softer side of his nature to her. She can have anything she wants from him, without even asking.

The Aries man likes to rule the roost, and he does. His Libran woman will make a beautiful and harmonious home for him, and welcome all his friends. She entertains very well, always takes trouble with her appearance and puts a great deal of time and money into making sure she always looks her best. The Aries man does not stint her; he is proud of her and willing to work hard so that she can shine.

They will entertain a great deal, and if he puts his foot in it, she will move in smoothly to defuse the situation. If they have children, he will be the lord and master and this allows her to give full sway to her femininity and to be a kind and loving mother. Their children will grow up with a firm but proud and doting father, and a mother who puts a lot of harmony and laughter into the home and keeps it running smoothly. This will be a happy couple. They will always put each other first, and their physical relationship will iron out any small problems that arise between them.

Libra Woman—Taurus Man. This is a good combination. He is dominant and stubborn; she is feminine and quite prepared to do what he tells her. If she doesn't want to, she will not argue with him, but use her charm to get her own way, without him even being aware that he has been talked round. Sometimes he does know—but she is so sweet, he will let her get away with it.

Their love life is good: they are very well matched. The Taurus man is sensuous, and so is the Libran woman. There is a lot of passion here, and a lot of love too, and when their love life is going well (which it usually is) the happiness they gain from it spills over into the rest of their lives, and they are very happy together. He is not too demanding, but he lets her know in no uncertain terms how attractive he finds her, and this is exactly what she loves to hear. She is loving and affectionate and will make him feel wanted.

He is protective and strong, and she wants and needs protection. She loves luxury and pleasure, and so does he, and they will be very happy in their home life, because she will create a beautiful home and he will give her the money to do it well. The only area of friction could be that she is very social; she likes a lot of friends on a superficial level and tends to have them constantly in and out of the house. The Taurean does not really like this. His home is his castle, and to tell the truth, he is a little jealous when too much of her attention goes away from him. She will see at once when he is getting to this stage, and will take a break from her friends and concentrate on him, charming and relaxing him until he is quite happy again. Any children will be secure and quietly happy.

Libra Woman—Gemini Man.

These two have much in common. Both are flirtatious, sociable, fond of luxury and beauty and both like to be part of a glittering social whirl— the more glittering the better.

Physically, their relationship is quite good, but only because they have so much going for them mentally. A Gemini man is quickly bored, and this applies in his love life as well as in other areas. He likes the style a Libran woman has, her attention to her appearance, and her taste in clothes. He can be proud of her. She knows how to mix well socially and he approves of that.

He pretends not to be very interested in the home, but in fact he is secretly pleased at the amount of money and effort a Libran woman will put into making it a luxurious and beautiful setting. He has many friends and needs somewhere suitable to entertain them.

He is not very fond of home life: he likes travel. She is happiest entertaining at home or being a guest of her friends, but she does want exciting and interesting vacations, and he will provide many of them. This is when they will have their happiest times, free to do just as they please, and just live for pleasure. They do not like roughing it, however, and will spare no expense to see that they don't have to.

The Gemini man is a great conversationalist, and very witty and amusing, and as the Libran woman loves to be entertained she will enjoy this side of him. He is not moody, but can be irritable, and when he is she will always be able to charm him into a good humor again. Any children they have will have to fit in with them.

Libra Woman—Cancer Man.
This couple will be very successful together in some ways, less so in others. She loves beautiful surroundings, harmony, luxury, and an easy life. He, in his turn, is very home-loving and will appreciate the home she has made and help her to make it exactly as she wishes.

Physically, they hit it off together, because she can charm the birds off the trees and is instantly attractive to the emotional Cancer man; he knows how to please a woman and will court her in a most wonderful way, with flowers, little presents and treats specially designed to please her. They are compatible and although she is more passionate than he is, he is more emotional and both have a great need to give and receive love.

Any difficulties are likely to arise from their difference in temperament. The Cancer man is extremely sensitive, moody and sometimes depressive. The Libra woman values equilibrium; she likes things to be positive. Her own moods respond very much to those around her and if she is in a depressing atmosphere, it affects her too. She hates gloom.

Her usual reaction to any sort of difficult situation is to try to charm her way out of it, smooth things over, get a little lightness into the proceedings and just carry on. Sometimes this does work with her Cancerian man, but more usually it does not: he becomes more and more gloomy because he thinks she is not taking him seriously. This is where the Libra woman scores. She knows instinctively when it is time to stop talking and, if she is wise, she will show him great affection and kindness, reassuring him of her love for him. Any children will have to compete with him for attention.

Libra Woman—Leo Man.

She is very feminine. She likes a man to take the lead and to provide for her and protect her. He does this and does it well. With her perfect taste and love of luxury, the Libra woman is quite a high spender and so is the Leo man. They both love nice surroundings: in fact he likes his home to be a palace and understands that this takes money. Provided she always allows him to be in charge, he will provide whatever she wants without complaint.

Physically, he can draw a response from her like no other man. He is fiery and passionate, she is loving and giving. If a Leo man is happy in love, he is a happy man and a joy to live with—when he is not, nothing else is right. She does make him happy and in return he adores her. She does not argue with him or cross him, she makes good use of his money to provide a beautiful home he can be proud of, and she lets him have all his own way—or so he thinks. Actually she is very good at getting her own way. She manipulates him into thinking he is in charge, but wheedles whatever she wants from him and makes him think it is his idea. He is not very fond of parties, but she is—and she, with her gentle voice and smiling ways, will make him actually want to escort her, if only to stop anyone else getting too close to her. She loves to entertain at home and so does he, so there are no problems there. Both are good hosts and hostesses: their guests want for nothing. It is a point of pride with Leo, and pleasure with Libra, to give them the very best. If they have children, she must remember always to give him pride of place; then all will be well.

Libra Woman—Virgo Man. A difficult combination. The Libra woman, with her love of luxury, ease and pleasure, is at odds with the basic character of the Virgo man, who is careful with money, hardworking, and dislikes ostentation. He may be drawn to her because she is such a charmer, and even he is not immune to that, but when he gets to know her, he will worry about her extravagance and her generally easy attitude to life and work. Work, for him, is a serious matter.

Physically, they are not well attuned. She is sensuous and feminine, he is inclined to be cold. His way of showing love is quite different: he is unselfish, seeking only to serve and work for those he loves, and although he can love very deeply, he has great difficulty in showing it, particularly in the ways that a Libran woman appreciates.

He does not have a large circle of friends; she has many, since she likes to be at the center of a social whirl. She likes giving parties and going to them and does not stint on the cost. To the Virgo man, who dislikes parties anyway, it seems a waste of money and this is something he really dislikes.

The Virgo man excels when it comes to steady, deep devotion. He is wonderful in bad times and will help her when she is ill or having some serious setback in her life, and his love will not waver. The Libra woman likes this part of his character; she learns she can rely on him, and she may see the real extent of his love for her and respond to it.

Libra Woman—Libra Man. These two will be happy together, with real understanding and mutual needs and goals. Libra is the sign of marriage and both of them function better in a partnership than in any other way. Neither of them will try to be top dog and they will amiably give way to each other, without a quarrel.

Physically they are well suited. Neither of them likes deep, heavy relationships, but both are quite sensuous, deeply affectionate and loving and have a great need to share love, so their love life should suit them both. They will give each other little surprise presents and in a hundred little ways, each makes the other feel wanted, needed and cherished. Libra LOVES to feel cherished!

Since they both love luxury and ease, little conflict here as they set about making home a lovely, warm, harmonious place, both to live in and to entertain in. They are excellent hosts and hostesses and will be at their happiest among a brilliant circle of guests—the more celebrated the better. They are both social climbers and like nothing better than to have a "somebody" as a guest.

Each will spend a lot of money. They like clothes, good living and nice furnishings. They also love going out and when they do, they like the very best of everything. Somehow, the money does seem to come their way, but they are not willing to exert themselves to earn it.

The only difficulty with this relationship, happy though it is, is that neither of them is really willing to face up to responsibilities and when the bad times come, there is a risk that they will let each other down.

Libra Woman—Scorpio Man.
He is a real challenge to her. He is everything she is not: intense, passionate, magnetic and intense. He is very attractive and knows how to reach any woman he wants to. He wants to reach her: her charm, wit and vitality attract him strongly and her happy personality, so different from his own, acts like a tonic to him.

She is a flirt and although she is just playing games, he suffers agonies of jealousy. He is very possessive and will do anything to stop the woman he loves being pursued by other men. The Libra woman is loving and affectionate and when she realizes, as she soon does, how much it upsets her Scorpio lover (and how angry he becomes with her) she will take care not to show this side of her nature when he is there.

Their physical relationship is very special. He is a very passionate lover, and he will be able to lead her to great passion too. She is loving and sweet, sensuous and feminine, but when she has a Scorpio lover, he will teach her to match him and they will share a lot of love. This is their great strength and the more negative aspects of the relationship seem unimportant.

She dreads his black moods. She has such charm and powers of persuasion that she can sometimes coax him out of them.

When she cannot, she becomes gloomy herself. His intensity finds no echo in her light, bright self, and privately she wishes sometimes he was not such heavy going. They can be happy; but she must not trifle with him. He is faithful; she must be too.

Libra Woman—Sagittarius Man.
The Libra woman, sparkling and charming her way through life and getting her own way with most of the men she meets, will find that in the Sagittarian man she has met her match.

They are both very social, and quite likely to meet at a party. He will be attracted by her charm and ease in company, and will like her popularity—this always attracts him to a woman. Her dress sense, like everything else about her appearance and home, is perfect, and he notices and approves of these things. She will be attracted by his humor and quick wit. He is a great talker, and can switch from subject to subject without effort, seeming to know something about everything. He will make her laugh, interest her—and then not telephone her when she expects it.

This sets the scene for the whole relationship. It moves in stops and starts, which she does not like. She simply cannot tie him down, not to a date for dinner, much less to marriage. What she likes is partnership; what he likes is freedom. She does not fret as much as most women would under these circumstances: she has her own system of getting her way and when she realizes what she's up against, she makes plans.

He is not really a jealous type, but, dressed up and flirting with others while being just a very little bit cool to him, she can give even him a twinge. He doesn't want to lose her, and if she starts to move away, he will quickly follow. The woman who intrigues him and charms him has the best chance. If they are good together physically too, he's hooked.

Libra Woman—Capricorn Man.
He has great difficulties in his love life. He finds it very difficult to show affection, and takes refuge in biting sarcasm and a patronizing attitude. Inwardly, he is desperate for love and capable of loving deeply. She attracts him, for she is as light as he is deep, charming and sweet, and usually the center of an admiring crowd.

She will know how to charm him and skillfully lead the conversation, smoothing things over, until he has relaxed enough to act more naturally with her.

With time, they should get on well. He is very suspicious and cautious, and she is rather impatient with this side of his character, but she does not show it and gradually, little by little, the real Capricorn man emerges: loyal, ambitious, hard-working and self-controlled. Once he is committed, he gives of himself without restraint, and will do anything to please. She loves comfort and luxury, he does not—he likes quite spartan surroundings. But if he loves her, he will give in about this and much else besides, because she is such a charmer that he cannot resist giving her what she wants.

Physically, he is a slow starter. He is so afraid of rejection that he will not make the first move, and will ignore quite obvious signals, just in case he's wrong. Once embarked on a love affair, he still holds back but the sensuous Libra woman can work magic with him and within a very short time they have a satisfactory and happy love life. This is a relationship that gets better and better. He counts himself very lucky to have met her—and he is.

Libra Woman—Aquarius Man. This relationship is well-starred. The Aquarian and Libran are in instinctive sympathy with each other—they are on the same wavelength. He is aloof, detached, and cool; but he is also intelligent and witty, and this she likes. As for her—she is charm itself, amusing and entertaining, and very sociable. He likes this, and will join the group of admirers that usually surrounds her.

Neither of them have really deep feelings: they like light, unstressed relationships, and do not want to mix with the more intense types. They loathe quarrels and rows, and will do anything to restore a good atmosphere. With each other, they can relax. Neither of them is going to make too much of a fuss about anything. Libra is a flirt, but he really doesn't mind—if he even notices. He seems in a world of his own a lot of the time. He has the same wish to live in beautiful surroundings as she does and loves her good taste. He has no real sense of money and will just let her go her own way on this, as in everything, and will expect her to let him do the same.

Aquarian men are very solo creatures. They are not looking for partnership, they don't like it. She is a marrier, and could ensnare him; he may drift into it through indifference, and because of this, she will manipulate him.

Physically, they are not very passionate. He is cool and much more interested in the mind and personality than in love; she is sensuous and capable of passion with the right partner, but it is not high on her list and she does not mind its absence.

Libra Woman—Pisces Man. He is sensitive, retiring,

moody and very easily hurt. She will find it difficult to build a relationship with him. She likes easy, undemanding people, who, though somewhat superficial, amuse or entertain her and don't cause her too many problems. She is bright and happy —and likes others to be likewise.

In her physical relationship with Pisces, the Libra woman will be drawn to his gentleness and kindness, and he is very loving and emotional, much more so than he appears to be. He loves seldom—and deeply. She is much more balanced than he is and will find it difficult to deal with so many emotional swings. She is loving and affectionate, so she expects love to be a happy experience; but it is often a trauma to Pisces. Their physical relationship can be surprisingly good, however, as each is a loving and giving person.

She loves parties, both giving them and going to them. He is quiet and retiring and doesn't really mix well. Nevertheless, he will play host happily enough because he likes looking after people, and she will sparkle away happily in the center, talking and charming the night away.

He likes comfortable surroundings, as does she, and both will make sure they have comfort and style. The Piscean man loves beautiful things, especially antiques, and the Libra woman will have such marvelous taste that he will happily live within the environment she creates.

If she controls her feelings of impatience with him and he takes on some of her sunny ways, they will settle well together.

Libra Man—Aries Woman. He is smooth and charming and she will find him very attractive. He knows how to draw her out, and get behind the abrasive character she sometimes presents, to the feminine woman who is longing to get out.

She is truthful, kind and loyal. She sticks to those she loves through thick and thin. She is tactless, though, and her Libran man will move in quickly to cover up for her and restore harmony. He is a very good mixer, and will take her out to nice places and show her how to enjoy life. The Aries woman is not mean, but she does sometimes wonder where all the money is coming from to support the extravagant lifestyle that the Libran man loves and needs. She is quite impulsive herself, however, so she will not nag him.

In their love life, he brings a touch of romance to the Arian woman, who, although more passionate than he is, is not known for romance. He will buy her little presents and knows how to court her. He has a great need to give and receive love, and once he has managed to make her understand that his interest and love are really genuine, she will be as responsive as he could wish.

he only real difficulty is that while the Aries woman is absolutely loyal and shines during adversity, the Libran man is a bit lightweight and tends to back away from situations that make him uncomfortable or angry. He may not stick to her as he should and she feels let down when he is less loyal than she is.

The lightness of touch that he brings to a relationship will make for happiness and harmony and she will teach him loyalty.

Libra Man—Taurus Woman. Not quite such a good combination as Taurus man–Libra woman, but quite good all the same. She may have a tendency to dominate the more lightweight Libra man. He will not resent this but she will. She likes the man to be in charge.

He is attracted to her for her peaceful and pleasant nature. He likes harmony and balance and so does she. Neither of them like arguments and quarrels, and a Libra man will run a mile to get out of an explosive situation or avoid unpleasantness.

She is placid, but once something angers her she has a formidable temper, and will not back away from a confrontation. Things rarely get to this stage between these two. He is a real charmer, and is so sensitive to the moods of his woman that he sees storm clouds brewing almost before she does and will step in to talk and charm and smooth things over before they get out of hand.

They share a love of luxury and comfort, and will happily spend lavishly to achieve it. He is more social than she is: he likes parties (both his own and other people's) and although she is not quite so keen on going out, she is very fond of entertaining and showing off her beautiful home, and is a good hostess as the Libran man is a good host.

Physically they are compatible. She is sensuous and passionate. He is sensuous too, but he is less passionate and more loving. He is very affectionate and longs to love and be loved. He does not want to assert himself, but if they are to be happy he sometimes must; she needs to know that he can, then all will be well.

Libra Man—Gemini Woman.
These two really like each other. They have a great deal in common, both fond of luxury and beauty, liking to be part of a glittering social circle. He likes to shine, which he does because of his polished charm and style, and she likes a lot of company because she is quick witted enough to be a marvelous conversationalist. She will never bore him—and he will never bore her. They are both rather superficial, they do not like deep or heavy relationships, and their companionship is mental rather than physical. Nevertheless, he has a strong need to love and be loved, and she will be able to hold him. She is loving too, but has a light touch. The heights of passion are not for this couple.

He loves beautiful surroundings. He likes his home to have every comfort and luxury, both for his own benefit and for those he likes to entertain so regularly; the Gemini woman is not fond of home life and this could be a point of friction.

What the Gemini woman likes is travel, and he is quite happy to go with her on many long and interesting holidays. They will get away together at every possible opportunity, and this is when they have their happiest times. They enjoy meeting new people all the time and his charm and her wit and humor ensure that they shine. They can live as they please, and his wish for a life of ease and pleasure is granted, while she, very rarely able to relax, is able to unwind. This is the lightest of romances, mixed with a strong friendship, and it can be surprisingly permanent.

Libra Man—Cancer Woman. This is rather a good combination. This couple will be quite successful together. She is a great home-maker. Creating a beautiful home to her is a work of art and the Libran man, with his liking for beauty and harmony all around him, will appreciate it and tell her so.

Physically they get on well together. He is rather lightweight in relationships, and never really involves himself, although he has many women friends, but with her it is different. She is very emotional and loving, and there is something in him that needs to love and be loved, so he is very affectionate and loving to her. Neither of them is very passionate—he because he dislikes heavy relationships; she because she is exceptionally receptive, and will only find passion with a partner who brings this out in her. She is the type of woman to intuitively be what the man wants her to be.

Both like the luxuries of life, and this includes entertaining and being entertained in high style. In the case of the Libran man, it also means going out a great deal socially, always to the best places. He is very knowledgeable about food and wine. She will go along with him and will really enjoy it, because although she is not as social as he is, she loves good things to eat and drink; in fact, she can be rather greedy at times.

He is a man-about-town. Occasionally, it will irk him to have a Cancerian woman clinging to him everywhere he goes. It is a small enough price to pay, though, for a happy and gentle love.

Libra Man—Leo Woman. Not a lot of natural sympathy between these two. The Libra man, though very charming and entertaining, is a bit of a lightweight. He won't stop to

argue the point, even with a Leo woman, because he hates confrontations, quarrels and sulks; he will just skillfully alter the course of the conversation, and smooth things over. She is usually attracted to him, particularly if she has been having a bad time emotionally just before they meet. He is so genuinely sympathetic—and he really understands women. He will draw her out and amuse her.

It is when the relationship takes a deeper turn that problems become visible. She appears to always want to be in charge—but she has a secret wish. Where her love-life is involved, she wants a man who is stronger than she is, who will lead so that she can follow. She is an intensely feminine woman, looking for a man who is masculine enough to make her feel secure. He likes nothing better than a partnership—he doesn't even want to lead and this will disappoint her.

They may well team up for a while. He is attracted by the golden glow she always has. He likes her vitality and life and he understands women well enough to be able to see through her mask of boyishness and pride to the real woman inside. However, it would take more strength than he possesses, and less laziness, to establish a really good strong relationship with her; in any case, he doesn't really like strong relationships—he likes flirting with a lot of women (he just cannot resist trying out his charm on them) and they are fated to be ships that pass in the night.

Libra Man—Virgo Woman.
An unlikely couple. There is not a lot of basis for attraction between them, other than his undoubted charm. He is attractive to everyone, and that includes her. When she gets to know him better however, she will realize that he is luxury loving, fond of a life of pleasure and ease, and disinclined to work very hard for it. This goes against her own character. She is a worker, through and through. She is careful with money and will not like the reckless way a Libra man spends money. If funds are low, she will become exasperated with him, but if there is enough money, although she won't approve, she will let him go his own way.

Physically, they won't spark each other at all. She is unawakened. She is not born with passion: she has to be led into it; and he, more loving than passionate and more flirtatious than he should be, is certainly not the man to bring her to life.

He likes luxury living. She likes thrift and can be mean. If she loves him, she will show her love quite differently to him —she will work hard for him, serve him, take wonderful care of him when he is ill or unhappy and stand by him no matter what. He, in turn, can charm her out of her serious moods, make her laugh, and show her a lighter side of life she never even knew existed, until she met him.

They may not be together for a lifetime, but there is something so irresistibly kind about a Libra man, so relaxing and charming and sweet, that she will never really forget the time they had together, and in his turn, he will remember her and miss her sterling qualities.

Libra Man—Libra Woman. Made for each other.
There is real understanding between them, and nobody is going to make too much fuss about anything. Libra is the sign of marriage; they like to run in double harness. They like the company and the back-up. They shine even better in twos.

Physically, they are very compatible. She is sensuous and knows how to draw a response from him—once he discovers that this relationship is going to be a happy one, with few moods, sulks, or rows, he can relax and be as loving as he wants to be. He is very affectionate by nature, and loving rather than highly passionate.

They love the sense of freedom they get with each other. Both are flirts, but neither really minds, quite admiring the way their Libra partner sparkles at parties, getting all the attention. They are rather superficial. Neither is looking for a deep or intense love. They like rather a good time, spending a lot of money, dressing well, and living a life of high style. They hate very earnest people, and they hate boredom. Luxury lovers, they will make sure they both have every comfort. She will create a beautiful and harmonious home, with no expense spared; he will take a close interest in it all and design some of it himself.

Together they can lead the good life. The only difficulty is that neither likes responsibilities and if things go wrong, neither is going to want to have to deal with a bad situation—their instinct is to melt away. There is a risk that they might let each other down—provided this doesn't happen, they will be happy together.

Libra Man—Scorpio Woman.
Any partnership with a Libran man will be pleasant and peaceful. He hates confrontations and will go to great lengths to avoid them. Libra is the sign of marriage, and he is very happy and makes a good husband, once he finds the right woman. The Scorpio woman tends to frighten him off. She is so intense, and he likes romantic flirtations better than passion; but she does attract him—and he attracts her. He is very charming, smooth and polished. He knows how to conduct a courtship.

She will love the charm and attention, and will use all her considerable powers to attract him. She may be happy with him initially, but their lovemaking is likely to be a disappointment to her. She needs a partner who will match her own passion; though affectionate and very loving, he will never do that. Physical love is not the most important thing to him. He is sensitive and refined, and prefers a different type of love, undemanding and light-hearted.

Emotionally, there is more compatibility. He is exceptionally skillful at handling women. He understands them, and he likes them. Even her moodiness and jealousy can be soothed by him. The one thing he cannot get away with is flirting in front of her. She is absolutely faithful, and insists he is also. He will not mind this. He is faithful and happy to be so—he is not looking for complications. He will try to please her, and usually succeed. She will keep him fully occupied. She makes an excellent wife and mother, loving, loyal and kind. Although he does not want to, it would be better if he made some show of taking the lead and being in charge from time to time; they both will be happier if he does.

Libra Man—Sagittarius Woman.
The Libra man, practised charmer though he is, has nothing on the Sagittarian woman. In her, he has met his match.

They are both very sociable. They like parties and a whirl of activity. He will be attracted to her vitality and wit, and she will love his charm and sense of style. She is popular, and so is he; they make a good pair. They are both great talkers, and good mixers and both like to have plenty of friends.

He is a flirt—but so is she, and he will find this amusing. He is very sure of himself, but she will make him less so; just as he thinks the courtship is going really well, she will drop out of circulation for a day or two. It is an on and off relationship and as he usually makes all the moves he will not much care for this.

She likes to be free; she is wary of being tied down and he likes a partnership better than anything else. Libra is the sign of marriage, and he is looking for an easy–going partnership and companionship above all. He understands and likes women, and is very good at manipulating them, and she will be no exception. She will soon respond to him if he withdraws from her a little; she doesn't want to lose him.

Physically they are well matched. The Sagittarian woman is passionate, though not possessive, and the Libran man is loving and affectionate. They have a lot in common and neither is subject to moodiness. She has a real temper though, and he will have to learn to handle it. He will do it by refusing to argue.

Libra Man—Capricorn Woman.

He may find her daunting to start with. She is serious and ambitious, and has not much sense of humor. However, like most other women, she cannot help responding to his charm. He is very easy to get on with and is very good for her as he encourages her to take a more lighthearted view of life; and she will enjoy his company.

Physically, her response may surprise him. She appears rather cold on first acquaintance, but this is misleading; she is shy, and not very sure of her powers of attraction. The Libran man, most of all the signs of the zodiac, has the power to soothe and reassure women, and once she is sure of his affection, and loses her fear that he will reject her, she is capable of passion and deep love.

With time, they should build a strong relationship. She has a great need for permanence, and once she is sure of him will be ready to make a commitment. Libra is the sign of marriage, and he really enjoys the companionship of a partnership. He functions best when he has chosen a partner.

Both are faithful. She is single minded, and once she has made her choice, is not interested in other men. He will always be a flirt, but she understands this and does not feel threatened by it. She was attracted by his charm, and she enjoys seeing him sparkle in company when she knows he is hers alone and that she has nothing to fear.

The only problem is likely to arise over money. She is very money conscious and does not like waste, and he is a big spender and a lover of luxury in all forms. She will control his worst extravagances and he won't mind too much.

Libra Man—Aquarius Woman. This is a very promising relationship. They get on well. They understand each other without the need of words. The Libran man is charm itself, and the Aquarian woman is very attracted to his light, bright personality. She does not like gloomy or intense people, preferring a light touch. She has a great sense of humor and is always ready for amusement. The Libran man likes her wit and intelligence and cool reserve, and she likes his easy manner.

Neither of them has deep feelings. They prefer light, undemanding relationships. They both hate quarrels and rows, and will go to great lengths to try to avoid them; he will back away from any confrontation and try to smooth things over, and she admires this approach and likes the harmony it brings to their relationship. She has no liking for scenes—they bore her.

He will always be a flirt, but she doesn't really mind. Passion does not play a very big part in her life; she is intellectual rather than physical, although she will respond to the loving and affectionate nature of the Libran man. He has a great need to give and receive love and although her need is less, she is caring and tender.

The real snag in this relationship is that she is a loner. Even when she is part of a happy, sociable crowd, she is very much on her own. Libra is the sign of marriage, and Librans are happiest of all in pairs. If he will give her sufficient freedom, she is more likely to settle with him than anyone. Companionship with privacy must be the goal.

Libra Man—Pisces Woman. He likes to be the center of attention, and she wants a man she can admire, so this relationship is off to a good start. He is very self-confident, charming and popular—he sparkles in company and is always in demand as a guest, and, shy and retiring, she will be flattered by his attention.

He understands women, and one of his most skillful ploys is to give them his undivided attention. He is very drawn to her gentleness and sweetness, and more than usually protective of her. Generally speaking, he is rather superficial; he likes light relationships without problems and happy confident people who do not suffer from moods. Most of all he hates quarrelsome, abrasive people. They turn him off. But the Piscean woman, although sensitive, is attractive to him. She is emotional, but he is so sweet to her and careful of her feelings that they are very happy together.

Physically they will get on well. She is emotional and loving, and this brings out the best in him. He has a great need to love and be loved, and feels able to express this fully with her. She is restful, quiet and content to let him take the limelight.

Both of them like the finer things of life and both are looking for a partnership. She wants it because she is insecure and can only thrive when she is certain she is loved; he wants it because he is happiest in a twosome. Libra is the sign of marriage.

VIII. Scorpio

The Scorpio Character

Scorpio men and women are magnetic, attractive people, with great strength of character. They are hardworking and loyal and expect the same high standards from other people. They love approval and will go to great lengths for praise, while refusing to do anything through force.

They can be charming when they are getting their own way, but surprisingly obstinate when they are not. Those in their circle learn to be diplomatic when they are dealing with them and Scorpio people are invariably courteous and willing in return. They rise to a challenge and will make supreme efforts, often with great self-sacrifice, to fulfill their obligations.

The Scorpio individual is fully conscious of his or her own merits and equally able to see merit in others and to set it before personal preference. They make remarkable critics, are very shrewd and possess keen judgment. Mentally, they are somewhat suspicious and skeptical and they love to probe all things to the core.

The typical Scorpio has a firm, controlled personality and is not given to constant outbursts of temper; however, if they are seriously offended or angered they will not easily forgive and they never forget. Their anger is cold, powerful and long-lasting and those who have crossed them usually regret it. They find themselves pushed out to the edges of the charmed circle that surrounds Scorpios, waiting to be accepted once again.

The Scorpio individual is physically strong and rarely ill. When they are, they have a great deal of internal force and recuperative power and they possess intuitive knowledge of the kind of medicine that best suits their requirements. They excel in nursing and often make a sick person feel better just by their presence.

Financially they succeed by adapting themselves to their work, by doing their best and working very hard.

They nearly always do well in life, having the will-power and determination to rise in the world. Success is very important to them: they are ambitious and whatever type of work they choose, they want to shine and to be the very best in their field. While they are high achievers, they are realistic and will not take on anything they are not sure they can do well.

Scorpios are tenaciously attached to the family. They are devoted and faithful sons and daughters, remaining firmly attached to brothers and sisters and always seeking to help and guide them. They stay closely attached to their families throughout life. As parents they take their responsibilities seriously and are as ambitious for their children as they are for themselves. They are very interested in their children's education and welfare and make excellent parents, loving and careful. The only difficulties they usually experience with their children are battles over independence, with the children anxious to make attempts on their own and the protective Scorpio parent unwilling to allow them to take risks. There can be some heated discussions when Scorpio, as always, insists that parents know best.

The Scorpio person meets life with courage whatever the setbacks, and quietly and patiently continues with the long term plan for making life better and happier for themselves and those around them; and, truth to tell, they usually succeed. They use the Scorpio strength of character as ballast, the magnetism and charm as levers, and the good sense as a defense against others who lack their honesty. They give their loyalty to those who deserve and return it and quietly prosper.

However, Scorpio people have another side to their nature. At the extreme of the sign they can be cunning and crafty and too keen to serve their own ends at the expense of others. There may be jealousy, both of people and achievements by others, and this is something most Scorpio people have to struggle against. The very magnetism that most strongly attracts others to them can equally drive them away when it turns to possessiveness and jealousy.

Fault-finding can also be a Scorpio trait and one which causes misery in their relationships. The achievement of perfection is important to them and they can be intolerant of others less able than themselves.

It must also be said that the Scorpio temperament does tend to be vindictive. They do not forget an injury, and will wait, sometimes years, for an opportunity to even the score. If they have not had a chance to do so, the hurt and anger rankles on and on, until a chance presents itself. Then they will take their revenge, often to the amazement of those who are the target, who had long ago forgotten what seemed to them rather a large fuss over very little. This is the proverbial sting in the Scorpio tail and virtually all Scorpio people carry it. Usually this characteristic does not alter with age: in fact it may become worse, because although Scorpios are not blind to their faults and are conscientious in trying to overcome them, in this case they feel that they are quite right and do not see it as a fault at all. Their sting is part of them.

How Scorpio Gets Along with Others

Scorpio with Aries

Money/Job. Scorpio makes a lot of money and uses it to live in lavish and comfortable style. They love beautiful things and best quality in everything. They are not careless with money; they organize it as they do everything else, to give them what they want. They hate waste but they are not mean and will not haggle over prices. They pay up without protest, unless they feel they are being cheated. If that happens, they will just walk away and refuse to deal with the person.

Jobwise, Scorpio and Aries people would not usually work well together. Although a Scorpio would value the truthfulness and loyalty of an Arien workmate the aggressiveness and lack of forethought and planning in the Aries partner would grate on the Scorpio—and both would want to be boss.

Home/Friends. Both Scorpio and Aries will want to be in charge here, so neither of them can have it all their own way. Scorpio has very good taste, so quite often Aries will give way over choice of furnishings and so forth, while insisting on having the last word over the house itself. This works quite well, as each thinks they have the best of the bargain: Scorpio is given a free hand to create confortable and beautiful surroundings, while the Aries partner feels in control having had the final say on the major investment.

Scorpio with Taurus

Money/Job. Scorpio and Taurus work well together. They understand and appreciate each other's quality of steadiness in work and will build up a mutual trust, letting the other work without constant supervision. They have similar feelings about money and success and are both methodical and hard-working. The difficulty lies in the instinctive dislike both have of working under anyone else; neither likes to be the underling. However, with so much else going for this team this can be overcome. Each respects the other; provided this continues, they can work in harmony, forgetting rank and achieving a great deal together.

Home/Friends. A happy combination. Both love their homes, and both enjoy luxury and quality. The home and family is the center of life for Scorpio and they will make it a great status symbol as well as a comfortable place to live. The Taurean will enjoy this and will help to achieve it. Neither enjoys socializing very much, but both like entertaining on their home ground, where they feel secure. This they do very well, making excellent hosts and hostesses and giving their friends the best of everything and their undivided attention while they are guests in their home. They both have a talent for design and decoration, which they put to good use. In the kitchen Taurus rules, because although Scorpio people love good food, it is the Taurean who is best at preparing wonderful meals.

Scorpio with Gemini

Money/Job. Scorpio is the heavyweight, Gemini the featherweight, in this contest: no question who is the boss—it's Scorpio. Gemini has a lightning mind and is usually engaged on several projects at once, quite a number of which are started but not finished. This enrages Scorpio, who is the opposite, working steadily at the job in hand and working for financial security. Gemini is also interested in financial security and if Scorpio can convince them of the need to persevere in one job and stay in one place until it is done, the partnership could work. Gemini is full of inventive ideas and labor-saving suggestions which actually do work: it is the constant need for change and diversion that is the trouble, but if Scorpio can organize them and keep them organized, a profitable partnership, led always by Scorpio, could result in benefit to both.

Home/Friends. Gemini likes lots of friends at a fairly superficial level: Scorpio likes fewer friendships, but deeper. They can compromise and have a happy social life with the chatterboxes who surround Gemini lightening the more intense relationships of Scorpio. In the home, Gemini will let Scorpio have full sway. All a Gemini asks is a home that runs like a hotel: constantly hot bathwater, food when required and a front door that they can depart from when traveling—which is most of the time.

Scorpio with Cancer

Money/Job. Scorpio and Cancer are on the same wavelength: they instinctively understand each other and will work together happily for a shared goal. They are particularly suited to work together in an artistic enterprise of some kind. The Cancerian respects the judgment and hard work of the Scorpio and will do whatever they can to help and take part of the load. In return, the Scorpio appreciates the many ways the Cancerian, working quietly in the background, supports them. The Scorpio is in charge, the Cancerian is happy to have it so. They make a great team.

Home/Friends. Scorpio and Cancer work hand-in-glove in creating a home to be proud of. For Cancer, it is mainly a wonderful chance for expressing creativity and making home a harmonious and happy place to be: for Scorpio, it is a status symbol as well, a place that shows the carefully chosen friends who are invited there that they have "arrived." Scorpio is selective about friends, only inviting old and trusted companions, and Cancer, who would like to have a wider circle, as always follows Scorpio's lead. They are both kind and hospitable to those they entertain, though they do not like sudden uninvited visitors and are not fond of being entertained in return, preferring home ground. They stay at home in preference to going out if possible, in comfort and style.

Scorpio with Leo

Money/Job. A difficult combination. Scorpio and Leo are both strong signs, but are usually to be found pulling in opposite directions. On the one hand, proud Leo is out to impress everyone and the primary aim of any business he owns or works in, he thinks, should be to show him as King. He is also very money-conscious, which is where he connects with Scorpio. Both want financial security and status, but Leo wants glory too. Scorpio would rather have approval and respect from those in working life and this can lead to friction, with Scorpio taking Leo down a painful peg or two in public. Very few people can dominate a Scorpio in any sphere: Leo can, and does. Workwise, Leo is boss. Emotionally, it is a different story.

Home/Friends. Scorpio makes an excellent friend, loyal and steadfast, but only to the chosen few. Leo is a good friend, but only on their terms and that means domination: of company, conversation and most other things. Their home will be a showplace, expensive and luxurious, but friends will not feel comfortable there because of the explosive undercurrents between Leo and Scorpio, as both silently battle it out. Leo will most often appear to win, but Scorpio is devious and will usually come off best in the end. These conflicts are about anything and everything: where to live, furnishings, even food. They are happiest going out: Leo never stints, nobody tries to be in charge, they have a wonderful time.

Scorpio with Virgo

Money/Job. Scorpio likes to lead, Virgo likes to serve. Job-wise, this combination works well. Virgo is as hard-working and cautious as even demanding Scorpio could wish and the result is prosperity and the fulfillment of Scorpio ambition. The Virgo aim is simply to do really well any job to which they set their hand, to give value for money; as such they make first class employees. The Scorpio boss appreciates such dedication and rewards it well and unstintingly, paying well and showing kindness and courtesy. Both are loyal to the other and both will work long hours without complaint when it is necessary. A satisfactory partnership.

Home/Friends. Home life runs smoothly. Scorpio makes the rules, Virgo keeps them. Scorpio sets the style, Virgo admires and maintains it. When they entertain, Scorpio draws up the menu and Virgo prepares it. Generally speaking they are liked by their friends, although some of them feel sorry for Virgo. However, their offers of advice or help are brushed aside: Virgo thinks it a privilege to carry out all Scorpio's many instructions to the letter. The result is a happy home with few arguments and little tension as both are admirably suited to their part of the relationship. They like a quiet family life, taking pleasure in their children who are their pride and joy.

Scorpio with Libra

Money/Job. Not an easy combination. Libra is intellectual and does not care to work too hard, Scorpio is a hard worker and expects others to be the same. Both are painstaking, however, and both will do a good job. While Libra likes the good things of life, they are less money oriented than Scorpio and there will be conflicts sometimes about this. Scorpio always wants to balance the books, while Libra works partly for pleasure in the job itself. If they can learn to compromise a little and meet each other half-way, it is a promising partnership, but if Scorpio is too demanding Libra will be unable to continue working with them.

Home/Friends. Libra finds some of Scorpio's friends dull, Scorpio thinks most of Libra's friends are shallow, but as both are very good hosts, the friends will be made welcome and will not realize it. Their home will be well-furnished and comfortable, and both like a good standard of living. Their combined taste is good and the general effect will be pleasing to both of them. Libra likes to socialize, particularly by going to the best restaurants and the theater, and will encourage Scorpio to do the same. Scorpio will enjoy the lively atmosphere quite a bit, though not so much as entertaining at home. Both enjoy this, especially if they entertain the two very different sets of friends, separately.

Scorpio with Scorpio

Money/Job. This is a good working relationship with few problems. They have an instinctive understanding of each other and usually agree about the best way to carry out work. They are both ambitious and highly motivated about money and will work hard and long to achieve their aims. The only conflicts that might arise are if they are in competition with each other in any way. Both are winners and neither likes to be second best. This also applies if one is senior to the other: both will want to be the boss and there will be a hard and probably unending struggle with each of them trying to outdo the other. They will each appreciate the contribution the other makes and this should make a business relationship a success.

Home/Friends. As Scorpio likes family better than friends, and old friends more than new ones, they will suit each other perfectly, creating a cosy circle for themselves out of mutually-liked people. Neither will ask the other to entertain acquaintances and they will like to spend a good deal of time alone together in their home, where they will be good companions.

Their home will be quiet, harmonious and beautiful and they will both take time and trouble to see that it remains that way. They will not stint the money that it costs to provide it and will give their children every advantage and comfort.

Scorpio with Sagittarius

Money/Job. Scorpio is hard-working, money-conscious, and painstaking. Sagittarius is not. Conflicts are inevitable. The Sagittarian is quick-witted, quick moving and inventive, but they become quickly bored with routine and are soon ready to try something new. Scorpio will keep on patiently working and it infuriates them to discover half-completed jobs, or to feel they are being left with most of the duller jobs, while Sagittarius shines, laughs and spends too much money. Scorpio is not mean and is always willing to pay for the job, but the books must balance in the end. Sagittarius likes money but is uninterested in bookkeeping. Also they do not like to be dominated or tied down. Scorpio cannot cope with this and their partnership will probably be short-lived.

Home/Friends. Sagittarius likes to go out, Scorpio likes to stay in and be cosy. Sagittarius has many friends and interests and although they like a nice home, it is mainly so they can bring a great many friends in and out of it and keep up a constant swirl of activity. To Scorpio the home is the center of the world, to be carefully chosen and then well-cared-for, shared only with their closest friends. It is easy to see that this would be a partnership with many strains. If there are children, Sagittarius will love them, but Scorpio will raise them.

Scorpio with Capricorn

Money/Job. Scorpio and Capricorn make a good combination, workwise. Both are steady workers, cautious and careful, both are ambitious and both know the value of money. They do not need to communicate to each other the necessity for doing a good job, because both understand it perfectly. They are painstaking and good at attending to detail. They both have tenacity and stamina. They rarely argue over matters of work, not even over who is in charge, because each trusts the other. If ever they do disagree, it is likely to be because Scorpio wants to draw some of their hard-earned money out and Capricorn wants every penny to stay where it is. These are not serious disagreements and the working relationship is a good one.

Home/Friends. Scorpio wants a home to reflect their personality: warm, comfortable and luxurious, a status symbol as well as a home. Capricorn's taste runs to the spartan and they dislike ostentation, although they are clean and tidy. Therefore, there is some conflict over the home. In most things Scorpio will listen to sensible Capricorn, but where the home is concerned, they will not, and usually the home reflects Scorpio. Neither of them make many friends, but those they have are permanent and will be invited to their home and pleasantly entertained. A rather cold, business-like relationship.

Scorpio with Aquarius

Money/Job. Scorpio will irritate Aquarius with demands for accountability, good timekeeping, application to the job in hand and attention to detail. In turn, Aquarius will absolutely enrage Scorpio by their complete disregard of all these things, by their lack of ambition, disinterest in money and boredom with the mundane. They are so unalike that they do not understand in the slightest the other point of view: Aquarius will work for virtually nothing if they are interested in what they are doing, or think it is worthwhile. Scorpio is ambitious and the question of money is uppermost in their minds. It is virtually impossible for them to have a worthwhile relationship where work or money is concerned.

Home/Friends. To Scorpio, the home is the inner sanctum, where they can relax and truly be themselves. They do not mind the cost and they will work hard to keep the home beautiful and welcoming—but only to their close friends. Aquarius, on the other hand, flits in and out, usually accompanied by several friends, most of them new. As these friends tend to be eccentric or artistic or both, Scorpio very much resents the intrusion of Aquarius' friends into their home. There is no real point of contact; Scorpio is lavish, Aquarius is thrifty and they differ in every way. They resent each other and if there are children, the resentment is doubled.

Scorpio with Pisces

Money/Job. Scorpio and Pisces make a good team in the world of work. Pisces loves money and an easy life, though they lack ambition. Scorpio has more than enough ambition for both and the same love of money, comfort and status. Pisces lacks drive, so Scorpio's strength of character is a positive help to them, preventing too much daydreaming and encouraging them to do well. There is a good deal of sympathy between them and they understand the need to work for the good things in life that they both wish to have. This is a good partnership, so long as Scorpio takes the lead.

Home/Friends. Both Pisces and Scorpio are interested in the home and fond of home life. They both enjoy creating a beautiful setting to live in, although Pisces enjoys it on an artistic level and as a comfortable buffer against the world, while Scorpio likes it to be visible proof of their prestige and standing in the world. Both will put time, money and effort into the home without counting the cost and it will be well worth while, as they will much prefer to stay in, usually alone, than go out. Everything they need will be there, and if there are children, they will be part of a peaceful, harmonious home, with proud and devoted parents who will see that they lack nothing. The only occasional problem may arise because both Pisces and Scorpio are very moody.

Love Mates

Scorpio Woman—Aries Man. The Scorpio woman is passionate, possessive and faithful. She asks for total commitment in a lover and when she has this will give a deep and lasting love. To the Aries man, passion is more important than love. It is just a part of his life and he may find the total dedication she needs too high a price to pay, even for such a wonderful love affair. Physically they are well matched: although both have strong wills, she will accept and even secretly welcome the domination of an Aries man in a love relationship. It is the only time she prefers someone else to take the lead. He will sweep her off her feet and her response will be all he could ask.

Emotionally, it will be less easy. She is complex and moody and much more emotional than the straightforward Aries man and sometimes his lack of sensitivity will hurt her deeply. She shows this in silences that he finds difficult to cope with. He likes everything out in the open; she broods alone.

Both are faithful. He trusts her completely and she gives him no cause to do otherwise. On the other hand she will still be suspicious of him, and her possessiveness extends to friends and hobbies, too. She will resent the time and attention he gives to them. He will find her restrictions irksome. Any difficulties they experience will be over this. However, apart from this, they have a very good relationship, and one that will last.

Scorpio Woman—Taurus Man. This could be a very happy and satisfying relationship. The Taurus man is sensual and appreciates the magnetism and femininity of the Scorpio woman. He is passionate enough for her and she is loving enough for him. His possessiveness matches her own—both accept it as a sign of their value to the other partner and do not resent it. Both are faithful, but he does like to flirt and can be very charming to the ladies and when he does this she becomes intensely jealous. Provided he does not do it too often, there will just be a lovers' tiff followed by a loving kiss-and-make-up, a little spice added to the relationship and no harm done; but if he does it too often he will see the full force of her fury. Her own jealousy makes her unhappy and moody and can result in his being kept on a tight rein. However, they do understand each other and will not usually strain the relationship over this.

Emotionally, they are well suited. They have similar aims, likes and dislikes and both are stable. He does find her moods baffling, but he accepts them as part of her and generally tries to ignore them and let them pass. He is not moody himself; he prefers a civilized talk to sort thing out if they go wrong.

The Taurus man is a giver of surprise presents, flowers or perfume perhaps; the Scorpio woman loves these little attentions. In addition to love, they like and respect each other and will be happy together.

Scorpio Woman—Gemini Man. This relationship

could be a problem. She is intense and passionate, he is light and flirtatious—and not just with her. He is a great talker, fond of socializing, and quickly bored. He can be passionate, but he cools off quickly and is then ready to move on. The Scorpio woman is looking for an intense love affair, with total commitment, growing into something permanent. It is not difficult to see the problems that exist between these two.

There may initially be a very strong attraction—even Gemini responds to that Scorpio magnetism—and she will respond to his charm and attentiveness. It is when her affections are deepening, and he remains a little detached, that the trouble starts. The more she restricts him, the more he will keep aloof. The more intense and jealous she becomes, the more he will flirt and charm. It is not done to hurt her, but to underline his freedom.

The Gemini man is a romantic—he will write a beautiful love letter and can make very pretty speeches. To her, however, actions speak louder than words. She is strongly dramatic, passionate and loving and she is looking for a man who will appreciate and respond to her. He has a light touch; he is not very passionate and so he disappoints her. When she retreats into tears or moodiness, he will treat her kindly, but inwardly he has no patience with emotional demands on this level. When the emotional atmosphere gets too heavy, he will gradually extricate himself (he doesn't like rows) and secretly, she will be glad he has gone.

Scorpio Woman—Cancer Man. A very good combination. These two understand each other. Both are sensitive and loving and they will be careful not to hurt each other's feelings.

The Scorpio woman is emotional and passionate. She will attract the Cancerian man irresistibly by her femininity and in turn, he will attract her by his capacity for love and emotion. He will understand her need for commitment and will give to her unstintingly. He makes her feel secure by the tenderness and attention he shows her and she will respond to him with a deep love.

She is very intense and moody and he is so responsive he will pick up her mood instantly and match it with his own. They communicate with each other without words and both find this a very satisfying part of their relationship.

He is very protective and although she is strong, she likes to feel protected. Both prefer long-term relationships and theirs will deepen as time goes by. They do not really need or want other people, they are happiest on their own. Both are faithful by nature and neither will give the other cause for jealousy, but she has a jealous nature and will sometimes be suspicious of him for no real reason and when this happens, it hurts him deeply. Both are possessive and will accept the possessiveness of the other partner in return.

They are well suited and their relationship improves all the time, as they become more and more secure in it.

Scorpio Woman—Leo Man. He sees himself as a king—and he will treat her as a queen. He is very masculine and responds to her great femininity. Both have great personal magnetism and both need a great deal of love and give as much in return. Physically, they are wonderfully suited. The strong

Scorpio woman is very passionate and responds to the Leo man because he is even stronger than she is and will take the lead in their love relationship.

Emotionally, there is some lack of understanding. He requires constant reassurance and flattery; she believes that actions speak louder than words. She feels he should be content with the obvious love between them. He may seek compliments from other women if he feels unappreciated and may stray into other relationships in order to boost his ego.

The Scorpio woman is very jealous and if he gives her the smallest reason not to trust him, he will face a fury far greater than he expected. As loving as she is, she will turn on him and it will take all the considerable charm, passion and strength that he possesses to calm her down and set things to rights between them again. She is one of the very few that can tame the proud Leo man and if he loves her enough he will not want to lose her. This is an explosive and passionate partnership which can work if each treats the other with respect. Together, they have great potential.

Scorpio Woman—Virgo Man.

At first glance, this looks like a very unlikely relationship. The Scorpio woman, with her intense personal magnetism, her need for physical love and her deep moods and jealousies, is very different from the Virgo man. He is controlled, reserved, selfless and not very passionate. Initially, she is not usually attracted to him, but strangely enough, he is often very attracted to her. Virgo loves seldom, but when he does, he loves completely, and nothing is too much trouble.

The attraction for him is like the moth to the flame: dangerous, but irresistible. If he falls in love with a Scorpio woman, he will quietly plan how to draw her to him. He usually does this by always being there, ready to help, advise, or carry out her wishes. He will be a friend when she needs one, or look after her when she is ill. Gradually she will come to rely on him and he will never let her down.

Physically, they are not especially well suited. She needs a strong physical relationship and he does not. He puts physical love a long way down on his list, but to her it is all-important. He will show her affection, but not so much as she would like.

He does however, have other qualities, by which she sets great store. He is faithful (a must with her), he loves her devotedly and unselfishly and he always puts her needs first. Whatever she wants, he will try to provide for her and usually he will succeed. He expresses his love in service and in taking care of her. To the surprise of many their friends, she sometimes builds a permanent relationship with him.

Scorpio Woman—Libra Man. Any partnership with

a Libra man will be harmonious and peaceful. Libra is the sign of marriage and Libra men make good husbands, once they find the right woman. The Scorpio woman, with her love of intrigue, passion and danger may be in danger of frightening him off: he is not that intense, himself, and tends to try to avoid heavy emotional scenes, arguments, or clashes. He is refined, in fact rather a snob and her dignity will attract him to her. He is charming and attentive and knows how to conduct a courtship.

She will be charmed initially and will use all her considerable powers of magnetism, but their lovemaking is likely to be disappointing to her. She needs a partner who will match her own passion and intensity and the Libra man, although sweet and affectionate, will never do that. In his turn, he expects refinement and sensitivity in a woman and prefers an undemanding kind of love and easy acceptance. Physical love is not a top priority for him. He would rate mutual interests and compatibility more highly.

Emotionally, the picture is better. He understands women and is very skillful at handling them. She, with her moodiness and jealousy, can be quite a handful, but he is charm itself, does not flirt in front of her and is faithful and happy to be so. He does not want complications. He will charm her into a better mood when necessary, try to please and usually succeed. In return she will prove to be a loyal and loving wife, and mother.

Scorpio Woman—Scorpio Man. Perfection—or claustrophobia for two, depending on how you look at it. These two will have a love-life that reaches the highest peaks and neither of them will play around with other people. Both are faithful by nature and each will be fully satisfied with the other. They will be instantly attracted to each other, as they both have great personal magnetism, and owing to the strength of Scorpio they have stability too.

They are both rather lacking in humor, but since this affects them equally, it won't matter. They will take themselves and their love affair very seriously and will want to spend a lot of time alone together to make plans (which will not include other people). They are both very strong-willed; the only thing stronger-willed than a Scorpio woman is a Scorpio man. Even so, he won't always win—she uses her femininity to get her own way and he is very susceptible to that.

They make a strong partnership and have a close bond. They don't need to talk to each other much and in fact they don't: Scorpios are not very talkative people and they are not too keen on those who are.

They will work steadily together for their future and he will provide the rather luxurious home she needs. He is a good provider and she will not want for anything. She will make him happy as nobody else can and enjoy the feeling of protection she gains from him.

They will sometimes clash and when they do, it will be head-on, with both refusing to give way; when this happens, they will resolve their differences by making love. They will be together as long as they are in love and they will be in love as long as they are together.

Scorpio Woman—Sagittarius Man. The Scorpio woman, with her jealous, possessive, passionate temperament, will have a very difficult time if she falls in love with a Sagittarian man. He is very attractive and can return and match her passion, but he will not be prepared to be restricted by her in any way. Any jealousy she shows would make him cool towards her and he, like no other, can make it only too plain that nobody owns him, not even those he loves. What she likes above all else is love and possession. What he likes best of all is freedom: to do what he likes, when he likes, to go where he likes and with whom he likes. This will not suit her—she will react with hurt, then fury, tears and tantrums: it won't make any difference.

Truth to tell, he is a bit of a flirt. Women tend to chase him and he is very happy to let them. He is very good at a party, sociable and friendly and with a marvelous sense of humor. As he is genuinely loving and caring, many women think they will be the one who will persuade him to settle down. In fact he has no intention of settling down, at any rate not until he approaches middle age, and often not then. His love is quite genuine while it lasts and he will not lie to her. He will always tell her truthfully that he does not intend to marry; the trouble is, she is so magnetic and attractive and so successful with the opposite sex, she simply does not believe he means it.

If she loves him very much and is prepared to wait and not put any pressure on him until he is ready to put down roots, he may settle with her in the end. Being a Scorpio, an all-or-nothing woman, she is unlikely to do that.

Scorpio Woman—Capricorn Man.

The Capricorn man is an unusual character and never more so than when in love. He is full of self-doubt, which he covers by being casual and sometimes bitingly sarcastic. He does not like to show his feelings because of a possible rebuff, and he has to be very sure of his welcome from a woman before he can trust himself to show her any affection. Yet he has a great need for love. The Scorpio woman, magnetic, passionate and attractive, often scares him at first, but she can be very good for him because she will be determined to unlock his feelings and will usually succeed in doing so.

She is subtle and so is he, and if she is attracted to him, she will be able to bring him out and help him to show his feelings as she shows hers.

Physically, they will have a good relationship. She is uninhibited and loving and will take the lead so that he can be sure of her. Emotionally, he is so self-controlled and cautious that it takes him quite a time to commit himself to a woman, but once he does she can be sure he will be faithful (which she insists on) and will do nothing to arouse her jealousy.

He is an expert at hiding his own feelings and is sometimes startled by the open way she shows hers. The Scorpio woman is moody and easily hurt when he is cold to her and he finds it difficult to show he loves her all the time.

They are both ambitious and have many goals in common. He does not always understand her, particularly her closeness to her family, and is sometimes jealous of this; but generally speaking they get on well alone together.

Scorpio Woman—Aquarius Man. There will be lit-

tle sympathy between these two. He is detached and aloof. He dislikes displays of affection or any other strong feeling and is drawn to people by mental affinity, not physical. She is magnetic, attractive and possessive, with a strong jealous streak. Love means a great deal to her. She has a lot to give and expects total commitment from a man in return. This the Aquarian will not be prepared to give.

He has many friends, often rather eccentric or unusual. He enjoys good conversation and interesting ideas and he would rather have a constant ebb and flow of acquaintances, with everything kept very light, than closer relationships with one or two people, which quickly bore him. The Scorpio woman needs love first and foremost in her life. She is looking for intensity and passion to match her own: she will not find it with an Aquarian man. The many other people he is surrounded with confuse and annoy her and she cannot understand why he does not want to be alone with her.

He is, to tell the truth, a little afraid of her. She is so complex and moody, demanding and possessive. He can of course see her attraction, but it is not one that appeals to him. It would require him to make too much of an effort and do too much in return. He prefers to settle for a rather solitary life, associating with those of his choice when it suits him. The Scorpio woman is not looking for an occasional playmate, but a partner, who will try to understand her and love her equally. The most that could come from this relationship would be friendship.

Scorpio Woman—Pisces Man. He is ultra-sensitive, withdrawn and very emotional. She is also very emotional and sensitive, but much stronger, much more positive. She will take charge of this relationship and it is better that she does.

The Piscean man is a dreamer, and the hard-headed back-up of a Scorpio woman is very useful to him. It can help him make his dreams a reality. She will boost his morale and encourage him to try harder when all he really wants to do is give up.

This outwardly confident woman has a sensuous, moody side to her nature which is in harmony with him. He is so sensitive to changes in her mood that he never hurts her, changing direction as soon as he feels the slightest change in her manner. He will do anything to placate her and keep her happy and while she will not be conscious of this, she knows that most of the time she is with him, she is tranquil and happy herself.

Emotionally, it is quite a good match; they are on the same wavelength. Physically, it is not so good. The extreme gentleness and softness of the Piscean man does not accord with the Scorpio woman's requirement of a forceful, passionate partner, who can match her intensity and love. She will instinctively try to draw this reaction from him, but the only effect it will have is to make him withdraw into his shell still further and to become very negative and miserable.

The Scorpio woman is kind, and does not wish to hurt anyone. She will soon realise that in him she has the makings of a wonderful and understanding friend and that she should look elsewhere for a lover.

Scorpio Man—Aries Woman. She could be very happy with him: he understands her inner need for someone stronger than she is in her love-life, and he makes her feel so secure she can stop holding back and give freely. He is a wonderful lover and physically they will be very compatible.

However, the Scorpio man has very decided ideas about what a woman should be, his woman in particular, and he will try to dominate her in every way and become furious when he does not succeed. The Aries woman is very independent and it is this that he does not like or understand. She is also lacking in tact and often hurts or annoys him by her outspokenness. Two very strong wills are engaged here, and neither will back down.

There is a lot of love in this partnership and what usually happens is that he, being much more subtle, gets his own way more often than not by the simple expedient of making love to her, when most problems will be forgotten—Aries never bear malice and usually cannot remember what an argument was about half an hour later, anyway. Scorpio is one of the few men who can see through her independence and bring out her true femininity and for that man she will be prepared to quietly give up doing some of the things he doesn't like. He appears to accept the rest—but he is quietly working away to change any little ways of hers that he doesn't like.

Such is their love that the relationship usually smooths out after a time, with the Scorpio man, who would be inclined to jealousy with most other women, trusting and relaxing with her—though he does wish she would stop dashing about sometimes and stay at home.

Scorpio Man—Taurus Woman.

This should be a very happy combination. He is magnetic and physically attractive; she is sensuous and feminine. She is passionate enough for him and he is loving enough for her. Both are possessive and neither resents it in the other. They see it as a sign of true love and would both be unhappy with partners who were too casual. The Scorpio man demands absolute faithfulness, and the Taurean woman has no difficulty in being faithful to him. He is a wonderful lover and she is content with him. Although she does like to flirt a little, mainly to reassure herself of her own attractiveness, she will know when to stop and give her jealous Scorpio lover no cause to suspect her. He will not allow her to go too far and each understands this and accepts it.

They are also well suited emotionally, having similar likes and dislikes and aims in life. He is moody, but she is quite able to cope with his moods peacefully and restore him to a good humor when necessary.

She will make a happy and harmonious home life for him and he will provide her with the material comforts she expects and needs. She will give him plenty of attention and always put him first and as this is his main requirement they will have a good relationship.

The Taurean woman can be obstinate, but the Scorpio man knows how, in a subtle way, to win his way on most things. There are no real points of conflict between them; he needs love, and she understands this and responds.

Scorpio Man—Gemini Woman.
He is attracted by her brightness and charm. She is attracted to him by his intensity and passion, so different from her own nature. She cannot resist seeing how far she can go with him, but it will not be long before she comes up against his jealousy and possessiveness. Since she is not jealous herself, she does not understand it and she does not take it seriously. The Gemini woman is a great game-player, and will flirt at a party while her Scorpio man fumes. If she does it too often, however, she will meet the full force of his anger. It makes him feel insecure and he is not going to put up with that.

He is possessive and it is when he attempts to restrict her that the difficulties start. She does not enjoy very intense relationships, preferring a light and undemanding love that will maintain her freedom. She likes to travel and she accounts to no one for her movements. This plunges him into agonies of doubt and he becomes very jealous indeed, even of her friends. The more she struggles to be free, the tighter he holds on to her.

The Scorpio man is, most of all, looking for a woman he can love unrestrainedly and who will give him the same love in return. He wants an exclusive relationship. Gemini does not. She becomes lonely without her friends and busy social life and inwardly exasperated by the moods and emotional demands for more and more of her time and attention. The more that Scorpio holds on, the more Gemini withdraws, until gradually she moves away from him altogether, leaving him free to find someone else to have and to hold—his dearest wish.

Scorpio Man—Cancer Woman. A near-perfect combination. These two understand each other. They will be careful not to annoy or upset each other, because they are both sensitive and loving.

She is very feminine and intuitive, and is very attracted to his similar nature, great magnetism and strength.

The Scorpio man is passionate and intense. He will attract the Cancer woman because she is sensuous and needs a man to take charge of her and their relationship. She needs to be able to trust him and expects his protection. The Scorpio man has a deep need to care for those he loves, watch over their interests and give great security, both emotionally and materially.

He will work hard to provide her with the means to maintain a truly beautiful home and she will happily use her good taste and color sense to make a home he can be proud of and enjoy spending time in. If they have children, she will be a perfect mother and he a proud and supportive father. He will not need to tell her how they should be brought up; her ways will be completely in tune with his and they will have the same outlook on most things.

The Cancer woman is eager to please and not very strong willed. Her Scorpio man will set the pace and she will follow. In only one thing is she likely to go her own way: spending money. He is far from mean, but he is careful to spend wisely, to get real value for money, and is not extravagant. He may lecture her about this from time to time, but the truth is that she can have just about anything she wants from him, just by asking for it. He loves her and does not want to disappoint her. This is a very loving couple.

Scorpio Man—Leo Woman. This partnership is happy in some ways and not in others. She is too independent for him: she goes her own way and will not accept guidance or advice from him—or from anyone else. This is very difficult for the Scorpio man to come to terms with: he likes to be in

charge of everything and has a strong need to protect and care for what is his.

Physically, they are very well suited and this is a highly com-bustible love affair. The Leo woman is outwardly strong and sometimes tomboyish and presents herself as being as good as a man at anything. Her real nature has another side, carefully hidden: she is looking for the man who is stronger than she is, who won't be frightened off—and in the Scorpio man, she has found him. He brings out her real femininity and she is secretly pleased to be swept along on a tide of passion and will give him a true and lasting love in return.

They do have some difficulty in communicating, however. She is a talker, a worker and extremely energetic so that even at play, she is doing something strenuous. He is silent and moody quite a lot of the time and she finds this hard to handle. Although he works hard, he likes a quiet life in his off-duty time. He enjoys music and home-life. He likes to be on his own territory rather than going out. She is soon bored with this and when a Leo woman is bored, everybody knows it. If they are to be happy together, she will have to tone down the parts of her personality that she knows really annoy him and he will have to allow her the constant activity that is essential to her and irksome to him. They should agree to differ.

Scorpio Man—Virgo Woman. A suprisingly good combination, often long-lasting. She embodies many of the things that he is looking for in a mate. She is always faithful —which suits him, as he has a very jealous nature—she is patient, hard-working, and will defer to him on everything. She is thrifty and meticulously clean and tidy, both in her home and in her person. Most of all, she appreciates him.

To her, the Scorpio man is the most attractive of all. She responds to his magnetic appeal, his dynamic personality. She does not mind the jealousy and can cope with any moodiness, because her love for him is truly selfless and she will go to endless trouble to see that things that upset or trouble him are simply not allowed to happen again. She will smooth his path.

He is very physical: he needs love and affection but most of all he needs passion and will give a strong love in return. The

Virgo woman's needs are less than his; nevertheless he brings her femininity to the surface and she responds to him. He knows she is not easily awakened and this pleases him, because she does not flirt and he is able to trust her to be faithful. In turn, he is faithful by nature and will remain so to her. One woman at a time is all he wants or needs; he is not the type to have affairs. He puts so much of himself into any relationship that he is simply uninterested in anyone else at the time.

They have a good chance of a long relationship. Both are conventional and they would be likely to put things on a correct footing, by marriage, when enough time had passed for them to be sure. Neither is impulsive. They are stable and this is a very steady relationship.

Scorpio Man—Libra Woman.

She is an absolute charmer. She is attractive, kind and a good conversationalist. He finds her gentle ways refreshing and relaxing and will seek her out. He does not talk much and has virtually no small talk or gossip; but she is skilled and the days of the courtship go well, as she keeps everything spinning along and does not allow long and awkward silences to fall.

She is attracted to the Scorpio man almost in spite of herself. He is everything she is not; intense, passionate, hard-working and serious. He has little sense of humor, but his personal magnetism and charm are so strong that she cannot keep away.

The Libra woman is loving and kind but a lot less passionate than he is. She likes an easy and undemanding kind of love, with companionship, jokes, and plenty of sparkling company. The Scorpio man, with his intensity and jealousy, is rather heavy going for her. However, he will teach her passion and love and she will show him how to enjoy company some of the time and take life a little less seriously.

She will charm him out of his moods, ease his worries and make home a pleasant place for him. He will be proud of her, as she takes great pride in her appearance and is a perfect guest and hostess and everyone will think he is very lucky. This pleases him, as, apart from anything else, there is always something of the status-seeker in him, in any field. The most important thing, however, is love. It is all-in-all to him. Their physical relationship will be decisive and affect everything else.

Scorpio Man—Scorpio Woman. These two will have a love-life that takes them to the heights. It is their greatest strength and will take them through the bad times when their two strong wills inevitably clash and they fight for supremacy. Most of the time, the Scorpio man will, after a struggle, win the day—but not always. The Scorpio woman learns early to use her femininity to get her own way—and he is so susceptible that he cannot resist her.

Irresistible force and immovable object. Both these things are basic in Scorpio. They have a great deal of drive, they are irresistible to each other—and they are immovable because they are both so obstinate. Fortunately, their viewpoint is usually the same; they combine forces to make an unbeatable pair. It is only when, very occasionally, they are opposed that trouble comes.

They are both capable of great anger, and deep moodiness—and they are both terribly jealous and possessive. They understand this streak in their partner's nature because they are the same, so it is much easier for them to get on with each other than with outsiders. Both are faithful by nature and neither will flirt or play around. They don't need to. They are both wonderful lovers and will make each other happier than anyone else.

When they do fall out, they will shout first, then sulk or cry, and then make love. They never tire of each other and will get the strength to recover even from their worst setbacks. They are both very strong and resilient, and together they are a force to be reckoned with.

Scorpio Man—Sagittarius Woman. She is fiery, attractive and sociable. At first glance she appeals to him. He likes her lively ways, her intelligence and wit and she in turn responds to his physical magnetism and the passion she senses in him.

Physically, they will not be disappointed in each other. She can return and match his passion and this will be the best part of the relationship. In other ways, it is not so good.

The great problem is that the Sagittarian woman does not like being tied down, AND she doesn't always want to be with her Scorpio man. This hurts him more than he will admit and when he is hurt, he retreats into deep, moody silences. She has no patience with this at all and hard words are likely to be spoken. As time goes on, he will try every way, devious and straightforward, to tame her. When this does not work (which it won't) he becomes angry and insistent and this makes her feel more and more restricted. What she likes best in the world is her freedom. What he likes best is love and commitment and a steady life.

The Scorpio man is very jealous and possessive and the Sagittarian woman is unquestionably a flirt. Sometimes she will flirt deliberately, for mischief, but even she will quail before his jealous rage and is not likely to do it again.

Because of these difficulties and differences, their love affair is likely to be short—but very, very sweet. They will have great pleasure from each other, but are unlikely to be a permanent fixture in each other's lives.

Scorpio Man—Capricorn Woman. This is a good partnership in some ways. Both are steady ambitious people: both value success and admire and respect the other for what they have achieved. They get along well together in general.

Emotionally, they are very different. The Scorpio man is dominant, intense, possessive and jealous in the extreme. The Capricorn woman is much cooler, inhibited and unwilling to risk everything for love. She is unlikely to be able to match his passion, though she is capable of a deep love and loyalty if her lover can help her to overcome her self-doubt. If anyone can do this, he can. He has the power to bring out the femininity of a woman in response to his own passion.

She tends to be a little frightened of life; she hides this behind sarcasm and coldness, but really she would like to be rescued, loved and protected. This, her Scorpio man will be only too delighted to do. He likes to protect those he loves and to direct their lives, and she will listen to him and take his advice.

He can be surprisingly good for her. Scorpio men have every strong characters, their only real weakness being the terrible jealousy and possessiveness they bring to all their relationships; but this will not be a problem with the Capricorn woman. She will be faithful and give him no cause for worry on that score.

Once she trusts him fully, she will have a great deal of love to give him and will look up to him and be content to let him take the lead. If they have the patience to overcome her initial reserve and coolness, they should be happy.

Scorpio Man—Aquarius Woman. She is too elusive to be truly attractive to him. She is aloof and cool, and rather reserved. He is passionate, magnetic and tenacious. The Scorpio man will be annoyed to find the Aquarian woman usually surrounded by friends. She prefers a number of light friendships to one or two intense ones and he is the opposite. She is not close to her family and he is. Most of all, she does not really seem to want to be deeply involved—and he does.

She likes good conversation and serene people. His moodiness and long silences find no echo in her nature. Emotionally, she is cool, though she makes a good friend. She likes amusing and eccentric people and they simply confuse him. He has a great need for intense and single-minded love and this is very difficult for her to give.

She will not arouse his jealousy, because basically she is as faithful as he is. But the passion he looks for in a woman is not a component of the Aquarian woman, and he will feel something is lacking.

She finds him too intense. His moodiness makes him an unknown quantity to her and although this intrigues her, she does not really know how to cope with him. He does not have much of a sense of humor and she has, so that he often thinks she is laughing at him when she is not.

The Scorpio man is complex and demanding and the Aquarian woman is not really prepared to make the effort to make this relationship work. This couple would be better as friends than as lovers, and any stronger relationship between them would be difficult to achieve.

Scorpio Man—Pisces Woman.

This combination has great potential. The Scorpio man, demanding, intense and passionate, can call up a wonderful response from the ultra-sensitive, emotional Pisces woman. She will let him take charge of the relationship and he will make her very happy.

Physically, they are very well matched. Both have a great need for love and when this is right, everything else falls into place. The Piscean woman, herself given to moodiness and introspection, will understand instinctively the needs of the Scorpio man and will attune herself to him without the need of words. She is eager to please and will do anything to make him happy, and he appreciates her and will take care not to hurt her feelings and to make her feel loved and cared for all the time.

Her gentleness is very good for him; it allows him to show the kindness and sweetness in his own nature. He is by nature dominant but with her he does not have to struggle to be so and therefore there is no clash of wills.

She is withdrawn and needs the support and protection of someone strong; he has this strength and she feels able to relax with him. Their weaknesses and strengths complement each other perfectly and she will never give him cause to be jealous. He is possessive, but so is she and she will understand it and accept it.

They have a great understanding between them and should have a happy and successful relationship lasting a long time.

IX. Sagittarius

The Sagittarius Character

Sagittarius men and women are the supreme optimists of the zodiac. No matter how black things look, they are hopeful; and since this is a very lucky sign, more often than not, their luck holds.

Sagittarians are active and enterprising. They love liberty, for others as well as themselves and will show courage in defending it. They hate injustices. The Sagittarian believes in free speech—sometimes too much of it. The Sagittarian woman, in particular, is often very tactless, and this can annoy friends. She will be forgiven, though, because her loyalty and kindness to her friends is very strong.

The Sagittarian character is very complex. They are law-abiding and they love order—but only when they think it is right and fair. If not, they are rebellious. They are so independent that sometimes people do not offer help or advice when it is needed, because they seem to have everything under control. This can be a completely false impression. Sagittarians are proud and do not like to show themselves in a difficult position; they find it almost impossible to ask for help.

Sagittarians have a ready wit, and although they call it discussion, they are actually very fond of arguing, on almost any subject. They are not quarrelsome—but they do like to persuade others to their point of view.

Sagittarians are ambitious and like to make their mark on the world. Their greatest enemy is boredom. They loathe routine and if they are forced by circumstances to stick rigidly to it, they become despondent. Given freedom, they will work hard and will not complain: they like no discipline except their own.

The Sagittarian has a quick, clear mind and is quick to learn things. They are adaptable and can make themselves at home anywhere and fit in with different people and customs. They like a simple life, with time and freedom to do what they want; they will sacrifice anything rather than lose their freedom of action and spirit.

The Sagittarian has a gentle nature, but quickly becomes cold and abrupt if treated without respect, either in personal relationships or in business. The company of unsympathetic people makes them irritable and they make no attempt to hide it.

The Sagittarian character is hail-fellow-well-met, but all is not as it seems on the surface. Inwardly, they are mistrustful of others, suspicious and watchful. Only when someone has passed through this early stage in friendship with a Sagittarian will they be accepted fully and after that, a better friend would be hard to find.

The Sagittarian man and woman have plenty of energy and are full of ideas and innovations. What they lack is the attention to detail and willingness to do the spade-work to make their ideas a success. They are very outgoing and will quite happily let other people take their ideas and put them to work for themselves; if they don't want to take something further, they are quite happy to let someone else benefit from it.

Sagittarians are givers in the truest sense of the word. They give very easily and never count the cost; whether it is in time, money or energy which could have been used for themselves.

They love children and get on very well with them, re-visiting their own childhood through them. Often they are happier in the company of children than adults. They will tell them stories, talk to them with real interest and restrain any tendency to lose their temper.

The Sagittarian temper! It is a drawback, to put it mildly. Sagittarians find it very difficult not to show anything they may be feeling and even more difficult not to say anything that is on the tip of their tongue. Often, while they are actually doing it, they are appalled; but they can't stop once started and will say exactly what they think. This can lose them jobs, as well as infuriate those in their personal life. When this happens, there is often an abrupt parting of the ways; but the Sagittarian has a secret. They are always, secretly, rather glad. They like things out in the open and if it means a rift—well, so be it.

This is the reverse side of the Sagittarian character. Combined with a natural impatience, and extreme dislike of restraint or control of any kind, the Sagittarian can be very hard to handle—and once everything seems to be settled and beginning to run properly, they are off again and in this they are exasperating. They will not work away patiently at anything, but pick up and put down many things, starting new projects with enthusiasm, then tiring of them and casting them aside.

Sagittarians are very restless people. They are always ready to move on and are not usually thinking about the life they are living today, but looking towards the future, which to them always looks promising and to which they are drawn very strongly.

How Sagittarius Gets Along with Others

Sagittarius with Aries

Money/Job. Aries and Sagittarius will get on well in business. The Sagittarian is an idea-man and the Arien has the application to work that the Sagittarian lacks, so they make a good team. The Arien likes the business sense of the Sagittarian, for while Sagittarians do not work nine-to-five, they are shrewd and astute in business and like making money. They rely on their luck a lot and this can give the more conservative Aries the jitters occasionally; but they soon begin to see results and after that all goes well. These two respect each other and will not tread on each other's toes. A good working partnership, with good money.

Home/Friends. Both Sagittarian and Arien are busy people with a lot of outside interests and activities, so they won't be in their home much. When they are, it will usually be in the company of some of their numerous friends; they like a busy social life. Their home will be comfortable and welcoming and friends will like to come there—and come almost too often. Aries likes company and likes entertaining, but Sagittarius is too much even for an Aries character, bringing people home at all hours of the day and night without warning. The Arien will not make people unwelcome, but will say a word or two in private to the Sagittarian when they have gone. Generally speaking, though, they suit each other.

Sagittarius with Taurus

Money/Job. The sparks will fly in this combination. Taurus is a strong sign used to having things their own way; they tend to push others around. Sagittarians don't let anyone push them around and Taurus will soon find this out. The Taurean works slowly and steadily and does a good job; the Sagittarian is fast and will work flat out when it suits them, but it does not suit them all the time. The Taurean will dislike the lack of routine and steadiness; the Sagittarian must be free or will not work at all. Both are money-motivated, but see different ways of achieving success. They can work together if Taurus will make sure all is done properly and can give the Sagittarian freedom to develop and do a good job.

Home/Friends. This can work quite well, as the Taurean loves the home and has a tremendous taste for luxury and comfort, sparing no expense and working hard to make a beautiful home, which they then spend a lot of time in. The Sagittarian loves beautiful surroundings, and does not grudge the money at all, but does not want to attend to the finer details of it all. They like a nice base where they can relax and the Taurean will give them this. If there are children, the Taurean will be the one to exercise parental control and the Sagittarian will aid and abet the children most of the time.

Sagittarius with Gemini

Money/Job. Both of these people will be full of ideas, but neither of them like applying themselves to the mundane spadework of actually developing the idea and making some money. They have far too much outward-going interest and neither has enough inner discipline. Gemini can settle down and work well, especially when motivated by the desire for security, which all Geminians want, but the Sagiattarian will not want to do this. Although Sagittarians like money and are actually successful in business through luck and intuition, nothing will make them put in a nine-to-five day—not every day, anyway. Both are spenders, but Gemini will learn to control it and teach Sagittarius to do the same. Success after effort in this partnership.

Home/Friends. They make a very sociable couple, liking friends and contact with the outside world. Neither of them is very interested in domesticity; the Gemini looks upon home as a place to recharge the batteries before setting off on more traveling and the Sagittarian looks on it as a hotel which is clean and comfortable and where everything is done properly. Whose job will it be to make the home and run it? Maybe both, maybe neither. Ideally they would prefer someone else to do it. Both good with children, they will treat them with kindness and interest.

Sagittarius with Cancer

Money/Job. Cancer people are careful with money and have the instinct to make every penny count. Sagittarius is careless and generous with money and this combination would be likely to be very worrying for the Cancerian who works quietly on trying to make a success of things. Although the Sagittarian is good in business and will make money, the Cancerian feels this is more by good luck than good management; and becomes more and more nervous, waiting for the crash. The Sagittarian will be irritated by what they see as lack of faith on the part of the Cancerian and will not submit to any form of control, nor listen to reason. If the Cancerian can manage to calm the doubts and let Sagittarius do what they want, all will be well. However, this is nerve-racking for the Cancerian, who shows it; and is an uneasy partnership.

Home/Friends. The Cancerian loves home-making and will create a beautiful home. The Sagittarian will like to live in it, but doesn't want to create it, so they will both be happy. The Sagittarian is out a great deal, but the Cancerian will not really mind: they are such home lovers they always have something to do and are happy alone or with their family. Cancerians are very good with children, loving and kind and caring. The Sagittarian loves them too, but will be glad the Cancerian wants to take charge. The Sagittarian parent is a friend.

Sagittarius with Leo

Money/Job. These two can go far together, provided Leo doesn't get too bossy and Sagittarius sticks to the job. Leo people are hard workers, efficient and painstaking, and they think the Sagittarian is slapdash. The Sagittarian rather admires Leo and is forced to respect them, because they are as clever in business as the Sagittarian but apply themselves to it better and make more money. The Sagittarian is money-motivated and is both shrewd and lucky, so they should do well. It would be best for Leo to take the lead; it is natural for them to do so and give the Sagittarian a certain amount of freedom of thought and action. This brings the best out of a Sagittarian and Leo shares the benefit.

Home/Friends. Leo will want a superb home and will spare no expense to get it. Sagittarius and Leo have similar taste and will not argue about furnishings or decor: both like comfort and both like the very best of everything. The Sagittarian is not quite so interested as Leo. They like life outside the home better than in it. Leo must be top dog and definitely will be; Sagittarians have no wish to dominate, but neither will they allow themselves to be dominated and if Leo tries to do this, the fur will fly. Both like children: Leo will be the disciplinarian, but not too often.

Sagittarius with Virgo

Money/Job. Virgo is a saver, Sagittarius is a spender. Virgo works quietly and conscientiously in the background; Sagittarians zip about, working hard for short bursts and then doing nothing for a time. They are opposites. This unnerves Virgo, who likes predictability and security. The Virgo is controlled, the Sagittarian is uncontrolled, starting new projects and dropping them rapidly and often. However, Sagittarians do have winning ideas and success and money does come to them. Virgo may worry while they do it, but will relax and work hard to help the Sagittarian when they have seen it proved that the system works and Sagittarians will share everything with them, so they reap the rewards.

Home/Friends. Virgo likes a very clean, tidy house, and works very hard to achieve it. A Virgo is not looking for luxury. The Sagittarian likes comfort. They like cleanliness but they are not tidy: far from it. They will get on each other's nerves. The Sagittarian will feel that the Virgo constantly nags and criticizes and the Virgo will feel the Sagittarian does not appreciate all their hard work. If they have children, Sagittarius will love them, perhaps more than anyone or anything else in life, but it is Virgo who provides the stability and who brings them up. Virgos are selfless parents.

Sagittarius with Libra

Money/Job. These two will have quite a good relationship. Both believe in live-and-let-live. The Sagittarian has their own way of working, hard and fast but not very regular, and relies on luck and shrewd business sense to see them through. The Libran works best without pressure or interference, so both are inclined to give the other freedom to work in the way most comfortable for them, and this pays off. The Sagittarian is good at making money and although Librans are not motivated by money for its own sake, they do like a very expensive and luxurious lifestyle and need the money to pay for it. The Sagittarian goes through a lot of money, being a big spender. Both will work together amiably in this set-up, trusting the other and being proved right.

Home/Friends. Both Libra and Sagittarius have many friends and value them. They like to entertain and they like a nice home to live and entertain in. The Libran has wonderful taste and will make a lovely home, which the Sagittarian will be proud of. The Sagittarian is not very domestic and likes to be out and about a lot of the time. The Libran loves going to expensive places where they can mix with a high level of society and have a very pleasant life. The Sagittarian does not always want to be with a partner and will go off by themselves; Libra does not mind at all.

Sagittarius with Scorpio

Money/Job. The Sagittarian lack of attention to detail and dislike of routine will enrage the Scorpio, who sticks to time-tables and the job in hand and expects others to do likewise. Each of this pair has something different to contribute; the Sagittarian has a bright mind and many good ideas, will work very hard from time to time (but at odd hours) and is clever and astute in business. The Scorpio is very good at making money and is very ambitious. Scorpios are better at planning and organizing and if they will do this part of it and utilize the skills of the Sagittarian, they could do very well financially together. Both are spenders and both like to get value for money.

Home/Friends. Sagittarius and Scorpio have little in common in the home. Scorpio has a home full of luxuries, partly because he or she enjoys them, but partly as status symbols, and the Sagittarian has no time for this. For Sagittarians, the home is there as a base, for them to use in between going away and going out, and although they like comfort and warmth, a good hotel suits them just as well. Sagittarians have many friends and they like light and amusing conversation when they entertain. They find the intensity and jealousy of Scorpio rather embarrassing. As parents, Scorpio rules, Sagittarius indulges.

Sagittarius with Sagittarius

Money/Job. Perfect understanding here. Each trusts the other, intuition and shrewdness is doubled and success is assured. Neither of them wants to do the donkey work and will probably give it to someone else. They will have a lot of good ideas, work will go through and money will be going in and out again so quickly it will be difficult to tell whether they are making a profit or a loss. They will be doing very well indeed, but spending so much that they may have a cash-flow problem from time to time. A peculiar feature of Sagittarians working together is that they often have their friends working with them and there is a good atmosphere. One note of caution: somebody must see to the running of the business and balance the books.

Home/Friends. Sagittarians are not very domesticated, though they like the comforts of home; and in the case of two together, they are unlikely to spend much time at home with each other. If they are not careful, it could quickly come to the point where they just pass in the hall. Each wants total freedom; each will be prepared to give the same to the other. They will have lots of friends passing through and enjoy entertaining. They will make good parents as they love children and find them interesting, although the curtailment of their freedom and the ties that children bring will irk them both.

Sagittarius with Capricorn

Money/Job. At first glance, this looks unlikely. Capricorn is steady and hard-working, very good at handling and budgeting money, cautious, careful and a planner. Sagittarius is intuitive, shrewd and good at making money, but works when he or she wishes and will not be controlled by anyone . . . and Sagittarians are also big spenders, which Capricorns are not. In spite of all this, they are a good combination, because Capricorn will look after the money and patiently work on the ideas

Sagittarius scatters along the way. Both will profit from the other: Sagittarius will make money and Capricorn will invest it and both will gain.

Home/Friends. Sagittarius is undomesticated. Capricorn will make a home but it will be spartan and rather cold and there will be no emphasis on luxury. The Sagittarian won't like this, but will be out so much of the time that it will only be a minor inconvenience. The Sagittarian is warm and friendly and likes plenty of company. The Capricorn is austere and cool, and they haven't a great deal in common. The Sagittarian will spend much too much money for the Capricorn's liking and it will go on things the Capricorn thinks are wasteful—luxuries that Sagittarians like. These two are much more likely to be business associates than friends—Capricorn is too aloof for Sagittarius, and Sagittarius is too overpowering for Capricorn.

Sagittarius with Aquarius

Money/Job. A lot of understanding here. Aquarians work for pleasure and for job satisfaction, and although they enjoy money and position, they put them second to working at something that interests them. The Sagittarian understands this perfectly, because although more money-conscious than the Aquarian, the Sagittarian also never does anything they do not want to do. There are many advantages. The Aquarian does not worry about the Sagittarian, but has faith in the bright ideas and skills that flow from them and is pleased to see they are doing so well with money; the Sagittarian is good at business and making money, the Aquarian will help to keep Sagittarian extravagance within bounds, without upsetting or annoying in any way. They can do well together.

Home/Friends. Sagittarians and Aquarians get along very well in the home. They like each other and have similar tastes, though the Aquarian has less love of luxury. They are kind to each other and have otherwise similar tastes. They enjoy the wit and conversation of their circle of friends. They build a pleasant life together. They are both very easy-going and do not try to prevent each other having a separate life. If there are children, they will all get along well together and the parents will discipline them with the use of reason rather than force.

Sagittarius with Pisces

Money/Job. Pisceans are artistic and creative and the Sagittarian will like this about them and harness it to their own shrewd and money making ideas, with good results. In this combination the Sagittarian needs to be in charge, as Pisces needs direction and without it will achieve nothing. The Sagittarian has to learn to control their own dislike of finishing a job before starting something else: they get so easily bored and hate to work to deadlines. If they can overcome this and use their very real intuition and luck, they will be successful in business and take the Piscean to success alongside them.

Home/Friends. The Piscean loves a beautiful home and the Sagittarian does not stint the money to pay for it, although Sagittarians spend more time out of the home than in it. It keeps Pisces very happy however, creating a lovely environment and making it elegant and comfortable. Sagittarians love to entertain and have a swirl of people in and out of their home, but the Piscean is more shy and retiring. However, Pisces likes looking after people, so will happily offer hospitality and will be well liked by all the guests, who have come to see Sagittarius but grow fond of Pisces too.

Love Mates

Sagittarius Woman—Aries Man. This is a passionate twosome and a very loving one, so long as she will let Aries take the lead. He is very dashing and daring and full of adventure, and the Sagittarian woman likes this in him. She is not interested in less active types of men, she likes a man to be a real man.

He is attracted to her because of her vitality and life. She is very spirited and he will not easily persuade her to do anything she doesn't want to, but this was one of the things he found so attractive in her. She is an outdoor woman and he is an outdoor man.

The Sagittarian woman is not bossy; to tell the truth she's not very interested in what other people do, since she likes living her own life to the full. She won't make the one fatal mistake in dealing with an Aries man: she won't try to take charge. She rather likes the feeling that he is the leader—but she won't follow him unless she agrees with him and wants to. From time to time he can find he is leading nobody, as she is going in a different direction.

Physically, they are very compatible. They both have a strong sex drive and plenty of love and warmth in their natures. However, for each of them this is just a small though important part of their lives together. They like to forge a real friendship and companionship and share activities and friends together. Neither of them wants to spend too long sitting in their own home on their own.

They have both got a temper and when they do quarrel it will be a real screaming match—but soon forgotten.

Sagittarius Woman—Taurus Man. The irresistible force (Sagittarius) meets the immovable object (Taurus). Nobody can budge the Taurean male—he is the most stubborn creature in the zodiac—but he is responsive to charm and the Sagittarian woman will wheedle all her own way out of him, while he thinks he is running the show.

He can be quite good for her. He will help her keep her feet more firmly on the ground and give her stability; and in turn, she will stir him up a bit. Without a bit of liveliness in the woman in his life, the Taurean man can be just the least bit dull. He works hard and plods purposefully on to eventual success and will be an excellent husband and provider; but he has another, hidden side to his nature.

He is very responsive to love shown to him and responds to feminine charm and to sex appeal. She knows how to charm him and amuse him. She will lift his moods with her good-humored ways and in spite of himself he cannot help being entertained by some of her escapades. He doesn't always strictly approve of her—but he does like her.

Their physical relationship will be good. The Taurus man is sensuous and this side of love is very important to him. The Sagittarian woman agrees and feels it makes a bond between them.

He is possessive and will be jealous of her friends and activities, who, he thinks, take up too much of her time. If she is sensible, she will notice the warning signs and give him her attention for a day or two.

Sagittarius Woman—Gemini Man.
These two really like each other. They have a great deal in common. The Gemini man is changeable, fickle, always moving on. The Sagittarian woman can outpace him and keep his interest. Their relationship scores on mental affinity. They are both very easily bored and like a witty and amusing companionship better than an intense love affair.

He is more flirtatious than physical and there may not be enough warmth to fill her need for quite a lot of heat in her love relationships. However, the Gemini man is such a perfect companion to her that she will accept it.

She is a great game-player—and so is he, none more so. Their courtship will be full of unspoken games, which will cause them great amusement, and both will always know exactly how the score stands. He is quickly tired of a woman with only her physical self to offer; he likes a challenge and the Sagittarian woman is a challenge, even to him.

Neither of them is jealous by nature—and it is just as well, as both are terrible flirts. Neither of them is possessive and in fact there is a real danger that their tie will be so light that it can lead to separate interests and separate lives. Freedom is terribly important to the Sagittarian woman and she will give up love rather than let it be taken from her—the Gemini man gives her her freedom and relies on the amount of interest she has in him to bring her back.

This liaison is likely to be temporary, but when they part it will be with no ill-feeling and a lasting affection toward each other for a happy and amusing time.

Sagittarius Woman—Cancer Man. He is a very

rare mixture: he is masculine and attractive, but he possesses an instinctive female intuition that gives him an insight into women and how they are likely to react. He sees through the independence of the Sagittarian woman to the very feminine person she is inwardly, and knows how to draw this side of her out.

He is very emotional and, after the first shock, she discovers that with him she is the same. He can make her feel things very intensely. All the same, their romantic path does not run smoothly.

She is very tactless and outspoken and the Cancerian man, so sensitive and vulnerable, is deeply wounded by this. It seems to her that he gets upset over very minor things and to tell the truth she is secretly rather impatient with this and wishes he would not brood so much about unimportant issues. He is cut to the quick by her sometimes very sharp words and withdraws back into that crab shell.

He is possessive and loving and she finds his clinging ways and need to be always with her rather constricting. Very soon she is trying to move a little away, to give herself space, and the more she does this the tighter the tenacious Cancerian man clings.

These two can really love each other, but they are unlikely

to have a long relationship. He would stay with her and teach her how to really love; it is she, in her need for freedom, who will break away from him.

Sagittarius Woman—Leo Man. A love match! These two are very well suited. They are both warm and passionate and are on the same wavelength. She is ideally suited to a Leo man because she will let him take the lead, and this is his prime requirement in any relationship. The difficulty will come when he tries to lead her in a direction she does not wish to go: nothing on earth will make her do it. She will not argue about it, she simply will go her own way as she always does.

He is bossy and she will find this amusing—until he tries to boss her. Then it will be a different story. She does not try to make him do anything he doesn't want to—and she won't stand for him trying to bully her. There will be some real screaming matches until he learns to respect her, as she already respects him. They both have real tempers, quickly up and quickly down, but neither of them bears a grudge and it will all be over in a very short while.

Physically, they are practically perfect together. There is a lot of heat in this relationship and they will always be able to resolve problems and difficulties through their physical closeness. She will come first with him and she will love him wholeheartedly in return.

He is possessive and she is not—and doesn't like to be possessed either. She will not change this part of his nature and he will keep a close eye on her. The Sagittarian woman must realize that this is how to discover how much she means to the Leo: he guards what he values, and he values her.

Sagittarius Woman—Virgo Man. These two are better as friends, rather than lovers. The fire of the Sagittarian woman finds no echo in the rather cold nature of the Virgo man. Her nature is outgoing, generous and impulsive; he is a fault-finder, critical and demanding, and she can become very depressed by feeling nothing she does is right. This is because she basically tries hard to please and becomes discouraged if she is not able to do so.

The Virgo man finds the Sagittarian woman altogether too much: too independent, doing just as she likes and taking little notice of whether he approves or not; too demanding emotionally, wanting responses and emotions from him that he finds very difficult to give. He wishes she would just settle down and not ask so much from life and from him; she wishes he asked for more and fought harder for it.

He is patient and perserving, unselfish in love, and wishing only to serve the woman he loves. He is in his element when she is ill, because then he has got her dependent on him and he can take care of her as he wishes to. He is reliable and dependable and will never let anyone down.

The Sagittarian woman appreciates all his finer qualities; she thinks he will make an excellent husband—for another woman! She, herself, is looking for someone more exciting.

She loves a man who makes her laugh and unfortunately the Virgo man does lack humor. She finds him stern and unbending. He is attracted by her very vitality and fire, but finds it different at close quarters. It makes him uncomfortable. They are best apart.

Sagittarius Woman—Libra Man. Rather a nice love affair. Both have a light touch in life and in love. The Libra man is very charming, a good conversationalist, and he really likes women. He will not like the bluntness and outspokenness of the Sagittarian woman: he likes harmony and peace and happiness and he likes life to run smoothly and cause him no problems. However, he does like her. She attracts him because she has much more vitality and warmth than he has, but without the intensity he dislikes in some other women. He finds her amusing and entertaining and will smooth over the worst of her tactless outbursts as long as they are not directed at him.

They are on the same wavelength mentally and they have a number of similar tastes. They are both cultured and like a life of high style. The Sagittarian woman will be proud of his looks and charm and will enjoy showing him off to her friends, while he likes taking her out because she is always good company.

This man cannot resist flirtations with other women, although they rarely come to anything more than that. He is not looking for complications, just amusing himself; the Sagittarian woman will not mind, as she plays the same game herself.

The only real problem is that she has a hot temper when she is roused and the Libran man absolutely hates fights or confrontations: he would rather leave. She likes to have things out; he likes everything to be smoothed over.

Physically he is a bit lightweight for her, since he is fonder of romance than passion; but they make each other happy.

Sagittarius Woman—Scorpio Man.

He finds her totally puzzling. He is most intense, ready to give his all to the right woman when he finds her; when he finds his Sagittarian woman, he is ready to commit himself—but she is not. What she likes is freedom and independence, and he wants to tie her down. He will not succeed.

The Sagittarian woman does what she likes when she likes and even a Scorpio man cannot change her. The intensity and passion in him appeals to her strongly: she is fiery in love herself. The jealousy and possessiveness do not. She is not possessive and cannot understand anyone who is. They may have a scorching love affair but they are not suited for a long-term relationship. He will want her to account to him, to be predictable and to stay put when he wants her to; she is a law unto herself.

She is rather flirtatious, and he will not stand for that; he is entirely faithful and if she is not she will have to face the intensity of a Scorpio rage; even she would quail before that.

The Sagittarian woman has a sunny nature. She doesn't like black moods in her partner and doesn't know how to cope with them. When someone upsets her she either loses her temper and shouts at them or becomes sarcastic; either way, it's out in the open. She doesn't understand the brooding silences and moods of Scorpio.

The Scorpio man finds the Sagittarian woman attractive and he is magnetic enough to make any woman interested in him: she will be, but not for long. She moves on.

Sagittarius Woman—Sagittarius Man. There is only one woman who can make a Sagittarian man think of marriage: a Sagittarian woman.

With her, he can relax. He knows he will always be free and she will not make boring scenes if he is late coming home. She will let him remain totally free—and will claim the same right in return.

Although both are flirtatious, strangely enough each stops the other. The Sagittarian man enjoys flirting the most when he knows somebody else is just a little bit jealous—the Sagittarian woman is not, since she is flirting herself and will not even notice. Also, he does not like his partner to be flirting too—he loses interest in the person he was charming and comes over to see what she is playing at.

What she is playing at is his own game, and she will win. He will find her more interesting than other women and, without noticing it, will become faithful to her. In exactly the same way, so will she become faithful to him.

The Sagittarian woman cannot be told what to do, not even by a Sagittarian man, but this is all right; he doesn't want to. He likes to see her as free as a bird and can always find something to do until she returns. He has many interests and many friends.

Physically, they are very compatible. Both are fiery and loving and quite romantic too. They will write each other love letters. Once they are in love, they are most affectionate with each other.

Both are tactless and blunt in speech; but neither is at all hurt by it. They are both the same in this way and take no real notice. Any quarrels soon blow over.

Sagittarius Woman—Capricorn Man. The Capricorn man has a very forbidding manner. This is because he represses his emotions violently, and although he needs and longs for love cannot allow himself to show this need, or to respond to a partner, until he is very sure indeed he will not be rejected.

He is attracted to the warmth in the personality of a Sagittarian woman and is very envious of the way she manages to have so many friends. He feels lonely and insecure and does not show his feelings to her at all. She will often, after being interested in him to begin with, write him off as not being her type, because of his total lack of reaction to her, only to find he is still following her around and appearing wherever she goes.

Sometimes a love affair between these two starts when the Sagittarian woman, used to attracting men and being successful with them, realizes he is not taking any notice of her. Then she will turn on her charm, coaxing him along gently and slowly until he finally shows his feelings. By this time, she has become really interested in him. The Capricorn man is fascinating.

Physically, they are fairly good together. She is full of fire and passion, while he is very sensuous and romantic. Still, he has enough passion for her and she is romantic enough for him.

The Capricorn man is full of secret fears and self-doubt. He needs a great deal of reassurance before he can believe himself truly loved, and only then will the best of him come out. The Sagittarian woman is really tactless and this, if unchecked, could wreck their relationship.

Sagittarius Woman—Aquarius Man. These two
are quite well suited for each other. Both have a light touch in romance. The Aquarian is very detached and remote, which the Sagittarian woman doesn't really mind because of the flattering amount of attention he pays to her. He listens to every word she says with great interest, and proves himself a great conversationalist and companion.

The Aquarian man tends to put a woman on a pedestal and the love affair is less rooted in what is actually going on between them than in what he dreams is going on. As dreams are often better than reality, he can become very disillusioned once he discovers what every day life is like with a woman. In the case of the Sagittarian woman, however, he is more likely to enjoy the relationship. She will never bore him and they will have many laughs together. They have a very similar sense of humor.

Physically, she may be a little disappointed in him. He tends to talk a lot about love, but is actually cool, and there is not as much fire in him as she likes. They are so compatible in other ways that she might be prepared to accept this.

They have many tastes in common; both are artistic and both like going out and keeping in the social swim. He has a lot of charm and flirts just as much as she does. Neither minds at all and they will often end the evening laughing together about those they have been dazzling all evening!

Sagittarius Woman—Pisces Man. Not an easy match.
He is dreamy and non-assertive and will not make any attempt to build a real partnership with her. He will let her go completely her own way, never argue with her or fight back, and lapse into depression and moodiness as a defense when her actions upset him.

The Sagittarian woman is a born fighter. She likes to have everything out in the open and will become very provocative in her attempts to make the Piscean man react positively. She will quickly lose patience with his weepy moods and although she is basically kind, her temper will often get the better of her as she tries in vain to make him a more equal partner. He won't do it. He doesn't want to and in his own more negative way, he is just as strong as she is.

He is imaginative. He is often clever and artistic and he loves all beautiful things. The Sagittarian likes this side of him and they will spend some time together happily following similar hobbies.

She is passionate, he is highly emotional, but they don't really hit it off physically. The Piscean man is looking for a much more gentle woman: he finds the Sagittarian passion rather too demanding, while she finds his hyper-sensitive nature and emotional needs very draining.

These two do not make a very loving couple together—but they can make a nice friendship.

Sagittarius Man—Aries Woman. Not quite so favorable as Aries man–Sagittarian woman. The Aries woman is always trying to take charge and can be bossy. She will want to organize the Sagittarian man and tell him what to do, and

he won't allow her to. He comes and goes as he likes and does not account to anyone. She is also very independent and resents a man trying to take the lead, but there will be no problem here. He doesn't wish to dominate; he just wants to run his own life.

The Sagittarian man is very easy going and will let his woman have a great deal of freedom of action, but he will claim the same in return. Above all he likes to be free and if the Aries woman has any dreams of marrying him, she had better learn this early on.

Physically they are well-suited; both have fiery natures and like quite a lot of heat in their love lives. Aries women can be miraculously changed by a very happy love life—they become gentler and much more loving. They give great loyalty to those they love and once they love the Sagittarian man will not hear a word against him.

Both of them like an outdoor life: he likes energetic hobbies and this suits her, as she is energetic too.

If she can try to hide her feelings when he is flirting and turning on the charm, and if he can learn not to tax her loyalty too far, they can get on fine together.

Sagittarius Man—Taurus Woman. The Taurean woman is not quite so stubborn as the Taurean man, but she is a lot more obstinate than the Sagittarian man and often gets her way through just steadily wearing him down. She is charming and sensuous and he will give in to her without complaining too much.

The only time she cannot push him is in trying to restrict his freedom to go out as much as he likes. She will be good for him, as she provides a stability that is missing in his character, but she will not try to dominate him.

She takes the right line with her roving man—she dresses herself up (and Taurean women love clothes and choose them well) and goes with him. He can flirt and play as much as he wishes—she is there to keep an eye on him.

Physically they should be well matched: he is passionate and she is very responsive. She has plenty of sex appeal too. Their love-life will be a pleasure to them and will create a strong, warm bond.

She must be careful never to show how possessive she is, or she will frighten him away. He values freedom above everything else and will even sacrifice love if he feels in danger of being trapped.

The Taurean woman likes quite a lot of money: she is fond of clothes and beautiful things and likes a very comfortable lifestyle. The Sagittarian man is very generous and will not stint her with money or material things. They should be quite contented together.

Sagittarius Man—Gemini Woman.

They have a great deal in common. She is flirtatious, fickle, changeable and easily bored. She will not be bored with a Sagittarian man: in him, she has met her match. Within a very short time of meeting him, she will spend quite a lot of her time wondering what HE is doing and thinking.

He is passionate, she less so, but she is loving and quite romantic. Both have a light touch in love affairs, and dislike a great deal of intensity, so they suit each other very well.

The Sagittarian man is very easily bored, as is the Gemini woman. Both of them need a strong mental affinity if they are to have a happy relationship, and these two have that. They also share a very quick wit and a sense of humor, and it is this that helps them through the occasional hard patches when they rub each other up the wrong way. They can both be irritable, but do not often become really angry with each other; they amuse each other too much for that.

Both lack much sense of commitment. They are not very likely to marry, but will stay together just as long as it suits them to do so, then move on without a great deal of upset. They are likely to remain firm friends. It is a feature of the Sagittarian man that he converts most of his love affairs into friendships in the end; with the Gemini woman there will be no difficulty in doing that. They are well suited to be friends and will retain a lasting affection for each other.

Sagittarius Man—Cancer Woman. This couple is going to have some difficulties right from the start. The Cancer woman is clinging and dependent, and needs love and reassurance. She is tenacious and will not easily let the man she is in love with have any sort of separate life. The Sagittarian man loves to be free above all else in life and he finds her ways difficult to live with.

At first, he is likely to be flattered by her constant presence and attention. She is very emotional and will make him feel very loved. After a time, however, he becomes uneasy and feels restricted and will start to make moves to break away, or at least to have some time to himself. The more he attempts to move away, the tighter she holds on. She feels insecure, he feels trapped; neither is happy and both show it.

The Sagittarian man is a flirt and the Cancer woman finds this deeply hurtful. He is also inclined to be tactless and sometimes says the very thing most likely to upset her. Her reaction is to become moody and depressed and he will have no idea how to cope with this. He likes everything out in the open and thinks a good row clears the air.

This couple can really love each other and she can teach him to really love and to want a deeper commitment than he usually does; while he can, if he loves her, coax her out of her insecurities and out of those black moods. It is not going to be easy, however, and this relationship, while sweet, will probably not be lasting.

Sagittarius Man—Leo Woman. Leo is used to having it all her own way. She is strong and rather bossy. The Sagittarian man is good for her because this is one man she will not boss: he will not try to dominate her, but he will go his own way and there is nothing she can do about it.

She likes a man to be in charge; she hides this feeling, but it is a deep rooted feeling. She needs the security of knowing she is with a man with real inner strength before she can relax and be as feminine as she wishes to be. He is a charmer. He has plenty of passion and so has the Leo woman and they will be physically very compatible. But the Sagittarian man does not wish to either dominate or be dominated; he wants to live his own life to the full and gives his woman the freedom to do likewise. She will argue with him to try to provoke him into taking charge of the relationship, but she will not alter him. There will be some real screaming matches between them, but at the end of it all, he is still living an independent life, keeping his freedom and doing nothing about setting a wedding date.

She is possessive and he will not be possessed. He thinks it cramps his style; he should learn that Leo women guard only what they value—it proves that she values him.

There is a lot of heat in this relationship and the physical love between them makes a strong bond; but in the end the Leo woman, who is absolutely committed herself, will probably decide that the relationship is not going anywhere. If she does, her pride will make her leave.

Sagittarius Man—Virgo Woman. They see life from basically different angles, and it is unlikely that they would be happy together.

She is serious, hard-working and honorable. She says what she means and she means what she says. She might be attracted to a Sagittarian man, as he is bright and entertaining and makes a charming companion, but it is an attraction that is unlikely to last when it becomes established on a more permanent basis.

He is passionate and loving and can draw a response from the Virgo woman that surprises them both; but her way of showing love is quite different. She is unselfish and her way is to serve and work and do everything she can to please and to make life easier for the man she loves. She is not very interested in physical love and is unemotional.

The Virgo woman finds it difficult to understand the independence and freedom a Sagittarian man values so highly. He is flirtatious and she disapproves strongly of this. She will try to make him settle down and be more steady, but she will not succeed.

She is a marrier; he is not. He does not like to be tied and domestic life bores him. She may have been attracted to him by his warmth and vitality, so different from her own character; but she is not comfortable with him and he makes her feel insecure. He dislikes her disapproval, since he likes to be praised and be well-liked. If he is ill, the Virgo woman will be wonderful and tend him with love; but when he recovers, he will be back as he was; the Sagittarian man never really changes.

Sagittarius Man—Libra Woman. These two are good together. Both are charmers: they like an active social life and although the Libra woman loves her home and takes a lot of trouble to make it beautiful and welcoming, she loves going out, too. The Sagittarian man will be proud of her: she always makes the best of her appearance and is usually the center of attention wherever she goes.

The Sagittarian man is very sociable too and likes to feel free when he is out, so he likes the way a Libra woman can take care of herself in company—it leaves him free to enjoy himself. He is rather blunt and outspoken and can be really tactless, so she is very useful to him; she will smooth things over and restore harmony when he has said the wrong thing—then gently rebuke him afterwards. He doesn't mind this; he is often horrified when he hears himself speaking, but it is usually too late by then.

They are on the same wavelength: they are both cultured and have a mental affinity. They get along very well together and share many interests. They do not spend a great deal of time alone together; they prefer to be in a social whirl, but they are compatible in their love-life. The Sagittarian man is passionate and the Libra woman is less so, but she is loving and this is enough for him.

His flirtatious nature does not worry her; she is the same herself and she knows that for both of them it is really just a way of socializing and adding a little zest to life. The real problem is likely to be his hot temper: she really loathes fights and confrontations and he will have to learn to control his temper if he wants to keep her.

Sagittarius Man—Scorpio Woman. She has a jealous, possessive and passionate temperament. If she falls in love with a Sagittarian man, life is going to be very difficult for her—and for him. He is very attractive and can match and return her passion, but he will not allow her to restrict his freedom or independence in any way. Her jealousy will make him cool off toward her and he will ignore her possessiveness and do and go where he pleases. The Scorpio woman reacts with fury, tears and tantrums as she feels him drift away from her; it will make no difference. Nobody owns a Sagittarian man, not even a Scorpio woman. He is quite strong enough to make it plain.

To her, love is the most important thing in life and she will sacrifice a great deal for it. He loves his freedom and will give up love in order to keep it. Many women think they will be the one to make him want to settle down: he is so charming to them all. But he is only flirting; he has no intention of settling down, not until he is approaching middle age at any rate and, often not even then.

His love is quite genuine while it lasts: he is a caring and loving person and he will not lie to her. Sometimes, she wishes he would! He tells her truthfully he does not intend to marry —but she is so magnetic and so successful with the opposite sex, she cannot believe he means it. If she really loves him and will wait patiently until he is ready to settle down, he may settle with her. But Scorpio is an all-or-nothing woman; this is unlikely.

Sagittarius Man—Sagittarius Woman. The Sagittarian woman is the only one who knows instinctively how to make a Sagittarian man think of marriage. She knows he wants to be free—so does she, so she will not pressure him or chase him. She will let him keep his independence and expect to keep hers. This will suit them very well.

They are both flirts, but become less so as they grow closer together; they are interested in each other—besides, she will retaliate if he overdoes the flirting and that will bring him back to her side, to see what she is up to.

She will play him at his own game—and win. This is because she really knows what makes him tick. She knows how she hates to be tied down herself and will not tie him. He can do what he likes; she has her own life to live.

The Sagittarian man will not try to tell her what to do, as

he is not bossy; he will admire her vitality and independence that strike such a responding chord in him. These two understand each other perfectly.

Physically, they are very compatible. They are both romantic and there is plenty of passion in their relationship. Once they are in love, they are affectionate to each other and likely to be faithful.

Both are tactless in speech, blunt and sometimes hurtful; this will not affect their relationship because they each give as good as they get. There will be a few screaming matches with those two explosive tempers, but their quarrels will be made up quickly and soon forgotten.

Sagittarius Man—Capricorn Woman. She will be very attracted to his easy wit and charm, but she will not show it. She represses her emotions violently. She has a strong wish and need for love, but will never show this until she is really sure of her partner, she so fears rejection.

She is attracted to the warmth of the Sagittarian man and wonders how he makes so many friends when she has such difficulty. She feels very insecure because of his popularity. He will often be interested in her to begin with, but loses interest when she keeps him at arm's length and doesn't seem to want to be friends.

The Capricorn woman will sometimes make some move towards the Sagittarian man when she realizes he is not taking any notice of her. He likes women and will not mind coaxing her out of her shyness once she gives him a sign.

After a slow start, this can be quite a satisfying love affair. The Sagittarian man is passionate and loving, while the Capricorn woman, once she is sure of her welcome, is sensuous and loving. She is more romantic than he is; still he has romance enough for her and she is passionate enough for him.

She is full of self-doubt and insecurity; unfortunately the Sagittarian man, with his roving, flirtatious ways and insistence on remaining free does not give her the security she needs. He is also blunt and outspoken and can be really tactless, and this could wreck their relationship. Harsh words really get through to a Capricorn woman.

Sagittarius Man—Aquarius Woman. Well suited. Their light touch of romance and similar sense of humor ensures that they have a good chance of happiness together. They both dislike heavy relationships and intense feelings in people: they are much more comfortable in a more free relationship.

She is cool, but she is witty and a good conversationalist, sociable and friendly. Some of her friends are very eccentric, but the Sagittarian man will not mind; he likes unusual people and will be charming to them.

The Aquarian woman looks up to the man she is in love with and thinks everything he does and says is right. She will put up with bad treatment from a man she loves because of this. However, the Sagittarian man will treat her well. He is rather a flirt but she doesn't mind at all, as she is quite confident of her ability to interest him and keep him; and she is right.

Physically, he is a lot more passionate than she is, but this won't really matter. It is the emotional bond that grows from being on the same wavelength that unites them. Gossips will report to her what he is up to when he is out of her sight, but she will take no notice. Against all the odds, these two tend to stick together. They are real friends, and they like each other very much.

Neither the Aquarian woman nor the Sagittarian man is very comfortable with marriage: they may live apart.

Sagittarius Man—Pisces Woman. He will quite enjoy this love affair; she will not. She will find the tactless and flirtatious Sagittarian man very hard to handle and is likely to suffer from bruised feelings. This makes her moody and he is less than patient with those who suffer from the moods he is immune to.

It is not only the Piscean woman who cannot bridle the Sagittarian man; nobody can do it. He is his own man, strong and independent, and he goes his own way. The only thing he is really interested in is freedom. Her loving and vulnerable ways make him feel guilty and this makes him want to move on to another partner who will flirt and take things less seriously.

The Piscean woman is loving and emotional and she can make him love her in return. He is more passionate than she, but she is responsive, and their love-life will be sweet. She is very feminine and this appeals to him. She will not try to change him, but will wish he would be more settled and want to stay at home alone with her more than he does.

She will give him plenty of room to maneuver and if she is patient he may settle with her in the end; but if he feels pressured and restricted in the relationship he will become restless and she will find it very difficult to hold onto him. The Sagittarian man finds the Piscean woman hyper-sensitive and emotionally draining and she find his blunt speech very hurtful. They are unlikely to stay together.

X. Capricorn ♑

The Capricorn Character

Capricorn men and women have a strong, fixed character. They are cautious but not timid, rarely proud or too independent, but they have a great deal of self-confidence.

They are painstaking and persevering, diplomatic and very hard-working. The Capricorn man or woman has fixed goals, and will work hard and long in pursuit of them. Progress may be slow, but it will be sure.

Extreme youth is the most trying time for Capricorns; as they grow older they become more and more successful. This applies in all areas of life, personal and business. They are achievers, and this becomes very obvious as they progress.

Capricorns are undemonstrative people, but they have very deep feelings. The Capricorn man and woman are slow to love, but when they do are devoted and loyal; they are steadfast and loyal through any adversity. They are sincere, and dislike those who are not.

The Capricorn woman is subject to depression, and it is this that causes most of her illnesses. Physically sturdy, all Capricorns have to fight against their own pessimism—the women in particular. They become despondent and give up too easily; the Capricorn man is subject to the same defeatist feelings, but he has more endurance. Capricorns are secret worriers; they worry about anything and everything.

Capricorns are very law-abiding and responsible. They are honest and trustworthy, and reliable in their dealings, even with those they do not like. They are always scrupulously fair in their judgments of people, and will think long and hard, weighing up every factor, before making decisions. They cannot be hurried; they will do everything in their own time.

Capricorn people are thrifty. They do not like waste in any form. They are economical in their ways, savers rather than spenders. Even so, they will always buy the best once they have made up their minds to make a purchase. They believe in quality, because it is lasting. They take care of their possessions, and prefer to repair things rather than replace them.

Capricorn people suffer from an inferiority complex. They have little confidence in themselves, and because of this they hold back from expressing an opinion or seeking out friendships. They fear rejection, and will take a long time to respond to any overtures of friendship directed at them. They are wary of placing themselves in a position where they ask for friendship and are snubbed; therefore they will let the other person do all the work at the beginning of a friendship, and have a reputation for being cold and unfriendly. On the surface they may appear aloof and remote, but inwardly they have a great need to be loved, and an even greater need to give love to someone else. It is just that they find it difficult to do so.

Those that they do extend their friendship to will find them loyal. They are good allies to have, especially in time of trouble. They respect and stay close to their relatives, particularly the older ones. Capricorn people are very good with old people, and they like them and are kind to them. The Capricorn person does their duty, no matter how inconvenient it may be. They do not duck out of their responsibilities, but see things through to the end.

Of course, even these well-behaved people have some faults. They can be cold and selfish when their interests turn solely toward themselves and leave other people's interests out of the reckoning. They love money and this can make a Capricorn person calculating and avaricious. There is also the undoubted fact of their ambition; they may be prepared to sacrifice personal relationships, and even the career prospects of another person, in order to succeed themselves.

Under circumstances of stress and strain, Capricorn people can be sarcastic and scornful. This often arises from hurt feelings or personal unhappiness concealed within themselves; but it does not make their harshness any easier to bear. Those who have been on the receiving end of a bitter outburst from a

Capricorn are usually shocked by the real dislike that seems to lie behind the words, and this can cause lasting damage to friendships and relationships.

Envy can also be a factor in undermining friendships. The fact is Capricorns find it much easier to show affection and support to those in need, than to those who are better placed than they are. It is that old insecurity showing again. Taken together, though, this is, on balance, a good person without too many faults.

How Capricorn Gets Along with Others

Capricorn with Aries

Money/Job. Capricorn will be a very steadying influence on Aries, keeping a tight hold of the purse-strings while not discouraging the Arien from making the most of their good ideas. Ariens gamble, Capricorns don't—they will make sure the books balance and take a lot of the workload off Aries, working patiently and perseveringly in the background. Both are ambitious and will be prepared to make sacrifices and work long hours to advance themselves. Capricorn pays attention to detail; Aries carves out the broad outline. The two can combine well and profitably.

Home/Friends. Aries people are rather slapdash and regard their home as something that has to suit them, rather than the other way around. They are not very tidy and are less organized than the Capricorn partner. A Capricorn runs a tight ship; the home is spartan rather than comfortable, though it is always clean and tidy. Capricorns do not make friends easily, but the Arien does and the Capricorn does rather enjoy socializing, provided they do not have to make the opening moves. Aries will introduce them to a nice circle of friends. Any children will be well cared for.

Capricorn with Taurus

Money/Job. A good combination. Both are steady, patient workers, and both have a proper regard for attention to detail. Their views on money coincide; both think it is important and will be careful with it, though the Taurean has expensive tastes and likes comfort and luxury while the Capricorn does not. However, the Taurean does not go into debt to finance his good taste, and the Capricorn will persuade the Taurean to economize if necessary. Both are prepared to work hard, and both are ambitious and want to succeed in the world and be respected by others for their achievements. There is no reason why they should not succeed.

Home/Friends. Not quite such a good outlook. The Taurean loves beauty and comfort in the home and does not mind spending hard earned money to get it; the Capricorn likes neatness and order but is not a spendthrift, and actually disapproves of luxury and soft living. The Taurean admires the thrift of the Capricorn person, but not the cheese-paring attitude. The Taurean is not wasteful, but the Capricorn, always on the outlook for savings, makes them feel guilty. If there are children, they will be good parents. Both provide well and the Taurean adds warmth.

Capricorn with Gemini

Money/Job. There will be some problems. Gemini has a quick, bright mind and can turn out a fantastic amount of work in a short space of time: Capricorn likes to work steadily, giving proper attention to all the details, and mistrusts the speed of Gemini, certain they have not done the job properly. They are always checking up. This will be very irksome to Gemini, and may cause an upset. There is one great link though; both fear poverty, and neither will want to spend very much money. The Capricorn balances the books; the Gemini is only too pleased to let them do it, and not to have to worry. If they can learn to accept that they work differently and trust each other, the Capricorn provides a very good back-up for Gemini and is a steadying influence.

Home/Friends. Capricorns are home-rooted people. Geminis are butterflies, out and about, socializing with their friends and going to as many different places as they can. The Gemini loves to travel, and will live out of a suitcase if allowed. Basically, the Capricorn will be left to manage things in the home; they will not mind this, because they are sure they can do it better anyway. If there are children, Gemini will stimulate them; Capricorn will restrain them.

Capricorn with Cancer

Money/Job. Capricorns are worriers—so are Cancerians. They will reassure each other. Both will take care with money. They both have modest tastes and do not spend much; they are good savers and good at cutting corners and making do. Cancerians have a flair for making money; and as Capricorn is so ambitious, they would be well advised to listen to the advice of a Cancerian when making investments. Capricorns trust nobody but themselves, but if they will respect the judgment of a Cancerian, they will make a profit. Capricorn works really hard, and they will help each other to succeed.

Home/Friends. Cancerians love their homes, and will spend money to give themselves pleasing surroundings. To a Capricorn, home should be functional and their surroundings, though always clean and tidy, need the caring touch of the Cancerian. The Capricorn will fret at money spent if it is on luxuries, but will pay up without a murmur for the best in the market for a large, basic purchase. They like quality. The Cancerian loves to entertain, and they make their home a pleasure to their guests and family alike. The Capricorn may be rather withdrawn to begin with, but will enjoy entertaining as long as it is not too much of an expense. Perfect balance as parents: Cancer gives love, Capricorn gives stability.

Capricorn with Leo

Money/Job. Leo is a shrewd and clever person in business and can make a great deal of money. Leo is a hard worker, but is careful to give the impression of it all being very easy, and this totally unnerves the Capricorn. So does Leo's big spending; frugal Capricorn nearly has a nervous breakdown over the bills. Leo brushes the worry aside; Capricorn spends a lot of time trying to balance the books. Leo will always lead; if Capricorn can take a deep breath and trust to Leo's wheeling and dealing, they can, with Capricorn's faithful background work, make a winning team.

Home/Friends. Capricorn's careful and money-saving ways strike no echo with Leo: Leo people hate economizing and would rather spend than save. They give the impression of being casual with money, but in fact they are not. The Leo person has a secret; they are terribly afraid of poverty. So although they appear to spend huge sums without turning a hair, in fact they always get value for money and do not go too far. They love a luxurious home and are very hospitable to their friends. They entertain lavishly; they are afraid of appearing mean. Leo will override the Capricorn's thrift and Capricorn will worry. Not a very good combination: if there are children, Leo will indulge them. Capricorn will steady them.

Capricorn with Virgo

Money/Job. These two will be fine. Capricorn is a worker —cold in manner perhaps but with fine sterling qualities. Virgo is very much the same. Both are economical, and dislike waste; both believe in good steady application to the job in hand and no risks taken. The difference is in ambition; Capricorn has strong ambitions, and Virgo has none. Virgo works in the background for the benefit of other people more than for their own good, and asks little in reward. Capricorn knows the value of money and work and will make sure they are properly rewarded for what they do. Virgo likes money; Capricorn will help them to make it.

Home/Friends. Good. They share the same aims, they want the same things. Neither of them likes luxury living, or indulgence in any form. They will have a rather spartan lifestyle but will be perfectly content with it; and while their friends spend on home and holidays, they will quietly watch their savings grow. They make good parents; they will make sure their children are given the best chances in life but will expect them to work hard and to achieve. Capricorn will help them with their homework and fire them with ambition; Virgo will teach them to work hard and be unselfish. Both Virgo and Capricorn need to relax a little and learn to laugh.

Capricorn with Libra

Money/Job. The Libran will drive the Capricorn person mad by lack of sustained hard work, and the Capricorn will make the Libran feel pressured and uneasy. Libras do not like to work hard. They like an easy life. They are not very anxious to make money, except as a means to pleasure and to buying all the lovely and expensive things they like to surround themselves with. They like to do just enough work to cover themselves, and they are experts at assessing this. The Capricorn, with hard-working ways, caution and ambition, is quite alien to them, and they do not like Capricorn's streak of meanness. They will not work well together unless both change totally; and they cannot do that.

Home/Friends. Libra likes a beautiful home as a setting for the glittering social life they aspire to. They like warmth and comfort and quite a bit of luxury. Capricorn likes a very modest lifestyle, nothing extravagant, and disapproves of luxury. Capricorn people will fret and worry inwardly about all the expense of the Libra lifestyle, and this will even prevent them from enjoying the company of friends. They are not suited to live together, and if there are children, will not agree about their upbringing. Libra will undermine Capricorn by telling the children life is short and for living. Life together will be a silent battle of wills.

Capricorn with Scorpio

Money/Job. Scorpio is not like Capricorn in character, but
as far as work is concerned, they understand each other and
combine well. Both will do a good job of work, and both understand the value of money and will be careful with it. They
will not argue over who is in charge, but will each do the
part of the job they are best at and have a team effort. Their
only real reason to disagree is that Scorpio is somewhat
more free-spending than Capricorn, though by no means careless; and Capricorn will want the money to stay where it is,
while Scorpio will want to use some of it. Scorpio will win,
in the face of the Capricorn's predictions of poverty. Scorpio
knows when to take notice, and will use common sense. Both
work very hard and deserve the success they will undoubtedly
achieve.

Home/Friends. Capricorn wants a home which is clean
and tidy and properly run, with bills paid on time and low
expenses. Scorpio wants a home that is luxurious and comfortable to live in, and a status symbol too, because Scorpio
believes the world will judge them by their possessions. They
cannot both be happy; Scorpio will have their own way. Although Capricorn will disapprove of the comfort and luxury,
Scorpio will not overspend, and gradually Capricorn will be
less worried. If they have children, they will each make a good
parent, but in different ways. Capricorn will teach ambition
and hard work, Scorpio will add warmth.

Capricorn with Sagittarius

Money/Job. Conflict here. These two are opposites, and opposites can either fight or realize that between them they have
absolutely all the aces. Capricorn will disapprove of the open-
handed, fast thinking Sagittarian and dismiss his moneymak-

ing schemes as being too intuitive and not having enough spadework put into them; and the Sagittarian will be irritated by the much slower Capricorn, who does not burn with his enthusiasm and who puts the brakes on all the time where money is concerned. This can be a good combination if each respects the other: Sagittarius will have the ideas, Capricorn will work on them and both will reap a profit; also, Capricorn will invest for both of them, for a rainy day.

Home/Friends. Capricorn is not much of a home-maker. They actively dislike luxury and will make sure everything is functional and as modest as possible. The Sagittarian does like comfort and pleasant surroundings—but is out so much socializing that they won't complain too much. Sagittarius and Capricorn don't have much in common; the Sagittarian is outgoing and warm, and loves company; the Capricorn is cool and reserved and does not like the constant coming and going of the Sagittarian's group of friends. These two make better business associates than personal friends: if they have children, they will be totally opposed on upbringing.

Capricorn with Capricorn

Money/Job. Not quite so good as it might look at first sight. Both having the same nature, they will each be cautious, rather slow, hard-working, ambitious people. They will also both lack vision, and the sense of adventure necessary to try something new, to trust to instinct, or to take a chance. This limits them severely, and they will have a long, hard struggle to make any advance at all. They will certainly wish to advance: Capricorns are very ambitious and very money-conscious. There will also be a lack of innovation and vision, though no lack of effort. They will take care of their money; they are both savers, not spenders.

Home/Friends. Here they will see eye-to-eye. The Capricorn home is clean and tidy, with anything useful or functional that is needed readily available, but no emphasis on luxuries. Capricorns do not like spending money, but they will spend on the best of a particular line, once they have decided it is essential. They like quality; they like things to last. Capricorns do not like debt or leasing; they are more likely to save for each thing, then buy it. If there are children, they will be well provided for, and having two Capricorn parents will make them totally secure.

Capricorn with Aquarius

Money/Job. An ill-assorted pair. The Capricorn will be utterly bewildered by the Aquarian's scatterbrained attitude toward business. Aquarians work when they want to, when they feel something is worthwhile, and not otherwise. They cannot be bribed or motivated by money because they are not primarily interested in money. They enjoy it when they have it, but they don't *worry* about it. Capricorns worry about everything, money most of all. Capricorns will try to organize Aquarians (and nobody can do that) and will lecture them. This does not bother Aquarius, who simply doesn't listen. Aquarians are very clever people, not usually extravagant, who like status but lack ambition. They have little in common with serious Capricorn, who considers them lightweight.

Home/Friends. Capricorn likes a spartan home; Aquarius likes beauty, and strange objects and people. It is an uneasy partnership. The Aquarian above all likes what is unusual, whether it be people, places or hobbies. The Capricorn is totally conservative and conventional, and will not like some of the people in Aquarius's circle. There will not be battles, because Capricorn shows displeasure by silence and coldness rather than quarrelling, and the Aquarian dislikes scenes and will just ignore trouble; but there will be stress. If there are children, Capricorn will govern but Aquarius will rule: children copy Aquarians.

Capricorn with Pisces

Money/Job. Capricorn is aloof and forbidding. Pisces is sympathetic and kind, and has a wonderful touch with people from all walks of life; therefore a Pisces person can be a very great help to Capricorn in relating to clients and customers, and is best left in charge of that side of the work. Pisceans do their fair share of any job, but it is just a component in their lives, and they lack the ambition of a Capricorn. Both like money, though for different reasons: the Piscean to spend, or give away, the Capricorn to save. It is best for Capricorn to balance the books.

Home/Friends. The Piscean is a giver in every sense. They are hospitable and give a lot of money away. The Capricorn nature is less open, and they will feel they have to keep a tight hold on the purse-strings. Pisceans like a lovely home. They are good home-makers and like to spend a lot of money on it, and once again, Capricorn will restrain them. Although the Piscean will not like this, they will appreciate it in one sense: they crave security, and Capricorn will give it to them and will stop others from taking advantage of their good nature. If there are children, they will be well taken care of—Capricorns are always mindful of their obligations; Pisceans provide the warmth they need and will welcome their friends.

Love Mates

Capricorn Woman—Aries Man. The Aries man may
attract the Capricorn woman by his drive, self-assurance and
energy, but she will not like the arrogance and brashness she
sees in him. If she is to love him, it will happen slowly, and
she is likely to try to avoid him in the early stages.

She uses her reasoning powers in love, as in everything else.
She likes security and power, and she is looking for a man who
is as levelheaded as she is, and who is ambitious and intends
to succeed.

As she grows to know the Aries man better, however, she
will begin to admire his loyalty and fixity of purpose: he is an
achiever, and she will like that. He is a hard worker and suc-
ceeds in most things he does; he shows signs of this at an early
age. The Capricorn woman needs time to mature; she improves
with age. She is insecure and introverted, particularly when
young, and often gives an impression of aloofness and reserve
when she is in fact very interested in a man and wishes he
would notice her.

The Aries man, with his passionate and loving nature, can
be the one who will get through to her. She is inwardly longing
for love and the Aries man, because he is so open and loving
himself, is a good lover and can give her the confidence she
needs to reveal herself as she really is.

Once her reserve goes and she really commits herself, the
Capricorn woman is as steady and faithful in her affections as
she is in other areas of her life; she will stick by him when he
gets into one of his occasional financial muddles and will give
him good advice which he will learn to trust. A good pair.

Capricorn Woman—Taurus Man. He is often very
attractive to her. She looks for stability and success and he has
both these qualities. He is attractive to women and is good at

managing them. He likes to take charge of a relationship and she welcomes this, because she has great difficulty in showing her emotions before she is really sure of her welcome and with the Taurus man, she does not need to do so. If he is interested, he will do the work for both of them.

The Capricorn woman is a contradiction: she longs for love but gives the impression of being cold and uninterested. She has a great fear of rejection and imagines herself to be inferior. The Taurus man is sensuous and loving and can be physically demanding, and she will find this reassuring. He will need her and will show that he does; and this will enable her to show her feelings with him. She is capable of a surprising response to passion, though she does not initiate it herself. She will like his stability and perseverence. He is an achiever and she is looking for an achiever, for someone who will be successful and who is ambitious and able to make money. Emotionally, she needs love and warmth and he provides this too. Both are careful about money and security and think alike about a great many things.

Once committed, the Capricorn woman is loyal and faithful, and loves truly. Before that, however, she lets her head rule her heart; she does not want to fall in love with the wrong man and will make every effort not to do so.

Capricorn Woman—Gemini Man. The Gemini man is charming. He lives for the moment, and is a bright and entertaining companion; for the Capricorn woman, this is not enough.

She is looking for an adult relationship, in which she can lose her own insecurities and blossom from her cold and reserved exterior. To do this, she needs a man who can give her sufficient security emotionally to show her true self. The Gemini man is many things, but he is not secure. He likes a pleasant and carefree life and he cannot be persuaded to take many things seriously.

To a Capricorn woman, most things are serious. She is an ambitious, hard working person herself and she is looking for a man who will be the same. She wants permanence—and she needs it. Although she has a deep need for love, she sets about finding it in the same way as she tries to achieve the other things she wants from life: she lets her head rule her heart. She does not want to fall in love with an unsuitable person and she will do her best to see that she does not, by mentally assessing the men she meets and not allowing a relationship to progress until she is sure something can come of it. Economy of effort is her watchword, in all areas of life. She does not waste time—or emotion.

It is as well that she does. Her feelings are so deep that she can be bitterly hurt by love and in the case of a Gemini man, she would be confused by his changeability, and hurt by his lack of commitment. He would not suit her—nor she, him.

Capricorn Woman—Cancer Man.
Both of this pair suffer from deep insecurities and both pretend to be something they are not in order to hide it. She hides a loving nature behind a mask of coldness and reserve; indeed she can give the impression of actively disliking a man she is really interested in. This arises from a feeling of inferiority and a fear of rejection.

He is full of secret anxieties and doubts, but he shows a different face. He is very masculine and hides his real sensitivity and fear of hurt under a casual exterior. If they would each stop pretending, they would find they had more in common than is obvious.

The Capricorn woman needs a warm and emotional man to give her confidence and persuade her to show her real feelings. The Cancerian man needs to feel loved above all. He is so sensitive he is wounded by quite trivial things and takes offense very easily.

Once he senses the real woman behind her don't-care exterior (and he is better than anyone at realizing how emotional women are), he will be kindness itself to her and drop his own macho act. Although they have very different characters, they could experience a deep and tender love. A Cancerian man knows how to make a woman feel cherished.

However, above all the Capricorn woman is looking for an achiever, someone who is ambitious and will be successful and offer her permanence and security, and a great deal will depend on whether the Cancerian man can come up to her demanding standards in this area.

Capricorn Woman—Leo Man.

She is restrained and reserved. She needs and wants love but finds it very difficult to show her feelings; and she also makes very sure, by using her head instead of her heart, that she chooses wisely before allowing herself to get even close to falling in love.

The Capricorn woman is looking for an achiever, a man who will offer her money, success and permanency. She does not want to waste her time or emotions, preferring to wait for the right person to come along. This may seem a rather cold-blooded way of dealing with love, but until the Capricorn woman falls in love, she IS cold, and will remain so until she finds a man she is sufficiently secure with to drop pretense and show her feelings. Because she is so afraid of being rejected, owing to feelings of imagined inferiority, she will often hide real interest in a man behind a formal, cool manner; and she is so good at this that the man may be driven away by her seeming coldness towards him.

To the Leo man, this is a real challenge. He will not be put off by her apparent indifference: his instinct is to find what he wants and then go all out to get it. As he is just the type of man she likes, successful, ambitious and proud, she is not likely to run too fast while he is chasing her! He is fiery and passionate in love and this is just what she needs to unlock her own response.

She will love and admire him and will be faithful. Once she gives her heart, her commitment is total. Leo thinks he has carried off a great prize—as, of course, he has.

Capricorn Woman—Virgo Man.

Not quite as good a combination as Virgo woman–Capricorn man, but still good. The Capricorn woman sees in the Virgo man many similarities to herself. Both are cautious, careful with money and hardworking; but although she is very much motivated by ambition, he is not—he is content to serve.

Their basic character is very similar, however; both are quiet and reserved on first acquaintance, both are restrained in their emotions and will not easily show their feelings, and both look for a partner with their head rather than their heart.

They are likely to regard each other as suitable partners, but it will be a rather cold relationship. She is capable of passion, but she is so afraid of rejection that she keeps her emotions under tight control and he is not the one to break through that control and make her show herself as she really is.

The Virgo man tends not to be very physical in his expression of love—though he can love truly and deeply. He is more inclined to express his love through devoted service and trying to please. The Capricorn woman will settle for this and they will be happy enough together, working for stability and a good future. She will want to motivate him to succeed, but it is more likely that she will be the driving force who will direct his hard work into the right direction to bring rewards.

She is loyal and faithful and he is the same. Both are looking for permanence and security, and will find it together.

Capricorn Woman—Libra Man. The Capricorn woman, though sensible and cautious, is not immune to the charm of the Libra man. No woman is. He is such good company, so easy to get along with, that she cannot help responding to him. He will encourage her to take a lighthearted view of life, and this is something new to her. She is serious and has little sense of humor.

She has a lack of confidence about her powers of attraction; he is wonderfully reassuring; of all men in the zodiac he has the most power to soothe and comfort women. Once she gets over her fear of rejection, she can relax with him, and then she is capable of passion and deep love. Although he finds her a little daunting to start with (owing to her more serious nature) he is fascinated to watch her flowering before his eyes—and all in response to his charm! He is a little conceited and cannot help congratulating himself. Once committed, she is loyal and faithful and so trusting of him that he finds himself more deeply involved than he thought and becoming protective of her.

They can build a strong relationship. The Libra man functions best in partnerships; Libra is the sign of marriage. The

Capricorn woman needs permanence and security to truly relax. The only real problem is over money. She is hardworking and ambitious and very money conscious; he is a big spender and not very work-motivated. She will change all this, but not openly: she will manipulate behind the scenes and he will find he is successful, without really knowing how he did it.

Capricorn Woman—Scorpio Man. This would be a good partnership in many ways. She will admire his success, and he will respect her virtues of hard work and economy. They get on well together.

Emotionally, they are different: the Scorpio man can do much to help to liberate a Capricorn woman. He is dominant, intense, possessive and jealous in the extreme. She is afraid of showing her feelings and keeps her emotions on a tight rein until she is positive there is no risk of rejection. He can bring out her femininity in response to his own passion and she is capable of a deep love and loyalty once she is committed.

She is a little frightened of life: she hides this behind an appearance of reserve and aloofness, but secretly she has a strong need for love and would love to be protected and cared for. In the Scorpio man, she has the ideal partner for this. He wants to protect and advise those he loves, and she will take notice of him and allow him to take the lead. Once she feels secure and loved, she becomes noticeably softer, and her tendency towards coldness and sarcasm disappears. She makes a loyal and devoted wife.

She likes men to be strong, ambitious, and successful. She wants the security that an assured future with enough money can give. She will have no worries on that score with him—he wants the same things. On his part, he will be good for her—his only real fault is the terrible jealousy he is subject to, and she is totally faithful. She will give him no cause for worry. They should be happy.

Capricorn Woman—Sagittarius Man. She is full of self-doubt and insecurity; and unfortunately, the Sagittarian man, with his flirtatious ways, does not give her the security and

permanence she needs before she can really express her feelings.

She will often be violently attracted to him, but is likely to give him a wide berth. He does not conform to her idea of the type of man she is looking for. She is looking for an achiever, someone who is going to be successful and make money. He often has money and is shrewd and clever in business, but she does not regard him as steady enough for her.

But she finds his warmth and friendliness very attractive. She has a lot of difficulty in forming friendships and she envies the ease with which he does it. He can put her at ease. For a woman to be on the receiving end of the total attention a Sagittarian man gives when he is pursuing a woman, is quite an experience; not many can resist it and the Capricorn woman is no exception.

For a time this can be a satisfying love affair. He likes women, and will happily coax her out of her reserve—and she will respond with a passion that will surprise him.

The trouble comes when she finds out that holding onto him is like having a tiger by the tail: he wants to be free—she wants to be sure. He will be very blunt in speech, and this could wreck their relationship. She can be really hurt by harsh words.

Capricorn Woman—Capricorn Man. Capricorn is a sign that is not best mated with its own sign. There is much that is negative in the Capricorn character, and a special warmth of manner and outgoing emotion in the partner is necessary to bring out the best, emotionally, in Capricorn people.

A Capricorn man needs a woman to help him show his feelings. He keeps them buttoned up tightly inside; he is afraid of revealing his emotions because he might be rejected, and this is his greatest fear. The Capricorn woman, with her identical hang-up, is frightened of him, just as he is frightened of her, and they could easily get off on the wrong foot and offend each other with sarcasm and hostility. They are unimaginative; they do not think for a moment that the cause of the other person's behavior is the same as for their own.

She is looking for a special somebody who will be "right" for her to fall in love with. He must be ambitious, persevering, hardworking, and prepared to achieve and make money: all the things a Capricorn man is. On this score, she will be pleased with him, and he finds a matching echo in her.

But she needs the warmth and spontaneity of a man who is deeply attracted to her, and shows it, to allow her to unlock her own feelings, and be as loving and giving as she really wishes. She will not get this from him, locked tightly away himself.

Both these Capricorns need to just trust a little, reach out—and discover what a good match they could be. But they won't.

Capricorn Woman—Aquarius Man.

She is not likely to seriously consider him as a suitable match. She is practical, with her feet well on the ground, looking to the future, ambitious and hardworking, and she is likely to be looking for a similar sort of man. She chooses with her head before making a commitment with her heart, and in this she is very wise; because with her emotional reserve, love is very important to her, and she becomes very hurt if she is disillusioned.

The Aquarian man is certainly charming, but he is neither serious nor ambitious. He is not very interested in making money, though he likes prestige and social success. He is often eccentric in manner, and the Capricorn woman, deeply conventional, does not much care for this.

Emotionally, he is cool, as she is, but with a major difference: he is not looking for deep involvement. He likes light, entertaining relationships and she is looking for the man who will give her such security and depth of love that she can relax her guard and give him the deep love and passion she is capable of.

The Aquarian man is likely to be frightened off by the intensity he senses in her, and by her somewhat humorless approach to life. Although she may like him (and who doesn't?), it would be better for them to be friends than lovers. Their goals are very different, and so are their personalities.

Capricorn Woman—Pisces Man. He is a dreamer, and he believes dreams can come true. He is loving and outgoing, sensitive and unworldly. He is not very interested in material things, nor is he very ambitious. He likes a peaceful, happy life, with no real ups and downs.

She is quite different. She is hardworking and interested in her career, and she is looking for a man who is an achiever, who will bring strength and security to her. He makes her feel warm and cared for, but lacks the strength of purpose to suit her.

A Capricorn woman hides her very real feelings, and need for love, and a Piscean man can do a great deal to make her lower her defenses and discover her own emotional potential. He has all the outgoing emotion, and can show her how to love. In the short term, this could be enough for both of them, but she is looking to the future—and she doesn't like short-term love affairs.

He loves very easily, and very often. The instability of his character will worry her, and she will not like his attraction to other women. The emotional Pisces man can be very hurt by a Capricorn woman. She has a streak of hardness and coldness he does not possess, and he is likely to come off worst in this relationship. If she is disappointed in him she can be very withdrawn, and he is too much of a dreamer, and too sensitive, to be able to cope with this. He is likely to let her go, and she will take this as proof that he never really cared for her. Nothing could be further from the truth.

Capricorn Man—Aries Woman. She has something special to give to him. He needs a great deal of help and support before he can show his feelings. The Capricorn man is restrained and reserved: he is looking for the woman who can unlock his heart.

She has the love and warmth, coupled with her own wholehearted fearlessness in love, to draw him out and show him how to feel. Aries women have great fire and passion, and the Capricorn man is passionate too, once his inhibitions are released. He is afraid of rejection: the thing he most dreads is a snub, and he will go to great lengths, even pretending a total disinterest, to avoid receiving one.

He will discover that she is trustworthy and loyal—both qualities he needs and wants in a woman—as well as loving, and gradually will learn to drop his defenses and be less guarded with her. Once he is committed, he is devoted and faithful, and makes a good lover and husband. His problem is that he does not know instinctively how to respond to affection: he has to learn. Who better to teach him than the ardent, loving Aries woman?

But she must be careful. His pride is very sensitive, and he will not like it if he thinks she is taking the lead. She can be aggressive and tactless, and anything like this will cause him to withdraw very quickly. He responds very well to kindness, and she will be surprised at how quickly he can be turned into a romantic.

Capricorn Man—Taurus Woman. He is drawn to
her sensuous, strongly feminine personality. She has great charm and diplomacy and will be able to get him to relax enough with her to drop his guard and gradually show his real feelings. He is a contradiction. He appears to be cold and unfeeling but actually is longing for love. It is real fear of a rebuff, or rejection, that restrains him. A Taurean woman is so confident in her own femininity that she is able to put him at his ease, and he can surprise her with his passion. He is devoted and loving once he is committed. He is looking for stability and permanence in a relationship, and once he has found it, will not easily let it go.

The Taurean woman likes permanence too. She will also like the feeling of security she gets with the Capricorn man. They are well suited: both like money and success, and she likes her man to achieve and to advance in life. This, he can and will do.

She is physically quite demanding in love, and he will be reassured by this. She needs him, and she lets him know it. This will enable him to show his love for her. Emotionally, he needs love and warmth, and she will provide it.

Both are faithful in love, and constant. The Taurean woman

does tend to flirt a little; she is so attractive she is always very much in demand, and this could upset and annoy the Capricorn man. He is possessive, because love is so difficult for him to find that he fears losing it again. This is a loving couple.

Capricorn Man—Gemini Woman. He is cold, reserved, and practical. She is a butterfly, light and free and with a gift for making friends that is envied by all. She attracts the Capricorn man, but she frightens and puzzles him. She seems to have no serious side to her nature at all: she is interested in a happy social life, and having enough money to achieve it; but she is not ambitious or persevering, and she is certainly not practical.

He appears to be self-sufficient, but in reality he is inhibited, and repressed with his emotions. He longs to meet someone who can make him forget his real fear of rejection so that he can drop his guard and fall in love. In order to do this he has to have great reassurance from her, and he will not get this from a Gemini woman. Her lightness of touch and coolness of approach do nothing to make him relax. He fears that she would soon become bored with him: and he is often right. She becomes bored very quickly; she is not really interested in getting deeply involved with anyone—she would rather have a series of light, undemanding relationships, more like loving friendships.

The Capricorn man, who is nobody's fool, soon realizes this; and although he likes her and will wish for her friendship, he will look elsewhere for a more suitable partner to receive his confidence and love. He is wise to do so; he would be hurt otherwise.

Capricorn Man—Cancer Woman. Surprisingly good. On the face of it, the emotional Cancerian woman and the rather cold and repressed Capricorn man may seem to have little in common: in fact, they are almost ideally suited.

He lacks confidence in his ability to give and receive love. It is because of this, and his real fear of rejection and rebuff, that he sometimes appears hostile and unfriendly, especially to aggressive types of women. She presents no threat to him. She is totally feminine, very receptive and kind. She is emotional and loving and can coax him to open up to her, and drop his defenses. Once he is able to realize he is capable of passion and deep love, she will be very responsive to him. This is because the Cancerian woman is, herself, very anxious and insecure, and she understands the Capricorn man, and sees through the exterior to the real nature.

Both have a deep need for security and permanence, and they will find it with each other. The only problem is her wish to make a beautiful home and spend a lot of money on it. He is a high achiever and will be successful in business, but he is a saver rather than a spender, and is quite happy with a very spartan sort of home.

The Cancerian woman will persuade him to let her have her way about this; and such is her power to make him deeply happy and contended that he will let her have what she wants. The Capricorn man will indulge her wishes, and be happy to do so.

Capricorn Man—Leo Woman. She has the fire and warmth to overcome his reserve and restraint in love, but she is abrasive and dominant and this could make him back away.

The Capricorn man has great difficulty in showing his emotional feelings; he does have them, and they are strong, but he can conceal them completely from other people, and he is often thought to be unfriendly and cold. He hides his fear of rejection and rebuff behind sarcasm and gives the appearance of needing nobody, though this is very far from the truth. He needs and wants love, but is afraid to ask for it, and has not learned how to respond to the needs of other people.

The Leo woman could help him; but his apparent hardness puts her on the defensive, and she is inclined to be sarcastic herself if she is provoked. He may hide real interest behind his cold, formal manner, but she sees him as he is on the surface, and it drives her away. If she can manage to get beneath the surface, she will find much that is in accord with her own character: he is an achiever, he works hard and is ambitious, and he will make money. She respects these attributes in a man, and will respect him for them. She is hard-working too, and has pride and dignity, and this appeals to him.

A Leo woman has great femininity, but she needs a man to make her feel totally sure of herself, and to be stronger in character than she is (very difficult!) before she can relax enough to show this side. This pairing is a stalemate.

Capricorn Man—Virgo Woman. This should be an ideal match: good for the Capricorn man, with his insecurities and fear of rejection, and good for the selfless Virgo woman, who has found someone who will appreciate her true value at last.

He is ambitious: he is going places. He wants power, money and prestige, and with the amount of hard work he will put into life, he will get everything he wants. She lacks ambition on her own account, but she will identify with her man and make his goals her goals; she will help him to achieve anything he is aiming for by doing her bit in the background, working without wishing for reward. This is the typical way for a Virgo to show love, Virgo women in particular. She is also receptive to his needs for emotional love. Although she is not passionate herself, she recognizes that within him there is a great deal of passion and emotion locked away. Her calmness and femininity help him to trust her not to reject him, and once committed, he is a good lover. The Capricorn man is one of the few who can awaken the Virgo woman and make her respond. They are very compatible and well matched: both are slow to love and appear rather cold and unfriendly to the outside world, but when they are alone together it is a very different story.

The Virgo woman needs time to learn to love, and the Capricorn man is patient and understanding. He knows from experience that they both are often misjudged by others. He will love and value her, and share with her all that they worked so hard to achieve.

Capricorn Man—Libra Woman. She attracts him with her light, happy manner, her charm and sweetness. The Capricorn man, with his great difficulties in his love life and

his fear of rejection, sometimes hides behind sarcasm and a patronizing attitude, and can drive a less observant woman away. The Libra woman is a social charmer: she knows how to lead the conversation skillfully, smoothing off the rough corners, until he is relaxed enough to act more naturally with her.

Given time, they get on well. She does get a little impatient with him in the earlier stages of the relationship; he is so suspicious and cautious and afraid of showing his feelings. She does not show her impatience, and little by little, the real Capricorn man emerges. Once he is committed, he is a devoted lover, and gives of himself completely. She is a luxury-lover, he is not: but he will give in about this and much else, if he is in love and loved in return by such a charming lady. He cannot resist giving her what she wants.

Physically, he is a slow starter. He is so under-confident he is very reluctant to make the first move, and she will have to lead him gently and patiently into the relationship they both want. She is sensuous, and can work magic with him.

The Capricorn man is very affected by love or the lack of it; he can be morose, cold and reserved when he feels unloved or unwanted but he is a changed man once he has found a woman to be happy with. He counts himself very lucky to have met a Libra woman—and he is.

Capricorn Man—Scorpio Woman. He is full of self-doubt, especially in matters of love. He covers his fear of rejection by a rather patronizing manner and often biting sarcasm. He must be very sure of his welcome from a woman before he will trust himself to show her affection—yet he has a great need to give and to receive love. The Scorpio woman is passionate and magnetic. She often frightens him off at first, but she can be very good for him. She will be determined to find out what is behind that cold and severe exterior, and will usually succeed in doing so. She will be able to bring him out, and help him show his feelings as she shows hers.

Physically, they will have a good relationship. She is loving and strongly sexed, and is willing to take the first step—so he can be sure of her; emotionally he is so self-contained and cautious that it takes time for him to relax and fall in love, but once he commits himself to a relationship he is devoted and faithful. He will do nothing to arouse the jealousy of his partner—and with a Scorpio woman, that is absolutely vital. Jealousy is her greatest weakness, and if a man is not faithful to her, he will be exposed to real fury when she finds out.

Because he is so good at hiding his feelings, it takes time for him to get used to the way she she is open with hers. The Scorpio woman is moody. She is easily hurt if he is cold to her, and he has to learn to show her he loves her all the time.

They have many goals in common; both are ambitious, so they will be united in their approach to life; and generally speaking they will get on well together.

Capricorn Man—Sagittarius Woman.

He is attracted to her warmth and vitality, and marvels at the easy way she makes friends. He is lonely and insecure, and has a very formal manner; he can come across as cold and unfriendly. In reality, he is longing for love, but so buttoned up are his feelings that he finds it almost impossible to show them, and people initially are put off by his forbidding manner.

Sometimes a love affair between these two can start when the Sagittarian woman, used to attracting and being successful with any man she wants, realizes he is not taking any notice of her. Then she will turn on the charm, coaxing him along gently until he finally warms to her enough to drop his guard and show those violently repressed feelings. By this time, she may have become fascinated by him. The Capricorn man is interesting to her because he is a contradiction: he seems to be one thing, then turns out to be quite another.

Physically, they can be good together. She is full of fire, and can awaken his passion. He is romantic and loving when he gives himself the chance to be, and will delight her with little gifts and attentions in a rather old-fashioned way.

The Capricorn man needs a great deal of reassurance from a lover. He is full of self-doubt, and is easily hurt when the Sagittarian woman, tactless beyond belief, expresses any dislikes or problems bluntly and forcibly. This could wreck their relationship. They may be interested in each other, but are not likely to stay together permanently.

Capricorn Man—Capricorn Woman.

Capricorn is a sign that is best mated with a sign other than its own. There is much that is negative in the Capricorn character, and they need the warmth of a more outgoing sign to bring out the best in them—particularly in the matter of their emotions.

The Capricorn man will find much to admire in a Capricorn woman: he will like her strength of character, her aptitude for hard work and perseverence, so like his own, and her ability to be single-minded in pursuit of a goal. However, emotionally they can get off to a bad start; they are both inhibited and both tend to hide their fear of rejection behind a somewhat sarcastic and patronizing exterior when they meet someone who really interests them. He is unimaginative: it simply does not occur to him that the cause of the other person's behavior might be the same as his own.

His feelings are buttoned up so tightly that he finds great difficulty in showing love for anyone at all. He needs the warmth and openness of a woman who is deeply attracted to him and shows it to enable him to pluck up courage and lower his defenses. Once he does this, he is a devoted and faithful lover, and the longer a love affair lasts, the better he becomes. He needs reassurance, but as she also wants to be reassured, without having to do the reassuring, it can be a stalemate, and they may never find out that they have much to give each other. Capricorns tend to be takers rather than givers: and where there are two Capricorns together, this tendency is doubled. If nobody will give first, how can they get started?

Capricorn Man—Aquarius Woman.

He is cold and calculating; she is cool and disinterested. This makes for a lukewarm partnership. The Capricorn man has a lot of intensity within, which he hides behind a rather hostile and cold exterior; he is so afraid of being rejected that he deliberately hides his feelings if he is interested in anyone—even if she makes it very clear that she is interested too. It takes time for him to gather up the courage to drop his defenses and trust a woman to accept him; once he does, he is devoted and loyal.

The Aquarian woman is as light as a feather; she is detached and remote. She will not give him the reassurance he needs, because she is too disinterested—not necessarily in him, but in the whole situation of having to draw him out and nurse him along. She looks for someone who will respond more easily—and not be so much work! She prefers light, witty people, and is not much attracted by the cold streak and gloomy outlook of the Capricorn man. True, he is an achiever, faithful and devoted: however these are not attributes that especially attract her. She turns her attention to more superficial, more socially easy men; and thinks that the Capricorn man will make a good husband—for someone else!

She is mistrustful of emotion; everything for her is in the mind. It takes a very special sort of man to attract her, and the earnest, worthy Capricorn is not really her type. It is unlikely she would be his type either; when he tries his sarcasm out on her he gets as good as he gives: Aquarians have a rapier wit, and make others feel very small on occasion. Not a likely couple.

Capricorn Man—Pisces Woman.

Her gentle charm and receptive loving nature are a strong lure to him. He finds it easier to relax with her and to show the more gentle and loving side of his nature, so different from the cold and indifferent front he puts on usually. He quickly warms to her and is able to relax with her, because she is so highly feminine and kind and so talented at getting along with people that she can draw him out and enable him to shine, without him even realizing it is being done.

All he knows is that he feels happier, more confident and more loving than he ever thought he could. The Piscean woman really likes him—and she lets it show. She is not deceived by his rather wintry manner; she is such a feeling person herself that she senses the feelings that are buttoned up in a Capricorn man, and very gently liberates them. He becomes much nicer once he meets her.

She is looking for something too; she is looking for someone to take care of her, someone reliable, capable, devoted and faithful—and someone who is an achiever, and can give her the financial security she needs if she is to fully relax and give her love. He will fulfill all these needs, and gladly.

The Capricorn man likes to protect and guide those he loves, and will achieve and work very hard to provide all that his woman needs: he is rather inclined to hold on to the purse strings, but she can get whatever she wants from him. He loves her and likes to please her, because she appreciates it—and him.

XI. Aquarius 🏺

The Aquarius Character

Aquarius men and women are loners. They enjoy the company of bright, interesting people, but even then they are in some way detached and alone within the group.

The Aquarian has an overwhelming interest in human nature. They find people fascinating, and like to study their character and analyze their motives. Aquarians make very good psychologists. They are humanitarian and want to help people; they will spend a great deal of their time and energy helping to sort out the problems that are affecting others, without any thought of reward. This is partly from a genuine desire to help, because Aquarians do not like to see other people in trouble and distress, but also partly from a pure interest in seeing how the situation will develop: Aquarians make good writers!

Aquarians need to conserve their energy; they are not the strongest of people physically, and over-tiredness can make them ill. Too many people and too much activity is very tiring to them; they rarely need medicines, but recuperate best with peace and quiet and being alone or with one or two very restful and undemanding people. They always respond very well to the beauty of nature; an ideal way for an Aquarian to recharge is in a remote cottage in lovely surroundings, for a day or two—without a telephone.

The Aquarian man and woman make good students: they are fond of study and will work hard to learn whatever they wish to know. In particular, they are fond of artistic and academic subjects: the more intricate, the better.

The Aquarian man and woman have sudden, violent enthusiasms—they work hard and long once they have decided they want to do something; and they put a lot of effort and self-sacrifice into it—only to drop it and waste all their efforts without a backward glance, if they become bored. Boredom is the worst enemy of the Aquarian: hard work, obstacles, even poverty, they can cope with, but they can't take boredom.

The Aquarian meets the problems of life in a rather typical way: they avert their eyes and wish the problems were not there; and after a time, the problems frequently disappear. This inaction on the part of the Aquarian is absolutely infuriating to other, more energetic signs; and the thing that is even more annoying is that this ploy very often works, in spite of dire warnings that it will not. Aquarians procrastinate; they put off until tomorrow what they do not wish to do today, and they do this in all areas of their life.

Aquarians are honest and ethical people. Having said this, it must be said that the ethics they are likely to observe are their own: they do not think things are right or wrong because of law or because others think so, and will just go their own way about this as in so many things. If they think something is wrong, they will not do it, even if nobody at all is looking. If they think it is right, and the law considers it wrong, they are quite capable of doing it with a policeman looking on. This can lead them into quite a bit of explaining, from time to time.

Aquarians are extremely eccentric individuals; they like unusual and interesting people and things, and their dress sense can be bizarre, as can some of the dishes they cook. However, they have a charm all their own and are not looked down on or regarded with suspicion, but are well liked, and get invited out a great deal. They are often a source of amusement to their listeners, but do not know why—or so they say: actually, they are very fond of playing to the crowd (all Aquarians are actors) and have a strong sense of humor. They are quite capable of acting up to get a laugh, while pretending to be innocent.

Aquarians are affectionate—but only if allowed to love at arm's length. They are undemonstrative and quite cold emotionally, and they loathe intense and very close relationships where they feel they are tightly bound, whether it is with family, lovers or friends. What to another person is a normal, loving relationship feels claustrophobic to an Aquarian, and they will withdraw.

This hurts those that love them unless they understand the true nature of the Aquarian, the more so because an Aquarian man or woman never explains and never apologizes: they just switch off the interest and disappear. Aquarians are sensitive and loving in a fresh, cool way; but they want people when they want them, and are quite ruthless in discarding them if necessary. The Aquarian wants privacy, and means to have it. Friends are welcome when invited—but they must learn not to intrude. Aquarians can be quite forbidding when provoked.

They can be mean. Aquarians do not find it natural to give —they have so many things they want for themselves—but they will contribute without protest for a decent present for a wedding or birthday or other formal occasion. They are not fond of giving surprise presents at other times, and do not always pay their way. Aquarians are takers more often than they are givers. This applies to their time as well as money and material things. As always, in all areas of life, they WILL give, and give freely—but only when, and to whom, they want. The Aquarian is complex, but more good than bad, and definitely unique.

How Aquarius Gets Along with Others

Aquarius with Aries

Money/Job. There is a basic difference in ideas and goals here. The Aries partner is interested in making money, and working to build up a secure future. They are so energetic and hardworking they can achieve anything they set their hand to. The Aquarian is not prepared to sacrifice their time, or their freedom, in order to toil for money. They like the prestige and the convenience of wealth. If it comes to them they are happy, but they only want to work at something they are interested in: this is more likely to be a profession than a job. Aries will find it difficult if not impossible to organize an Aquarian; Aquarians don't argue, they just walk away.

Home/Friends. They will live together fairly harmoniously, but this will be due mainly to the efforts of the Aquarian, who hates arguments and refuses to have them. Aries will seethe because they like everything out in the open, discussed, and sorted out. But the Aquarian will give Aries their own way most of the time, just to avoid trouble. Aquarians like all sorts of people as friends, a lot of them unconventional or eccentric; Aries is conventional and won't care for them. Children will learn about life from Aquarius; about love from Aries.

Aquarius with Taurus

Money/Job. Taurus and Aquarius are both quite careful with money—Taurus is the big spender of the two, but Taureans are never careless with money, so the Aquarian will have no cause for alarm. Taureans are very hard workers, steady and consistent; Aquarians work flat out in a burst of enthusiasm —and stop just as suddenly when the enthusiasm burns out. The Taurean will quickly realize that they have to set the pace and make sure of a certain amount of steady work from the Aquarian, otherwise all will be chaos; and Taureans cannot stand that. They are not an ideal team, and will irritate each other at times, but can jog along all right.

Home/Friends. Taureans like a beautiful home, partly because they love comfort, and partly because it is the outer evidence of their ability to be good providers—which they certainly are. Taureans love possessions, and even when they have outgrown their use would rather lend them than sell them or give them away. The Aquarian has perfect taste, and will help the Taurean spend all that money! They will make a beautiful home: Aquarius is artistic when given a free hand, and Taurus will not stint on paying for it. The Aquarian circle of friends may not be to the taste of conventional Taurus, but they quite enjoy the frequent comings and goings in the home. If there are children, Aquarius will teach them; Taurus will provide for them, and discipline them.

Aquarius with Gemini

Money/Job. Geminis and Aquarians get along. They understand each other without any difficulty and chatter to each other non-stop, amuse each other, and interest each other. They are both exceptionally fast thinkers, and can do their work in half the time anyone else can. When the two get together, the effect is doubled. They will have some wonderful ideas, and work hard in short bursts towards success. The difficulty is that although Aquarians like money, and Geminis need security, neither of them is interested in doing the day-to-day routine work, or seeing to the books: they should let a third person do that, and carry on with what they're best at.

Home/Friends. This should be a successful team effort. Both Gemini and Aquarius have a light touch in life, and both dislike boredom above all. They will like each other—and have a lot of laughs up their sleeves at other prople. Aquarius likes unusual friends and bizarre clothes and food: Gemini loves anything new and will join in and enjoy it all. Gemini travels a great deal, and both like to be as free as the air, so they will extend the same courtesy to each other. They make a very compatible pair of friends; it is more difficult to see them as husband and wife; neither has the commitment. Both like children—but not necessarily their own.

Aquarius with Cancer

Money/Job. Cancerians are not at their best with Aquarians; they are too different. The Cancerian likes to be close to people: the Aquarian does not. The Cancerian likes to amass money, which they need to do because they are high spenders —the Aquarian is not very interested in money or material things, but in the work itself, provided it is of interest. If it has anything to do with people, it will be. A Cancerian will work hard in pursuit of financial success; an Aquarian will not, and will turn and walk away when the Cancerian tries to find out why. The vagueness of the Aquarian maddens the Cancerian: the materialism of the Cancerian is alien to Aquarius. Not a likely team.

Home/Friends. The Cancerian is a real home lover. They spend a great deal of time and energy on their homes—and a great deal of money. The Aquarian has good taste, and will enjoy shopping for things to make the home nice. After that, it is different. The Aquarian is not domesticated, nor even especially interested in the home, once it is finished: the Cancerian carries on improving and polishing, and is annoyed at the lack of reaction from Aquarius. Aquarius looks to the future, to the next thing—Cancer clings to the past, to old friendships, old loves. The more the Cancerian clings to the Aquarian, the more the Aquarian pulls away. If there are children, the Cancerian gives warmth and love—and claustrophobia; Aquarius gives learning and light affection, and will enter into their games.

Aquarius with Leo

Money/Job. Aquarius will be like a red rag to a bull where Leo is concerned. Leo runs a tight ship, works hard, and expects everyone else to do likewise. Leo people abide by the rules: they work hard and play hard, and they are very organized. The Aquarians drift through life and in spite of all Leo's efforts at organizing them (and there will be many) somehow manage to continue being disorganized and not working when they don't want to or aren't interested. If Leo can use the talents of the Aquarian with people, and not try to motivate an Aquarian with acquiring material possessions, it may be possible. Leo is clever and shrewd, and can see how best to use talents: Aquarius is clever, and can be useful.

Home/Friends. This is likely to be difficult. It will not be a battleground, because although Leo likes a fight, Aquarius does not, and will simply turn away from trouble or temper. Leo tries to organize in the home the same as at work, and the Aquarian is very difficult to organize. Aquarians do not like tackling things; they like to leave them alone and see if they will just resolve themselves. Leos like everything under control. A Leo home is perfectly ordered. Aquarians are not very domesticated and don't wish to be; they are untidy. With children, Aquarians educate them, and otherwise leave them alone; Leo teaches respect and love.

Aquarius with Virgo

Money/Job. Virgo people work hard to advance in the world; they love money and know the value of it. They are savers, not spenders. They get on surprisingly well with the vague Aquarian, because an Aquarian is careful with money, too, and will work hard if they are interested in the job, though not as consistently as the Virgo person. Virgo is unselfish in work as in other ways, and will do the work for the Aquarian on the odd times they slip away; this builds up quite a nice relationship between them, and Aquarians won't let them down. They will work rather well together.

Home/Friends. Home life is likely to be happy and harmonious, though rather cool. The Virgo person does not want close relationships, and this suits the Aquarian fine. Aquarians are not domesticated and do not wish to be, but Virgo is a worker at home as much as at work, and they will uncomplainingly work in the background to keep the house as sparkling as they like it. Aquarians tend to be takers rather than givers, so they will take the service the Virgo person gives as no more than their due. Neither are givers financially; neither expect it of the other. They are undemanding of each other, and can relax without being questioned as to what they are thinking—they are not being asked to open up. If there are children, they will have a remote relationship with them, though Virgo will provide and Aquarius instruct.

Aquarius with Libra

Money/Job. These two are very well suited: they will live and let live. Both are clever, and both work best without pressure: if too much pressure is put on a Libran, they just do less and less, disapproval paralyzing them. Aquarians are the same, except that the reasons are different. Aquarians are perverse, and the more they are told what to do, and how fast to do it, the more they drag their feet and dawdle and do the opposite. This is their way of asserting themselves and refusing to be driven. They appear weak: they are actually very strong. They are clever, particularly when working in the professions or with people, and they are artistic, as are Librans. They will put their heads together and have a happy working partnership.

Home/Friends. This will be a success. They both have similar requirements. Neither likes a lot of close or intense relationships: in fact, not any, really. They like superficial relationships with bright, amusing people, and Libra loves celebrities. Aquarius pretends to be unimpressed—but likes them too, and will cultivate them. They will have a pleasant home and a pleasant life with no quarrels: both absolutely loathe rows and unpleasantness. Children will have a harmonious home with plenty of interesting people in and out.

Aquarius with Scorpio

Money/Job. Aquarius will enrage Scorpio by being unpunctual, unaccountable, and interested in the job at hand only if it is something they really enjoy doing. The Scorpio person takes work very seriously, and will irritate the Aquarian by demanding that they take it seriously too. Aquarians lack ambition in the usual sense: they do like money and status but are not prepared to work at something they don't enjoy to get it. They will work for virtually nothing if they think what they are doing is worthwhile. Scorpio is ambitious, with the question of money always uppermost in their mind. They just can't see each other's point of view and it would be virtually impossible for Aquarius and Scorpio to co-operate at work.

Home/Friends. The home is very important to a Scorpio person. It is their inner sanctum, open only to those they are very close to. Aquarians, flitting in and out with their rather eccentric or artistic friends, seem to Scorpio to invade their place, and they do resent it. Scorpio puts most of the work and money into the home, and regards it as mostly his. There is no real common ground between them: Scorpio is lavish, Aquarius is thrifty. They differ in every way, especially emotionally. If there are children, Scorpio will be a proud and possessive parent, and Aquarius will be a friend.

Aquarius with Sagittarius

Money/Job. Aquarians get on well with Sagittarians. Both are enthusiastic and will work well when they are interested in what they are doing. The Sagittarian is more motivated by money than the Aquarian; the Aquarian wants to feel that what they are doing is interesting and worthwhile, and money is a secondary consideration. Neither will pressure the other; the Sagittarian values the contribution that the Aquarian makes, and respects the cleverness and inventiveness they bring to the job. The Aquarian likes the speed and capability of the Sagittarian. Sagittarius is a spender, Aquarius a saver, but neither of them is interested in routine, and will have to use self-discipline to see it is carried out.

Home/Friends. This is a good combination. Neither of them is very domesticated. They see the home as a place to be comfortable in, and to entertain their friends. The Sagittarian likes to be free, and spends a lot of time going out; the Aquarian does not mind this at all, as they like and need privacy and will enjoy having the home to themselves when they want it. They form a good strong friendship, and Sagittarius is amused and entertained by the strange and artistic friends that Aquarius brings home. If there are children, they will live in a free atmosphere, and be allowed to develop their own characters without interference.

Aquarius with Capricorn

Money/Job. Aquarians work when they want to: when they are interested, and feel that what they are doing is worthwhile. Capricorns work because they are ambitious and money-motivated, and they always do their best at the job in hand. They are disciplined in their attitude to work, and are bewildered by the scatterbrained attitude of the Aquarian, who cannot be motivated by money, or other people, to work when they do not wish to. Capricorns worry about everything, and they will certainly worry about the lack of application to work in the clever Aquarian. They will continually lecture them, but this will not affect the Aquarian, who just won't listen. They are not suited to work together.

Home/Friends. An uneasy alliance. The Aquarian likes the beautiful and unusual; the Capricorn is conventional in the extreme, and likes the home to be spartan and utilitarian. Capricorns do not approve of the eccentric people Aquarians like so much, and they do not like the fact that the Aquarian is undomesticated. Capricorns feel a home is to be worked at; Aquarians think it is to live in: both are right, and both are wrong. They will never agree. If there are children, Capricorn will teach them discipline, and Aquarius will teach them to think.

Aquarius with Aquarius

Money/Job. When is a partnership not a partnership? When they are both Aquarians. Aquarians are always solo: they may occupy the same space but they will not work together. They will each work independently and singly. They will, however, have sympathy with the aims of the other. Neither is money-motivated, nor ambitious; they like to feel that what they are doing is interesting and worthwhile, and when they do, they will work hard. Otherwise, they do the bare minimum necessary to make a living. Together, they can achieve much that is good and helps people.

Home/Friends. Home life will run smoothly. Neither of these two Aquarians likes scenes or confrontations; Aquarians find emotions tiring, and avoid them wherever possible. They will settle happily together, doing the minimum domestic work they can to keep the home in order, because domesticity as such bores them. Together, they can happily entertain their somewhat eccentric circle of friends, and indulge their artistic natures in making beautiful surroundings. Both need and want quite a lot of privacy, and each will allow the other to have it, by never questioning where they are going or what they are doing, and by peacefully entertaining themselves while the other Aquarian does the same. Children may not get enough attention.

Aquarius with Pisces

Money/Job. Pisceans start things, and are sensitive, and artistic. Aquarians are academically clever, humanitarian in their attitudes, and artistic too. There is more sympathy between these two than may be visible at first. The Aquarian does not like to work a routine day and keep to time, but neither does the Piscean. If they are working together in an artistic enterprise, they could do well together, encouraging each other and each letting the other go their own way. Pisces is much more money conscious than the Aquarian, and this is just as well; Pisces will look after the books, and the Aquarian will not waste money.

Home/Friends. Pisceans love a beautiful home, and spend a lot of time and money on making one. Both will enjoy furnishing it and making it a welcoming place to entertain. Aquarius has lots of friends, and although Pisceans are shy, they do enjoy company and like looking after people. Aquarians are not very domestic, but Pisceans are, and to tell the truth they prefer to run the home themselves: they are quite fussy and don't really like the way anyone else does things. This suits the Aquarian, so both are happy. The one problem is that Aquarians like to be free, and to be alone in privacy quite a lot of the time; Pisces may irritate them with their constant desire for company, while they hurt Pisces by their withdrawal. Children are loved by Pisces, educated by Aquarius.

Love Mates

Aquarius Woman—Aries Man. She has a little quirk in her personality in relation to love. She wants most what she cannot have. If she is attracted to an Aries man, he is likely to be disinterested in the beginning. She will not especially appeal to him on a physical or emotional level; she is too cool for that; and mentally, there is not a great deal in common. He is intelligent, but her mind is really subtle.

He is dynamic and attractive; and this, coupled with the fact that he is not interested in her, will often be enough to make an Aquarian woman think she is in love. She may well not be at all; she has such difficulty in sorting out her emotions that she can and does often mistake love for friendship, and friendship for love.

In the beginning, the unavailable Aries man will attract her very powerfully, and she will do all in her power to capture him. She has little pride, and when she is in love will give up the little she does have. She asks so little, and is so adoring, that frequently he begins to become interested; soon he will be headlong in love. He loves without counting the cost; and his love is long-lasting and devoted.

It is at this point that the Aquarian woman, now that she has him for her own, begins to discover that there are some things about him she doesn't like. They are not compatible physically; she is much less ardent than he is, and as she does not have strong emotional feelings herself, she soon becomes bored by those who do.

If he really loves her, he can begin to woo her. Just when he thought the battle was over, it is beginning. But she should be cautious: if she is too elusive, for too long, or not sufficiently loving, he will look elsewhere. This almost always causes her to adore him all over again!

Aquarius Woman—Taurus Man.

Here is where the Aquarian woman can meet her match. She looks up to a man if she is interested in him; she thinks he is perfect, and the more off-hand he is with her, the more she longs for him. In the case of a Taurus man, he has quite a pronounced sense of his own importance, and her passive acceptancy just goes to prove to him that he is very much in demand, and a good catch. He will probably patronize her, and she will look up to him all the more.

Once they have fallen in love, there is a change. All men have feet of clay, and he is no exception. She is disappointed: he is not what he seemed. The true situation is that he is exactly what he seemed, but an Aquarian woman suspends her very good powers of judgment when she is interested in a man. Once he is hers, she sees him clearly, and will often fall out of love with him quite as hard as she fell in. A Taurean man has deep emotional feelings, and once he is committed it is much harder for him to switch off. He will not let her get away so easily; and he can capture the heart of any woman when he turns on the charm. It hurts his pride to be rejected, so he holds on to her. If she can be kept with him a little longer, she may begin to fall in love properly, with the real man this time instead of an illusion.

She lives in dreams. She is really much more interested in friendship than love, but tends to confuse the two. A Taurean man is a loyal friend and a good lover; he can teach her true emotion. Love matters to him; he is quite sentimental, and he will find her coolness and the way she dismisses love really hurtful. If she remains too detached, she will lose him.

Aquarius Woman—Gemini Man.

He will be enchanted by her. She is everything he likes in a woman; refined, witty, clever—and a little reserved. She has a cool charm all her own, and he will find her very attractive. Gemini men like understatement; they can't stand obviously sexy women, and they like attraction to be subtle, even a little mysterious.

The Gemini man is an ace game-player; and he will notice her slight withdrawal when he shows interest in her. It is part and parcel of the Aquarian woman that she wants the man she cannot have; the cooler he is to her, and the more unattainable he is, the more she wants him. She will sacrifice her pride, and her peace of mind, to continue to run after him. He is clever, and after sparkling to make her interested in him, will mysteriously withdraw—and hide his interest.

The Aquarian nature being what it is, she will obligingly run after him, and slowly, reluctantly, he will let her persuade him how happy they can be together. This is usually the danger point in her romance: once she has the man she wanted, she doesn't want him any more. The Gemini man is an exception. He has drawn her to him all the while he has held her at bay, and he never quite makes her feel secure with him. The fear of losing him keeps her on her toes and keeps her in love; his amusing and light character holds her attention.

Physically they are compatible: both are cool lovers, both are detached. Mentally they will be very close, and will amuse and entertain each other so much that they do not realize what a permanent couple they have become.

Aquarius Woman—Cancer Man. She should not be romantically involved with him. He is not her type, and she is certainly not his. He is loving and gentle, extremely sensitive, and emotional. She is detached, aloof, unsentimental, and cool.

However, the Cancerian man understands women better than most men, and can be most attractive to them. The Aquarian woman, if she is attracted, will blind herself to all the reasons they are not compatible, and pursue him with such skill he will not even realize it until he finds himself hopelessly involved.

As she really wants only the men she cannot have, it is at this point that she may well decide the romance is off. She does not like a settled love affair, or marriage; she is basically a loner and is happiest on her own, with friends available when she needs them, and nobody when she doesn't.

The Cancerian man with his emotionalism and his clinging ways irks her, and makes her feel tied. She does not know how to deal with his moods, and is usually unsympathetic to them. She doesn't suffer from moods herself, and doesn't like those who do.

Aquarian women are much more comfortable with friendship than love, but they frequently confuse the two emotions, and end up as lovers with those they should have reserved for friends. This is what happens with this couple.

It would be best of all if they would change their love affair into a friendship; however, Cancerians are clingers, and they don't give up easily. In this case, it is in vain, and he is likely to be badly hurt at her hands.

Aquarius Woman—Leo Man. He likes to be adored; she likes to put those she loves on a pedestal, and worship at their feet; therefore, they would seem to be well suited. In the beginning, all goes well, but owing to a strange quirk in her emotional nature it falls apart.

Aquarian women are blinded by love; they lose their very considerable reasoning powers, and for a time believe the man to be right about everything, including what they themselves should do or should not do. However, idols do have feet of clay, and when the relationship slides into a day-to-day one, problems will soon become all-too-visible to her, and she will become disillusioned. It is her pattern in all her love affairs. Boredom sets in, and the Aquarian woman, with her in-built aversion to close partnerships or marriages, breathes a little sigh of relief and moves on, belonging to herself again.

As this usually happens just when the Leo man has reached the peak of his feelings for her, he will be amazed and unbelieving of the change in her. Leos do not look for faults in themselves, so he will assume that either she has met someone else, or there is something wrong with her, emotionally. The truth is that the Aquarian woman is perverse; she wants what she cannot have and who she cannot have. When they become attainable, their magic is gone.

Aquarian women do not have a great need for love, but are self-contained and cool. They like their own company and they like privacy; they also like friendships with compatible people and falling in love with dream lovers. If the Leo man wants to turn this dream into reality, he must learn to always keep a little distance, always to hold something back and keep a little mystery: this can work.

Aquarius Woman—Virgo Man. She has quite a bit in common with him, and they will get along well.

She's cool, not liking heavy emotional scenes, either good or bad. She likes peace and quiet, privacy and congenial companions. So does he. Neither of them is competitive in the slightest; they are virtually totally lacking in wordly ambitions, though Virgo knows the value of money and will work hard to gain enough to save.

She falls in love with the unattainable lover; the more unsuitable and unavailable he is, the better. Secretly, she would rather worship and dream about love than experience it. Once her love affair becomes reality and is downgraded to a day-to-day business, it loses its appeal and ends. With a Virgo man, this is unlikely to happen. She is much more likely to like him and have a normal friendship with him than worship at his feet; and from this can grow a real and enjoyable relationship.

He is chilly emotionally, but the Aquarian woman is much the same and will be pleased to be allowed to grow in a cool climate. He is faithful and devoted, selfless and considerate: he is not too demanding for her. Their partnership will turn slowly from a friendship into something more permanent. They can live together without friction, because both will allow the other the essential areas of privacy in their lives, without even needing to discuss it.

It may seem a remote relationship to some, but it will give them a nice stability and the feeling of one to share with, while still remaining self-contained, that they like. Aquarian women would rather write about romance than live it.

Aquarius Woman—Libra Man. They are both cool customers. Both dislike scenes and quarrels, and so their relationship is likely to run smoothly.

The Libra man is a charmer and the Aquarian woman will be instinctively drawn to him. He is quick-witted, and they will be likely to share a light and quick sense of humor and enjoy their conversations. If they develop a friendship that turns to love, it should go well.

If, on the other hand, she falls immediately in love with the Libran man, who is often very good looking and polished, she will turn him into a dream lover that she worships as faultless; and this inevitably turns to disillusion when she discovers that he is not. She makes a habit of doing this, and therefore most of her relationships are short-lived. She is easy to capture, but difficult to hold.

He is more likely to hold her successfully, however, than most other men. She is easily bored, but he will hold her interest, and she will interest him because she has a striking personality, clever and original, and because she is not too intense.

If they strike up a friendship, it can turn to love naturally and gradually, and they can build a permanent relationship. He will like her rather eccentric friends and the light sociable atmosphere around her.

Aquarian women are loners, however. They do not take readily to marriage or to partnerships, and Libran men do. Libra is the sign of marriage. Libra likes a lot of togetherness; Aquarius does not. He must let her feel free—and she must not make him feel unwanted.

Aquarius Woman—Scorpio Man. She finds him too intense. He is moody and she does not understand moods. Her own temperament is level and she is not given to extremes of emotion.

She is too elusive to really suit him; he likes a few strong, intense relationships, while she likes a number of light friendships. The Scorpio man is passionate, magnetic and single minded; he is looking for commitment. The Aquarian woman likes to be free. She is basically a loner, who only wants company when she feels she needs it and then on her terms. It is unlikely she would be willing to invest the amount of time and single-mindedness that the Scorpio man would want.

However, she has one quirk of character that could see her falling madly in love with him: she prefers dreams of love to the real thing and will often fix on the most unsuitable and difficult-to-attain man and worship him. It is only later, when a love affair is on a day-to-day footing, that she gradually realizes her idol has feet of clay; then disillusionment sets in and she will move on.

This is absolutely baffling to him. When this happens, he thinks she has been pretending to love him all along and can be very hurt. The truth is much simpler: she loves what she THINKS a man is—and often, not the real man at all.

Any romance between these two very different people would be likely to be short-lived; she is too elusive and uncommitted for him, and he is too demanding for her.

Aquarius Woman—Sagittarius Man.

This pair are well suited. They have a light touch in romance and similarly sardonic sense of humor. They both dislike heavy and intense relationships and feeling tied; they are comfortable with each other in a basically free relationship.

The Aquarian woman is a cool customer: so is the Sagittarian man. Both are good conversationalists and they are very much on the same wavelength. Neither will make the other feel constricted; in this relationship they can be together, but still feel free. This is perfection for them both.

She looks up to the man she has fallen in love with and thinks he is right about anything and everything, for as long as her love lasts. This is likely to be until things get onto a more mundane footing. She is the first to fall out of love—she gets bored with the routine and soon sees her idol's feet of clay. In the case of a Sagittarian man, however, this will not be so likely to happen. He does not take himself seriously and his faults, which are flirtation, unreliability and telling lies, will be apparent to even a love-struck Aquarian woman from the very beginning. She is very tolerant and accepting, and as long as she sees the disadvantages and falls in love with the real man, instead of, as so often in her case, a dream figure, all will be well.

He is more passionate than she is, and he notices the lack of passion in her. However, he is also very accepting of people, and as she is affectionate and kind, he will take her as she is. She will always be cool and less emotional than he is, but they can build a good relationship onto a solid base of friendship, liking and mutual respect for the freedom and privacy of the other.

Aquarius Woman—Capricorn Man.

This is likely to be a lukewarm partnership, with not much real sympathy between the two. The Capricorn man is cold and calculating, the Aquarian woman is cool and disinterested. He has a lot of intensity, but it is hidden behind a façade. He pretends to be hostile and rejecting, because he so much fears a rebuff himself: he will make sure he rejects others before they have a chance to reject him.

In a love affair, he needs a very special type of reassurance from a woman before he has the courage to drop his defenses and show how much he needs love—and how much he longs to give love to someone else. She will not give him the reassurance he needs: she is not interested enough. She does not like to have to pay very much attention to the needs and moods of others; she is self-contained and self-controlled and likes others to be the same.

The Aquarian woman is light and cool; she likes beautiful surroundings, peace and quiet—and her own company, quite a lot of the time. She is a dreamer: for her, everything is in the mind. She would rather worship a dream lover than build a relationship with a real man. She falls easily in love—and just as easily out again.

The Aquarian woman is not likely to fall in love with a Capricorn man: if she does, it will be as a result of one of her attacks of love which happen irrespective of whether or not a man is in any way suitable for her, or even available to her. Once she has him, and sees the real man, she will drop him just as quickly: to him, this would be a disaster. They are best apart.

Aquarius Woman—Aquarius Man.

This relationship is so tenuous, it is difficult to see anything linking these two remote, self-absorbed people at all.

Yet Aquarians are attracted to each other, both as friends and as lovers: you will find that any Aquarian has more friends who are also Aquarians than of any other sign.

All Aquarians are very individualistic and very difficult to understand; therefore, as these two are both the same, they stand to gain a flying start. They know what makes each other tick. They also know exactly how most to annoy the other partner when they wish to, and will use this to pay each other back; Aquarians do not quarrel as a general rule. They hate rows and upheavals.

He is an original thinker: for him everything is on a mental level and he is much more likely to notice what she is talking about than her looks (though Aquarian women have a particular type of beauty that is unusual—their great beauty is their eyes, which are often exceptionally lovely). She has a tranquility about her, and a barbed wit, which make an irresistable combination to an Aquarian man.

She will like him. He will not hem her in or bother her when she wants to be alone: he will disappear frequently too and she will understand perfectly. There is little passion between these two. At best, they have a friendship which ripens into a loving companionship. This suits them very well. At worst, they are strangers who meet occasionally in the hall—and don't stop to talk. This can lead to separate lives—and a stronger link with a closer lover.

Aquarius Woman—Pisces Man.
He is loving, sensitive and needs and gets a great deal of attention from those who love him. He is always looking for security, whether financial or emotional, and it is this constant search for reassurance which gets on her nerves. She sees it as self-indulgence: she likes people as detached and aloof as she is herself. Clinging personalities scare her away: besides, no Aquarian woman values anything she has come by easily. She likes to worship a man and dream about him—even though, when she finds he has feet of clay, she loses interest.

She likes a man who is unattainable: the more unavailable he is, the greater her wish to make him love her. While she is in love, she is blind; she thinks that everything he does and says is right, and can be badly treated as a result of this. If she falls in love in this way with a Piscean man, he will not treat her badly. He is loving and good to a woman who cares for him: it is only later, when her love has faded to nothing in day to day contact, that this could change.

He is very emotional; while love is shown to him he loves

greatly in return and will do anything to please a woman. If she ceases to show him that love, he will not quietly put up with it, but will find someone else very quickly and leave her flat.

If this happens to an Aquarian woman, it can have a very strange effect: he becomes unattainable again and she can find her love genuinely rekindled and go chasing after him, trying to get him back. But this combination will never really work. She is too cool for him; he is too emotional and too demanding for her.

Aquarius Man—Aries Woman.

This looks like an unlikely combination. She is direct, aggressive, and loving: she wears her heart on her sleeve. He seems cold and unfeeling to her. An Aries woman is not likely to attract an Aquarian man; he likes mystery in a woman, and a very light touch in a relationship. She is loyal, loving and devoted; she is also passionate, both in love and in anger. When things are not right, to her the best way to resolve the situation is to have it right out in the open, and if it leads to a quarrel, even a serious one, that is all right with her. Quarrels clear the air and then there can be a loving reconciliation.

However, it is not all right with him. He is unemotional. He does not like a lot of feeling or passion, whether in love or otherwise. What he likes is reason, and civilized solutions. The heat in an Aries woman drives him even more into himself, and she will find him inaccessible. The hotter she blows, the cooler he grows.

She will do anything for a man she loves, and ask very little in return. She is a most devoted lover. But she does need to feel absolutely sure that he really does love her: a lack of love makes her look for someone else—and she could stray away.

The Aquarian man, self contained, introverted, with his love of privacy, and his often quite eccentric circle of friends, is not very suitable for her. He will not give her the love she needs and deserves, and she will often think, not without reason, that he is laughing at her. This would be the last straw to her: her sense of humor is never strong, and love is a serious business to her. Not a long-term love.

Aquarius Man—Taurus Woman.

He is attracted to her because she is different from him, but in a way he likes. She is sensuous, feminine, and refined. She takes great care of her appearance, and has a very nice style of dress. She is not loud in any way, and yet she is positive and warm. The Aquarian man approves of her; he thinks she is very stable, and she is.

She is not given to extremes of mood; this makes her a restful companion, although she is not dull. Aquarian men tend to irritate women; they are so quick on the uptake and such original thinkers that in any gathering they tend to shine, and women become neglected. In this case, she is not overlooked. Even though she cannot match his quick wit and humor, she is quite capable of socializing well with many different types of people—and she is not easily overshadowed. She has confidence in her very different personality.

She is sensuous and loving, and he can be a little too cool for her. He is affectionate, but he lacks passion. However, a Taurean woman, more than any other, adapts herself to the type of man she is in love with; and she will get more of a response from him than would most other women.

Aquarian men are not very interested in marriage or long partnerships; the Taurean woman likes stability in love as in everything else. She is a marrier. If she decided to marry him she will make sure the path of life runs very smoothly. She is peaceful by nature so there would be no real quarrels, and their life together will have a restful quality he will gradually become used to and not wish to give up. This relationship may turn out to be less temporary than he thought.

Aquarius Man—Gemini Woman.

A very good combination. She is a flirt; she has had a lot of men-friends, but none of them have really lasted. She wants the impossible in a man—he must be loyal and loving of her, utterly devoted to her interests, always there when she wants him—but willing to disappear when she says the word, and leave her free to travel wherever, whenever, and with whomever she wishes. A Gemini woman can be breathtakingly selfish, but she doesn't see it that way, and such is her charm and wit and style that there is no shortage of willing victims coming forward to be "the one."

In the Aquarian man, she may have met the impossible: the perfect man for her. He has a very light touch in relationships, and he doesn't particularly want a woman on a day-to-day basis anyway. He has his own life and his own friends and interests, and a love affair or partnership takes up a very small proportion of his interest. He likes privacy, and quite a bit of time to himself, so she is a good match for him.

They have such good mental communication, and get along so well as friends, that they will amuse and entertain each other whenever they are together. Neither of them make heavy weather out of any difficulties they may experience; both are likely just to let things lie and smooth over the occasional disagreement, or agree to differ. He likes the speed of her mind. Neither of them is very interested in intense and passionate affairs; to tell the truth, they are quickly bored by them. Aquarius will let Gemini spread her wings and go where she likes: Gemini will let Aquarius walk alone, without questioning where: and such is their delight in each other that he will often accompany her on her travels. They suit each other down to the ground.

Aquarius Man—Cancer Woman.
The Cancerian woman is a good and loving woman, perfectly suited for marriage and motherhood—but not with an Aquarian man! Her clinging and possessive ways, and dependence on him, will drive him mad, and he will become so cold and abrupt in his manner at the curtailment of his freedom that he will hurt her, make her feel insecure, and make her cling more tightly than ever. It is a vicious circle.

He can be attracted by her feminity and air of helplessness: he likes to help people, and doesn't feel threatened by her. She is easy to fall in love with; she is attentive and kind, gentle and affectionate, and always defers to her man. She is not argumentative or aggressive; so, initially anyway, the Aquarian finds her very pleasant female company.

However, her grip tightens as time goes on, and to the Aquarian man, insistent on being free and retaining privacy, this can become suffocating. On her part, she cannot understand why he is becoming colder and colder, and less and less forthcoming about where he is going and with whom: he just won't tell her anything—and no matter how much she cries and pleads (and a Cancerian woman can turn on the tears like no other) he becomes more and more remote, until he breaks away altogether.

He does not like hurting people: this does not mean that he will weakly do what they want to avoid it. He will hurt someone if it is necessary to survive, but he will suffer guilt about it. He feels very guilty about her, as she means him to. He bears no malice and prefers to part friends; it won't be possible in this case.

Aquarius Man—Leo Woman. He can be attracted to
her; he cannot resist the pull of her vital and magnetic personality. She is a very sunny person, and he knows he needs some of her warmth. However, she has better sense than to be too interested in him.

A Leo woman is sensible, even about love. She knows exactly what sort of man she likes, and who will suit her, and she does not waste her time on those who would not be compatible with her. She does not like the coldness, and the superficiality, of the Aquarian man. She is passionate and loving herself, and she is looking for a man with a similar temperament. She likes achievers: as he has little or no ambition, he is not an achiever in the accepted sense of the word, though he is clever and can often be an academic. She is not too impressed with the more high flown types of "cleverness" and she does not like people who pose. The Aquarian man, it must be admitted, DOES pose. He knows he does it—but he doesn't like anyone else to realize it.

He is cool and uncommitted, and wishes to remain so. He is a loner; he likes time to be by himself when he wishes. He does not wish to account to anyone for his movements and he is not suited to the double harness of marriage. He likes freedom and friendship—in that order.

Leo women like strong men, and the Aquarian, with his detached and remote manner, gives the impression of weakness. Nothing could be farther from the truth; he is actually extremely strong—he always does what he wants, and goes his own way. She will grow to respect him, but this will not be enough to bind them.

Aquarius Man—Virgo Woman. A compatible pair.

Both have a cool attitude to love and marriage. She is a marrier, and he is not. He likes time to himself, freedom, and privacy; but as she will not interfere, but will peacefully allow him to come and go as he likes, he could well think of her as a permanent partner.

The Virgo woman likes the quick mind and cleverness of the Aquarian man. He is remote and detached, but so is she, and she is relieved not to have to cope with anyone very possessive or demanding. She will look after him very well and make him comfortable, which he enjoys, as he cannot be bothered to do it for himself. For him, everything is in the mind; he does not much care for domesticity, but likes everything to run smoothly. She will see that it does.

The one real difficulty could be the Virgo tendency to criticize and nag. She is hyper-critical; she thinks she knows the best way for anything to be done, and Aquarians do not like critical people. They are very good at dealing with them: they just switch off and stop listening. He does not get angry, and neither does she; but it could make her feel put out to think her advice is being ignored. He is perverse: he always does the opposite of what is wanted of him, unless he is gently maneuvered into thinking it is his own idea, and he can be very stubborn.

If this can be overcome, however, they have the opportunity of a pleasant and lasting relationship, in which each is grateful for the opportunity to develop independently of the other, sharing at the same time.

Aquarius Man—Libra Woman. Aquarian men tend to talk down to people; she will not allow him to do this. She stands her ground, but in such a pleasant and charming way that he does not feel threatened; he will find her an interesting and charming companion.

He is not very good at one-to-one partnerships; he quickly gets bored. She likes company and will socialize well with his friends, who are often eccentric and nearly always clever, as he is himself. He shines in such company, and she will appreciate his qualities of intelligence and wit.

Libra is the sign of marriage; she likes permanent relationships and is looking for a man to marry. The Aquarian, with his dislike of close relationships and his fear of losing his independence in marriage, is a difficult proposition for her. She will not be daunted by this: she is so very attractive and successful with the opposite sex that she is sure she can marry anyone she chooses.

Even with an Aquarian man, she could succeed. She is very fair and just in her relationships and not especially possessive and she will see no reason why he should not have privacy when he wants it and continue to socialize with his friends. She likes company too; she entertains very well and is happy to do so. She will not pressure him in any way and he could gradually come around to her way of thinking.

Neither of them likes very intense or passionate relationships; they are both quite light and superficial and like entertainment and amusement. They are likely to have a very happy, romantic friendship, perhaps leading to marriage.

Aquarius Man—Scorpio Woman. If a Scorpio woman falls in love with an Aquarian man, she will be unhappy. His lack of commitment and emotional coolness is absolutely foreign to her nature: she is deeply loving, loyal and passionate. She has no time for half measures.

She is intense and magnetic and she is capable of attracting any man she wants to, even an Aquarian: but she would be wise not to do so. He simply hasn't the depth of love and commitment to give to her in return and is bored by displays of emotion. She is jealous; he cannot stand any form of possessiveness, and the more tied down he feels the more determined his efforts to go his own way and continue mixing with his own circle. She will give up everything for him: he is not willing to give up anything for her.

The Aquarian man finds deep emotion somewhat embarrassing. He does not quite know what to do about it. He likes a light, romantic touch in affairs of the heart. He hates scenes and there will be plenty of them if he is involved with a Scorpio woman. Aquarian men are very stubborn: because they are not aggressive it should not be thought that they are weak. On the contrary, they are very strong. They go their own way in spite of everything and everyone. Anyone who has ever tried to budge an Aquarian knows that.

The more she tries to pull him to her ways, the more aloof he becomes; the more emotional scenes she makes, the more he withdraws. He will not fight or argue; he simply walks away. If she continues to do it (and with her nature, she cannot stop) he will walk away for good—she may not like it, but it is best for her.

Aquarius Man—Sagittarius Woman. She can fascinate him. She is bright and vital, quick-witted and amusing, and she clings to her freedom and independence even more than he does. He can find himself in the utterly novel position of trying to persuade her that sometimes it is nice to have a permanent partner: she doesn't really believe it, but may be tempted with him, as she can see she really will be as free as air.

She has warmth, much more than he has, and he knows he needs this from her. His own nature is very cool, and he is undemonstrative; however, he is affectionate and romantic at heart, and he does like her very light touch in love. She is not very intense; she has many and varied interests and friends and she is so fast-moving she keeps him on his toes and keeps away his deadliest enemy—boredom.

He may be rather a disappointment to her physically: Sagittarian woman put quite a bit of heat into a relationship, and they find the Aquarian rather unresponsive as a lover. Passion is not everything to a Sagittarian woman; she values friendship and compatibility and she is accepting of different types of people. She can see his good points and overlook his deficiencies.

There will be a wonderful atmosphere in their home: there will be a feeling that anything is possible. She is the supreme optimist and her happy nature influences everyone around her. She will keep him happy—except when she is angry. Sagittarian women really do lash out when they lose their tempers and Aquarian men hate trouble. Otherwise, they will get along very happily together.

Aquarius Man—Capricorn Woman.
This is a chilly relationship. He is light, cool and romantic; she is intense and needs and wants love, but she is very cold until she finds exactly the right man to unlock her emotions. He will not take the time or trouble to do this.

The Capricorn woman is afraid of rejection and failure: she takes refuge in often biting sarcasm and putting men down— she will regret it if she does this to an Aquarian man, who will respond with a wit far more devastating than hers. If she can show him that she is afraid and uncertain, he will be kind to her. Aquarians are kind to people who are in distress, or who are inadequate in any way; they don't like hostility and won't accept it.

She is very ambitious and is looking for a man who is an achiever and a hard worker. He may in fact work hard, in his own way, but as in everything else in his life he makes light of it, and may appear to do less than he does. He is often an academic, not very often interested in making money, and she is. She may at first be interested in him even though he appears to be cold and remote. She knows that she appears like this herself, and that it covers a personality quite different.

In his case however, it is the true personality she is seeing: an Aquarian never bothers to hide what they are. People may take them or leave them, as they wish. In her case, with her deep insecurities and need for committed, steady love, she would be well advised to leave it. She would never feel secure with an Aquarian man and he would be bored by her insecurity.

Aquarius Man—Aquarius Woman. Mirror image.
They will fascinate each other. Aquarians do not wish it to be
known, but they are narcissistic—they love in other people
something of themselves. A lot of their friends tend to be Aquarians. There is an unspoken sympathy and liking between them.
Introduce an Aquarian man to an Aquarian woman and watch
their eyes light up and the conversation take off, as if it was
being spoken in shorthand! They understand each other perfectly.

All Aquarians are very individualistic and original. They like
people with bright minds and quick wit and they find this with
each other. Of course, there are drawbacks.

For one thing, Aquarian women are so detached and solitary
that they become really nervous and irritable if they don't get
some privacy and quite a bit of time to themselves. The Aquarian man is not quite so bad as this, but he suffers from the
same thing. If they both need to be alone at the same time—
fine. If not, although they are each quite happy to let the other
live a free and independent life, when are they likely to see
each other? Aquarians don't often need other people—but
when they do, the other Aquarian is not likely to be around.

This can lead to the gradual break-up of their relationship.
It is so light and tenuous that it hardly exists at all, and if one
of them is going through a period of needing somebody, it is
quite likely they will turn to someone else: someone who is
prepared to give them more time and attention. Of course,
when the emergency is over, they won't want it any more: but
that is a different problem, to be solved another day.

Aquarius Man—Pisces Woman. She is fascinating:
enigmatic, delicate and emotional. He likes mystery and it is
her air of stillness, or something concealed, that will attract
him to her. He will use all his considerable skills and interest
in people to draw her out and uncover her secretive nature.
Because she is so multi-faceted, she will hold his interest.

Whether or not he will interest her is another matter. She is
very responsive; she usually likes those who like her, who show
affection or interest in her. In his case, she senses that his

interest is almost curiosity and the coolness of his emotions, which she senses, rather puts her off.

To tell the truth, he is too detached and cool for her to have any serious kind of relationship with. She likes peace and security. She wants someone to settle down with, someone she can look after and pamper who will cherish her in return. Aquarian men can be irritable and abrupt when confronted with what they see as too much sentimentality, and this hurts a Piscean woman very much. She will not get the emotional love and deep feeling that she is looking for with him.

He does not appreciate her. He is so busy analyzing her that he overlooks her loving nature. He is affectionate in love, but nothing like she is; what she regards as deep love he sees as restricting and claustrophobic and what he sees as love (freedom from question or possessiveness, companionship) she sees as little more than friendship: she is quite right.

XII. Pisces 〓

The Pisces Character

Pisces men and women are very intuitive. They seem to sense things in a totally different way than other people: in a strange way, they "know" things. They are often referred to as "walking encyclopedias" because they are rarely at a loss to explain anything and know something about practically everything.

One very strong feature of this sign is a love of dumb animals. Piscean people are sensitive to the needs and problems of others and the same sensitivity applies to animals: they make marvelous veterinarians and can also often be found working for voluntary organizations that help animals and animal sanctuaries.

The Piscean man and woman have very strong emotions: their lives are ruled by their feelings, both negative and positive. Their emotions are very much affected by those they come into contact with: Pisceans are not self-starters, but are mirror images of those they are with at the time.

Pisceans are very undecided and very changeable. They often act on impulse or whim and cannot be predicted in any way. They always do what they feel at the time, even if logically they know they will regret it later. Pisceans, more than any other sign, live for today and live for love.

Pisceans are negative in every way; they do not like arguments or fights, and will often allow other people to get the better of them rather than make a scene. This causes them to be badly treated and to be regarded by some as spineless. They will sometimes stand up and be counted, but it is much more likely to be in defense of a cause than for their personal advantage.

Piscean men and women are inclined to put on a better front than they can maintain for any length of time; inwardly they fret and worry about hard circumstances. They fear failure and have a great fear of poverty and of the consequences of their actions. Pisceans worry a great deal and it is this constant anxiety that causes them to be delicate in health; worry is bad for them. They are high-strung, emotional and nervous, and need to be understood and treated with great kindness.

Pisceans are kind: they are hospitable and their guests will love to come again because of the genuinely warm welcome they receive. They are especially kind to those who are helpless and dependent; in fact one of the few times they will stand up and speak out will be when someone unfortunate is being bullied, or cannot speak up for themselves. Pisceans understand and love children, and are usually loved by them in return. They demand very little; they love people for exactly what they are and do not ask them to change, or to improve. They are the same with children—they allow them to go their own way, and do not criticize them if mistakes are made. They will help without comment or thought of reward.

Piscean men and women are dreamers: they are very well suited to be actors or artists, because then they can express themselves in a world as they think it to be or wish it to be and not as it really is. Reality is often too hard for the Piscean and they turn away from it. Basically, they are good people and if they do anything wrong, it is usually because they lack stamina and will. It is rarely for gain and never for cruelty. Pisceans are incapable of deliberate cruelty. They are sensitive and gentle, loving and tender. They are forgiving by nature, because they are so tolerant; but they never forget.

An action which seemed to them cruel or unfair stays with them always; the wound heals but the scar is carried throughout life. A Piscean can look back to early childhood and still weep over the things that happened then. Because of this, they are unable to leave bad times behind them and start again with optimism. They carry all the bad times with them, throughout life, like a snail carries a shell. Everything that happens to them, stays with them.

Pisceans can be tricky and devious. They are very subtle

people, and because their emotional feelings are so overwhelming, they will sacrifice anything for love. They often get themselves into serious trouble because they cannot say no to someone they care for, even when asked to do something they know is wrong. This is the basic weakness of the Piscean character; and it does not take long for other people to find out about it and trade on it. The Piscean man or woman wants love above all else and if they think they will get it by doing something they have been asked, they will go ahead, even while dreading the consequences.

The Piscean man or woman is therefore largely at the mercy of who happens to come into his or her life: if it is someone of good character, who treats them well, there will be no problem. If it is a darker character, they will be only too easy to lead astray and will take appalling risks.

It is therefore necessary for all those who are close to, or love, a Piscean to protect them from the harsher aspects of life, to give them a chance to dream and keep them away from bad company.

How Pisces Gets Along with Others

Pisces with Aries

Money/Job. Pisceans need the security that money brings. They love the material comforts of life and they love to have enough money to indulge themselves, and to give away. Pisceans give a great deal of money away—they give away their possessions too. Pisceans feel guilty if they have more than other people. Aries is open-handed too, but has loyalty to Pisces: the Aries person will put Pisces first—and stop them being taken for too many rides. They will work together quite well, because Pisceans are docile and will do what Aries tells them to do, while Aries has a good head for business and will make sure that the Piscean is rewarded well for effort.

Home/Friends. Pisceans create a beautiful home. They adore home-making, and Aries is generous and will make sure there is enough money available to do it in style. Aries don't want to make the home, but they do like nice surroundings and a place that they can ask their friends to, and Pisces will not let them down. They will be proud of their home. Although Pisceans are very hospitable and welcoming, the Arien will tend to have too many people in and out and too many aggressive characters: the Piscean needs time alone, and time to be silent. The Aries partner won't like this; silence makes them uncomfortable. If there are children, Aries will lead and protect them; Pisces will love and nurture them.

Pisces with Taurus

Money/Job. Pisces and Taurus have totally opposing ideas on money. Taurus is very money-conscious and will not understand the way Pisces gives it away, or wastes it. Taurus loves luxury, but cannot bear waste. In this type of combination, it is best for the Taurean to be in charge of the money, and of the general running of things: they are orderly and organized and will make a good job of it. Pisceans are wonderful at dealing with people; they are kind and sympathetic, and people will open up to them. They are best at dealing with the public, selling, and public relations. Let Taurus do the rest. Pisces will, as always, try to please; left alone to work in their own way they will be useful. Taurus will be surprised and pleased.

Home/Friends. This will be a lovely home. Pisces loves home-making; so does Taurus, and no expense will be spared to create a beautiful and relaxing place for them to live and entertain their friends. Their home will be luxurious and their friends welcome. They will tend to like the same types of people: rather conventional and good company. If there are children, the Piscean is a child too, and will understand them without effort, and get on with them. They will need the more adult Taurean to discipline them, and teach them right from wrong.

Pisces with Gemini

Money/Job. Both want financial security, so they will be united in their efforts to make money. However, there is not much in common apart from that. Gemini has a quicksilver mind and keeps up a fast pace at work; Pisces is slow and dreamy and not very successful in business. Both are extremely changeable; the two together would find it difficult to maintain the same direction for more than an hour at a time, and neither would tell the other of their changes of plan! It is chaos all the way. Pisces has a natural talent for dealing with people; Gemini has a lively mind and a flair for business—if they both stick to what they are best at and try to remember to tell each other what is on the agenda, they may succeed.

Home/Friends. Pisces is home-centered and home-loving; Gemini is just as happy in a hotel room, and likes to use the home as a base between travels. Obviously these two are not best suited for each other. Pisces will want to discuss and compare and fuss with the furnishings; Gemini will be interested in the beginning, but very quickly will get bored. If there are children, Gemini will show them how to broaden their horizons; Pisces will teach them love and caring for people. Both Pisces and Gemini retain a lot of the child in themselves, so neither of them will guide the children; they will grow up in a free atmosphere, and have to find their own feet.

Pisces with Cancer

Money/Job. These two understand each other. They will work well together, and not pressure each other at all. Cancerians and Pisceans both need material security and both like the things money brings: Cancerians are not as generous as Pisceans (who will give away the coat off their back) but they are good at business and will coax the impressionable Piscean into working in a more organized way. Pisces is always anxious to please; the Cancerian is appreciative, so it is a nice, harmonious combination.

Home/Friends. Cancerians love home—and so do Pisceans. These two will never want to go out! They will have a beautiful home, furnished with great style and taste, and will spend an alarming amount of money on it all, adding to it all the time and making improvements. They will entertain those they like—but will shy away from aggressive, noisy people, and keep them out. If there are children, they will be tremendously loved—and rather spoiled! Neither Cancer nor Pisces will want to correct them or upset them; however, Cancer will probably be the one to give any absolutely essential guidance, because Cancer does like good manners and good behavior, so they will grit their teeth on rare occasions and attend to discipline. Pisces never will.

Pisces with Leo

Money/Job. Pisces and Leo are both big spenders, and they will need to be careful of their finances. Pisceans are negative, Leos are positive: they can be a surprisingly good combination. Leo will be given their head to rule; Pisces will follow their lead whole-heartedly—Pisceans are very trusting, but this will not matter because Leos are trustworthy. They will organize the Piscean and make sure they organize them properly, and make full use of the talent of the Piscean for any form of art and for dealing with people.

Home/Friends. Leo likes a lavish home, luxury, and everything of the very best. Pisceans are very good home-makers, fond of beautiful things and kind and hospitable to friends. Home to a Leo is partly a status-symbol; to Pisces it is security. Both will value their home. Leo has to be the boss and Pisces is more than happy to let them.

Their only real difficulties will come because Leo is very outgoing, strong and outspoken, and Pisces is shy and impressionable and subject to intense emotional moods which Leo finds difficult to deal with. If there are children, Leo will discipline them and shape them for life. Leo is a proud parent. Pisces will love them and care for them, and be less demanding. They will make a good balance.

Pisces with Virgo

Money/Job. The Piscean is dreamy and vague. Virgo is precise and hardworking: the Virgoan will find Pisceans irritating because of their emotionalism and find it difficult to get them to settle into the routine of a job. Pisces will not like the way the Virgoan thinks of work, first and last, and will not like the pressure that Virgo puts on them. If Pisceans are not happy, they do not work well; they become even slower. Neither is very ambitious, but the worst difference between them is over money: Pisces is interested in money only because they love spending it and giving it away—Virgo is a saver, not a spender and will try to stop Pisces.

Home/Friends. Not a lot in common. Pisces loves a beautiful home and will spend a great deal on it; Virgo likes a home to be functional and not luxurious, and they will not let Pisces have a free hand. Virgo is too cold for emotional, loving Pisces, and the sensitive Piscean is given to black moods and depressions if they feel they are being criticized too much. Virgo is unemotional and doesn't understand at all. If there are children, Pisces will love them; Virgo will control them.

Pisces with Libra

Money/Job. Pisces will fit very well with Libra: both love luxury and beautiful surroundings. If there is enough money, they will find little to disagree about. They can work together well because they both manage their time to fit the projects before them, changing as the situation changes. Pisces needs direction; Libra's artistic talents can channel Pisces into mutually satisfying works. Pisces can inspire Libra. They make a good team, as neither will try to take charge.

Home/Friends. Pisces will arrange a pleasant place for Libra to throw the parties that make life worthwhile. But Pisceans win too; caring for Libra's friends will let them feel nurturing. Libra's desire for a busy social calendar may upset Pisces, but neither will ever know; both hate scenes. This makes for a life that both find very pleasant. If there are children, the Libran will help them develop at their own speed while the Piscean gives them the love and support they need. The children will be happy and active.

Pisces with Scorpio

Money/Job. Scorpio is much stronger than Pisces and will take the lead. This suits them both. Tender, dreamy Pisces will do their best to please, and Scorpio is excellent at making money and will put in the hard work that produces results. Pisceans are artistic, and very good at coping with people. Scorpio can always see natural talent and put it to good use and will not expect the impossible of the Piscean. Scorpio likes money, and so does Pisces; both are spenders, but Pisces spends on others, Scorpio on themselves.

Home/Friends. Both like a really nice home. To Scorpio, it is a status symbol, a public sign of what they have achieved, so they like luxury and everything of the highest quality and style. This suits Pisces; they like a lovely home and will put a lot of work and money into it, but it is for themselves and for their friends. Pisceans do not care what the world thinks. They are governed by their feelings, wants and needs, and they would always rather live for today than for tomorrow. If there are children, proud Scorpio will see they have the best of everything and will bring them up properly; Pisces gives affection and understanding. Between them, they provide a happy home and make good parents.

Pisces with Sagittarius

Money/Job. The Sagittarian likes the Piscean and puts just the right amount of pressure on them to make them achieve. Pisceans need direction or they will achieve nothing, but a fine balance is required. If they are pushed too hard they become unhappy and then are not able to work at their best. Pisceans are artistic and creative. The Sagittarian will like this about them, and is shrewd enough to harness their talents to their own money-making ideas. Sagittarians will be successful in business, if they can just learn to finish what they start, and will take the Piscean along with them to success and financial reward.

Home/Friends. The Sagittarian spends more time out of the home than in it. They love comfort, but are not too good at putting down roots. The home keeps Pisces very happy, however, because they are very home-centered; they love to create a beautiful environment, and the Sagittarian will be quite willing to let them have a free hand to do so. The Sagittarian likes living with the results; Pisces like the creativity involved. The home-loving and moody Piscean may make the Sagittarian feel hampered and tied, however; and the Piscean may be hurt at the lack of interest in the home Sagittarius shows. Children will be loved and wanted, but not guided.

Pisces with Capricorn

Money/Job. Pisces is sympathetic and kind, and has a wonderful skill for putting people at their ease and dealing with their problems. Since Capricorn often appears cold and forbidding, Pisces should look after the money—which Pisces will be very careless with, given half a chance. Work is a necessity for Pisceans, just to earn enough money to be able to have the material things they crave: they work only to acquire. Capricorns work because they are ambitious, and although money is very important to them, they are happiest saving it, and investing and building toward tomorrow. It is best for Capricorn to oversee everything, and keep an eye on the amount of money Pisces is spending.

Home/Friends. Pisceans are good home-makers, and will have a lovely home. They like to spend a lot of money on their home, and again Capricorn will restrain them. In one way, Pisceans are prepared to accept this: they need security and they know that with a Capricorn, they will have it. They may not be able to have everything they want, when they want it, but there will always be something behind them for a rainy day, and they will be less worried generally with a Capricorn taking charge. Children will be secure and loved.

Pisces with Aquarius

Money/Job. There is more sympathy between these two than would at first appear. The Aquarian is clever and artistic. The Piscean is artistic too, intuitive, and very skilled at dealing with people and problems; neither of them likes to work a routine nine-to-five day, and neither will insist that the other does. If they are working together in some sort of public relations or artistic enterprise, they could do well, encouraging each other but basically working independently. Pisces is more money conscious than the Aquarian. Pisceans love luxury and material things; Aquarians like them but do not strive for them. Pisces will look after the money—but Aquarius must make sure they are not spending it!

Home/Friends. Pisceans love beautiful surroundings, and spend a lot of money and time on their home. Both will enjoy furnishing it, but Aquarius will not be very interested in continually maintaining it and modernizing. To an Aquarian, home, once it is complete, needs no more. A nice comfortable place to relax and entertain friends is enough. Aquarians are not domestic, but Pisceans are and will delight in taking over. One problem could be that Aquarians, although sociable, do need quite a bit of time for privacy and thought, and Pisces could irritate them with their constant need for company; while Aquarius hurts Pisces by withdrawal. Children will be loved by Pisces, educated by Aquarius.

Pisces with Pisces

Money/Job. These two talented and artistic people will work very well together. They will understand each other without words, and work in harmony. Their only real difficulty is that neither of them is good with money: both are good at spending it and giving it away, but neither of them is a saver. They could get into real trouble with money unless they guard against it; and as they are quite materialistic, and like security, they probably will. The answer for them is to let a third person hold on to the purse strings—and if they are wise, they will do so.

Home/Friends. Pisces loves a beautiful home: how much more do TWO Pisceans love a beautiful home! They will spend all their free time and money in making it a lovely place to live and to invite their many friends to, and all will find a warm welcome there; Pisceans are very hospitable. Friendship and love are very important to Pisceans: they will like each other best of all, for the lack of difficulty in communicating—but they will not shut other people out. If there are children, they will be loved and cherished, and everything that can be given to them, will be. There is a risk of them being so indulged that they become spoiled, and perhaps lazy. However it is no good expecting Piscean parents to be disciplinarians: the children will be loved, and must find their own feet.

Love Mates

Pisces Woman—Aries Man. She needs protection from the harshness of life; he is strong and likes to protect those he loves. He will look after the Piscean woman and shelter her from those who would take advantage of her good nature. She is kindness itself: she is always receptive to a hard-luck story, because of her trusting nature. He will make sure she is less exposed to them.

The Aries man is generous too; but he is not quite so trusting as she is. He is a giver, and so is she; he will not stint her, but he will take care of her.

The Pisces woman is extremely emotional; she is prone to great changes of mood. He is much more consistent, and he finds it difficult to cope with her changeability. However she is so loving, and so loveable, that he is willing to make efforts to understand her.

He is passionate and loving; she is not so passionate, but deeply loving and loyal. She takes her lead from the person she loves: Piscean women are like mirrors, they reflect the emotions of others. The Aries man, with his loving ways, will draw a strong response from her, and they will have a happy and satisfying love life.

Their problem could be that he speaks first and thinks second: he can be very blunt and outspoken. Harsh words hurt a Piscean woman as much as a blow, and he will have to be very careful of her feelings. It is difficult for him to do this, because he is impulsive, in speech as in action. It will be very necessary, however, if they are to be happy.

Pisces Woman—Taurus Man. He is solid and dependable, and he will give her the security she so badly needs. He is also a romantic, so her deeply emotional feelings will have an outlet. The Taurean man responds when love is shown to him, and the Piscean woman has a deep need to give and to receive love. She will bring out the best in him; he will protect her and cherish her—but he will not understand her.

Everything is black and white to him. He operates on pure logic. She is instinctive and intuitive—there is very little that is logical about her. She is very changeable, and has a lot of difficulty in making up her mind. He solves this simply: most of the time, he makes it up for her. Far from resenting it, she relaxes with him.

The Taurean man likes to be in charge; it makes him feel nervous and insecure to be dependent on anyone else. He is not suited to women who want to take the lead. He can be very obstinate. The Piscean woman is very pliable: he will not have to test his strength against hers.

She loves luxury and material comfort. So does he, and he will indulge her and please her. Physically, they should be happy. He is sensuous and she is as responsive as he could wish.

The only difficulty is that she is very moody, and often there is no apparent reason for it. Taureans like things to remain the same, and her unpredictability does throw him off. He will accept it as part of her, however, and think she is worth it.

Pisces Woman—Gemini Man.

It is difficult to see how there could be much common ground between this couple. He likes light, superficial relationships that are full of mental stimulation and fun. She is looking for a strong, emotional link with a man who will care for her and protect her, and allow her to bloom and give the great love of which she is capable.

The Piscean woman will be hurt and bewildered by the impatience the Gemini man shows her. He is a great charmer, and she can be very attracted to him; he is often attracted to her because of her air of mystery. He is always looking for a woman who is out of the ordinary, and mystery is a powerful attraction to him. However, emotionalism bores him, and he is soon ready to move on.

The Piscean woman is not good at superficial relationships;

she always gets hurt. She puts a lot of love into her love affairs, and is not a flirt. The Gemini man is—and he can be as hard as nails when it suits him.

He always wants to be free; he finds it irksome to have the responsibility of making another person happy. When that other person is a Piscean woman who looks to him for friendship, love, companionship, and protection, he is likely to think it is all getting too heavy. He won't want to hurt her—but unfortunately, he will.

She is not normally jealous; as long as she has basic security with someone and feels loved, she dreams her way through her relationships, and is happy. Because she is insecure, the flirtations of a Gemini man can cause her agonies of jealousy.

Pisces Woman—Cancer Man.

A near perfect combination. The intense emotional love of the Piscean woman finds an echo in the Cancerian man. He, too, is intensely loving and very emotional. They are both subject to moods that most other people find difficult to understand. Not with these partners, however: he understands her perfectly—and vice versa.

The Cancerian man is old-fashioned; he knows how to court a woman. He pays her many small attentions, and gives her many little gifts, carefully chosen. This delights the Piscean woman: she is very feminine and loves all the attention. He makes her feel totally secure, tells her he loves her, and spends a lot of time with her. He doesn't seem to need other people, and she is able to really relax with him, and give him her heart and her innermost confidences. She will tell him things she has never told anyone—and he will keep her secrets. They find each other absolutely fascinating.

Physically, they are very compatible. He is a good lover, sensitive to every slight change of mood. She responds to him strongly; she is very loving, and she is single-minded: she won't be interested in anyone else while she is in love with him. The Cancerian man will keep her love, because he is the same. He will be loyal to her.

Both of them find the world rather a harsh place; both are dreamers, and tend to withdraw into make-believe when they are unhappy or having a bad time. This is when they feel lonely. Once they have found each other, they will withdraw together, and shut the front door on their troubles.

Pisces Woman—Leo Man.

At first sight, it looks as though proud and bossy Leo would steamroller the delicate Piscean woman, but in fact the reality is different.

The Leo man is king. He always wants to be boss and will fight very hard to be the dominant person in any set-up. The Piscean woman is so feminine, and so loving, that she will turn the tables on him: what could not have been achieved by force will be achieved by love—he will give her just about all of her own way.

When he is secure in being allowed to rule, he is generous and loving, and she makes it clear from the start that she is glad he is strong, because he can protect her and care for her. This he will gladly do. Physically, he is passionate, more so than she is, but she is so responsive and loving that he is more than happy with her. A Piscean woman is like a mirror where feelings are concerned; her deeply emotional nature makes her respond to those feelings shown to her. If she is with someone cold, she remains emotional but her glow is subdued; when she is with Leo she is as loving as he is.

He does not understand her emotional moods and changeability, but he accepts that it is part of her nature. She is often tearful, and this DOES get on his nerves. He is embarrassed by tears; he doesn't know how to cope with them, so he can be very abrupt when confronted by them. The Piscean woman, with her gift for responding to what is wanted of her, will learn to laugh more and cry less: it will not be difficult, as the Leo man will make her happy.

Pisces Woman—Virgo Man.

Love is at the bottom of the list for a Virgo man; it is at the top for a Piscean woman. These two are complete opposites. He lives for tomorrow, when all his efforts and savings will pay off; she lives for today, and for love.

He shows love quite differently from most people. He sees

it as much more important to be devoted, and to serve and care for his woman, than to make pretty speeches. He is dependable and true—but he is not romantic.

She longs for romance and attention. She lives in daydreams, and would rather be unhappy in love than be without it. She is love personified. She loves the poor and the weak in society, she loves animals who cannot protect themselves; she is in tears at a sad film or book, so completely does she identify with it. She has so much to give, and he doesn't want it. Emotion, he thinks, is a waste of valuable time. There is a lot more to life than love.

The Piscean woman can never be happy in these circumstances. Sometimes her eyes can be opened to how much the Virgo man does love her, if she becomes ill or is in serious trouble of some kind. He will stand by her and take care of her devotedly. She will be grateful to him and he will have her lifelong friendship and concern. But she needs, above all, a man who loves her and shows that he does—and it is only when she is securely loved that she can blossom and be at her best. She will move on.

Pisces Woman—Libra Man. Libra is the sign of marriage, and Libra men are happiest in a partnership. The Piscean woman is looking for security and love, and will respond to the Libra man. He understands women, and one of his most skillful ploys is to give them his undivided attention. This is exactly the right technique for her. She is shy and gentle, but she loves attention; she cannot have too much of it.

She finds life harsh, and is looking for someone who will protect her and care for her. He is not usually very protective by nature, but he will be with her. He is very drawn to her gentleness; he hates aggressive and quarrelsome people, and with her he can have complete harmony. She brings out the best in him. Generally speaking, he likes light, superficial relationships and happy, confident, witty people.

The Piscean woman has more extremes of mood than he likes, but she is sensitive, and he is attracted to her. He needs to love and be loved, and he senses her capacity for gentle, giving love.

She is restful, quiet and content to let him take the limelight. She does not compete with him, so he can relax with her.

Both of them like the finer things of life, and they will have a very happy and pleasant relationship, both at home, which they will both appreciate and make beautiful, and with friends. Libra is very sociable, Pisces not quite so much so, but she will be very popular with his friends. This is a good match.

Pisces Woman—Scorpio Man. Great potential. She responds wonderfully to this magnetic, demanding, intense man. She is everything he likes in a woman: feminine, emotional and loving. She is also ultra-sensitive, and he will have to be careful not to hurt her feelings.

Physically, they are well matched. When their love-life is right, everything else falls into place. For both of them, love means everything. The Piscean woman responds instinctively to the Scorpio man; she is eager to please and will do anything to make him happy, because he makes her feel so loved. If they have difficult times, it is their physical relationship that will pull them through: It is their strength, and the rock on which their relationship is built.

The gentle Piscean woman is very good for the Scorpio man; she allows him to release the kindness and sweetness in his own nature. He hides this so as not to appear weak, but with the Piscean woman he has no need to try to dominate. There is no struggle, or clash of wills. He leads, she follows.

She is quite timid: she finds life harsh and difficult on her own. She needs the support and protection of someone strong: the Scorpio man has this strength, and he will willingly take care of her—he likes those he loves to be under his protection. He is possessive, but so is she; she will understand it and accept it. It is another proof to her that he loves her.

They have a great understanding between them, and should have a happy, loving and successful relationship. It will last a long time, and they may well marry.

Pisces Woman—Sagittarius Man. This will not be a happy love affair for the sensitive, easily hurt Piscean woman.

The Sagittarian man will enjoy it, because he enjoys all conquests. She will find the flirtatious and tactless Sagittarian man very hard to handle. He is easy to capture—but almost impossible to tie down.

She needs security and a sense of being deeply loved. She senses that he is not really committing himself, and she is right. He is a charming companion, and will court her and be as romantic as she could wish, but there is no feeling of security or permanence there. The gentle and sensitive Piscean cannot help showing her bewilderment; she is vunerable, and he feels guilty, and wants to move on to more light-hearted and flirtatious female company.

The Piscean woman is loving and emotional, and their love-life will be sweet. Both are loving. He finds her femininity very attractive. She will not try to change him: she is the most tolerant of all the zodiac signs. A Piscean woman is uncomplaining and patient—and this may just capture him in the end.

If she will wait, and give him room to maneuver; if she is willing to let him make the decision to settle down with her at his own speed (and it may take a long time) he might end up with her.

She could make him happy—but would he make her happy? Probably not. He finds her emotionally draining, and she finds his blunt speech and uncaring ways hurtful.

Pisces Woman—Capricorn Man.
He needs a very special sort of reassurance from a woman before he can relax his cold and forbidding exterior, and show her how much he needs to love and be loved.

She is the most kind and loving woman in the zodiac. She can draw him out and she is so talented at getting along with people that he immediately feels at ease in her company. The gentle charm and strong loving and receptive nature of a Piscean woman is a potent lure to the Capricorn man. With her, he can show the more gentle and loving side of his nature.

He is very much drawn to her gentleness and femininity. She is such a feeling person herself that she is not fooled by the mask he wears. He fears rejection, and she takes care never to snub him. He find himself trusting her more and more, and opening up in her company. She really likes him—and she lets it show. She is the woman he is looking for.

The Piscean woman is looking for someone special too. She is timid and finds life harsh; she longs for a special someone to protect her and take care of her, to cherish her and love her. She also needs her man to be an achiever, who can give her the financial security she needs. The Capricorn fills the bill— and will gladly give her whatever she wants. He does not like giving money, or spending it: but he finds her irresistible and will give in to make her happy. He thinks he is lucky to have found her—and he is.

Pisces Woman—Aquarius Man.

She is very responsive; she usually likes best those that like her. She is very put off by emotional coolness or unkind words.

In the case of the Aquarian man, she may not know quite what to make of him. She senses that his interest, which he makes obvious, is superficial. It is little more than curiosity. He is drawn to her by her air of stillness and of mystery. He will use all his considerable charm to draw her out. Because she is so multi-faceted, she holds his interest.

He is too cool for her to have any real relationship with. He is detached, and not looking for any kind of deep love or involvement. She will not be especially drawn to him; everything for him is of the mind. For her, it is of emotion; to a Piscean woman, love is everything. The Aquarian man would not understand her needs and would make no attempt to meet them.

She likes love, security, and peace of mind, in that order. She likes a man who will protect her and care for her, and shield her from the unpleasant side of life. In the Aquarian, she has a footloose charmer, more interested in preserving his freedom than in falling in love.

The Piscean woman is completely intuitive and instinctive: she does what she feels, she says what she thinks. The Aquarian analyzes all the emotion out of everything. Even when he is involved in a passionate affair (and it can happen) he is mentally analyzing it even while it is going on. He has a cold streak.

She makes him feel claustrophobic; she loves him too much. He makes her feel unloved and unwanted: he loves her too little.

Pisces Woman—Pisces Man.

Near perfection. These two understand each other perfectly. They will not hurt each other, or let each other down.

She needs love above all else: so does he. They will have a wonderful and emotional love-life. Both of them would sacrifice anything for love. Physically they are well matched; they know each other's needs instinctively, and are so sensitive to the slightest shift of mood that they have a superb wordless communication. There is a deep security between them that they both need and although they are both moody, who better to understand and soothe them than another Piscean, who knows exactly what they are feeling?

The difficulty with this relationship is that the Piscean woman is looking for a strong protector to shield her from life—and so is the Piscean man. She wants him to look after her—but he wants her to look after him. Neither of them wants to take any responsibility and both are impractical dreamers. They are unlikely to be able to give each other the financial security and stability that they both so desperately need.

However, even if this is not a permanent relationship, it will be an extremely loving and rewarding one. Neither of them will ever forget the other and there will be a lasting love and bond between them.

While it lasts, they will both give freely and completely to each other. When they do move apart, each subconsciously seeking more security with someone stronger, they will often remain loving friends.

Pisces Man—Aries Woman.

This is a difficult partnership. She tends to be too strong and too demanding for him. He is dreamy and indecisive; she is aggressive and makes up her mind in a flash—then sticks to it.

He has a lot to give her, however. The Aries woman feels that she has to battle her way through life—she will not have to battle with him. He is not going to try to dominate her, and this will help to relax her.

Unfortunately, she will try to dominate him, and will try to make him stronger. This can be very difficult for him. He is a dreamer, kind and sweet and very loving, but he is not a fighter. She is sometimes abrupt in her manner and speech, and though she doesn't mean to upset him, it hurts him. A harsh word to a Piscean man is as bad as a blow, and he will brood about it. He is moody, she is not. She will not understand his emotional moods, and is inclined to be impatient with them.

However, the Aries woman is loving and loyal, and she will defend him from people she feels are trading on his good nature. She is less trusting than he is, and will make sure that people don't take more from him than he can really manage easily to give. The Piscean man is a real giver, with money, with time, and with emotions. A hard-luck story always gets to him.

If she loves him, she will have to accept early on in the relationship that she cannot change him: all she can do is love him, and let him love her and give her the tenderness she needs but is unable to ask for.

Pisces Man—Taurus Woman.
He can have a good relationship with her. She is feminine and receptive, and will not scare him off by being aggressive or argumentative. He is dreamy and sensitive, and she likes this in a man. Both love beautiful things, and both are artistic.

The Taurean woman has a stability that the Piscean man is drawn to. He knows he is indecisive; he likes the way she has her feet firmly planted on the ground. She will talk him out of his most impractical schemes, and as she is ambitious herself will gently push him in the right direction. She will not attempt to dominate him—but she can coax him to do what is best for them both.

Physically, they should get along well. The Taurean woman has quite a lot of passion in her make-up; the Piscean man has less, but is so loving and responsive to her that she is more than happy with him. He is kind and loving to her and anything she wants that is within his power to give her, he will give her gladly.

She is tranquil and peaceful. He loves this in her; there will not be quarrels or upsets between them, and when they do not agree, they will be able to compromise without either of them resenting it.

He is moody; she is not. She will not encourage his occasional fits of depression and despondency, nor will she argue with him. She will just gently change the subject and soon he will have forgotten what was worrying him. She is a pleasant companion, and they should be happy.

Pisces Man—Gemini Woman.
He will never know where he is with her. He is always insecure anyway, and this makes him much worse. He will worry constantly, and will not be really happy.

The Gemini woman is a butterfly. She does not settle easily with one man or in one place. The Piscean needs emotional as well as financial security, and he just cannot cope with this. He wants a woman who loves him totally and shows it. She wants to preserve her independence and, although she is looking for romance, she is looking for lightness and brightness. She does not like heavy or deeply emotional relationships.

She likes mental stimulation. She likes clever, witty people and rather superficial relationships. These leave her free to move on when the fancy takes her, without having to feel guilty. She does feel a bit guilty about him. Although he is not normally jealous, he is quite possessive; he needs to know the woman he loves is really his, and the Gemini woman is a terrible flirt.

The Piscean man is a giver—he gives love freely and unselfishly and the Gemini woman is a taker and does not really give back enough to make him happy. He puts love at the top of his list: he will sacrifice anything for love. She is more comfortable with friendships than with deep love.

A love relationship between these two is not really likely to last long. She finds it too intense and will move on. She will try to do this without hurting him too much and will breathe a sigh of relief when she does. In this relationship, it is the Piscean man who is the loser.

Pisces Man—Cancer Woman.
She is the answer to his prayer. She is loving, kind and has deep feelings. She is as

sensitive as he is and is very feminine. He responds to her immediately, as she does to him.

Their physical love-life will be very good, and neither of them will want or need anybody else. Both are faithful and both are quite possessive. The Cancerian woman doesn't mind the possessiveness of the Piscean man; she accepts it as proof that he really loves her. She can be driven to infidelity if she feels unloved or unappreciated, but when she knows she is loved without reservation, she will not stray.

He will be faithful to her because she is everything he could ever want in a woman. A Piscean man can stray, but it is only in search of reassurance. With her, he doesn't need to do this.

He tends to be weak; any hard luck story will produce results from him, even the most far-fetched. He cannot refuse a favor to anyone, even when it is very awkward for him. The Cancerian woman has a stronger sense of self-preservation than he has and she uses that same sense for those she loves: she will not allow people to take advantage of him.

These two can build a very happy and long-lasting relationship. They are very well suited, will make a nice home together and give each other no cause for worry. A loving couple.

Pisces Man—Leo Woman. It is very unlikely that he would be attracted to her—and even less likely that she would be attracted to him. The Leo woman looks for a man who is even stronger than she is—and that's REALLY hard to find. The gentle, dreamy Piscean man is not strong enough for her; he couldn't hold her and would not even want to try.

He is loving and caring, but he is looking for a much gentler, more feminine woman. A Leo woman would scare him off. Inwardly, she is highly feminine, which is why she needs a man stronger than she is, but she gives the impression of being very dominant and this scares off a lot of men, especially Piscean men. Also, she likes an achiever; he is not ambitious and tends to drift through life, doing whatever comes along. He is not particularly motivated to work, though he wants and needs money to make himself feel secure.

Leo women are very cut and dried; they know where they are going, and they know what they want. The indecisive, drifting Piscean man is not their type. He is just about impossible to pin down to anything; he will say anything for peace, and then go back on it.

If these two do meet and, against all odds, fall in love, it is the Piscean man who will come off the worst. Love to him is the most important thing in the world; he will give up anything for love. To a Leo woman, love is important too—but only as part of the rest of life. She would soon be impatient with his tender ways and he would be wounded by her. Her weapon when she is not happy is scorn; nothing could be worse or more hurtful to him.

Pisces Man—Virgo Woman.

She makes a wonderful wife. She is a hard worker, utterly devoted to her man and will show her love by helping him, working for him, and serving him in every way she can. She tends to be confused about love, though, and it is love that is the most important thing to him.

She is not a self-starter where love is concerned. She is unawakened, and it takes a special type of man to reach her and teach her how to love. The Piscean man can be that man. He is all love, all feeling and all dreams. The practical Virgo woman is a good balance for him, and he will be loving and tender toward her. If she can respond to him, they could have a good relationship. It must be said, though, that Virgo women have a cold streak, and no Piscean man can live with this.

It all depends on the love there is between them. She looks to her man for a lead; he doesn't want to lead. However, she is very practical and will soon be gently edging him in the direction he ought to go.

The many people who take advantage of him will get short shift from her; she will not encourage them and will protect him and look after his money. This is where she really shines. She is absolutely loyal and committed, and at all times she will stand by the man she has chosen. If bad times come, she will still be there, and he can rely on her absolutely. He needs that security and will value it. If he can teach her how to love, and she can learn from him, they could be very happy.

Pisces Man—Libra Woman.

She will be drawn by his kindness and gentleness, which she shares. Libra women are very loving and emotional physically, and their love relationship is likely to be surprisingly good.

Apart from this, however, she likes happy, uncomplicated people. She expects love to be a happy experience and so often, to a Pisces man, it is a trauma. Pisces loves seldom—and deeply. She is more balanced than he is and will find it very difficult to cope with so many moods and emotional swings. She likes easy, undemanding people who are amusing and somewhat superficial. She finds him too intense for real comfort.

However, she is a kind and loving woman, and will bring stability to the dreamy and drifting Piscean man. She will direct him gently in his career and this will be to his advantage. Both need and want money to finance a rather luxurious lifestyle. He will work in order to gain security, but he is never quite sure which path to take. She is a great help here. She knows what suits him and is quite successful at making money herself.

She loves parties, both giving them and going to them. He is rather shy and retiring and doesn't mix well; but he is kind and hospitable and will happily entertain her friends while she sparkles in the middle of an admiring group. She is very popular.

He is possessive, but he is not jealous. He is proud of this woman who loves him, and admires her more than anyone.

Pisces Man—Scorpio Woman. The intense and emotional Scorpio woman will take charge of this relationship, and it is better that she does.

He is ultra-sensitive, loving, with very deep feelings. He is a dreamer and her hard-headed back-up is very useful to him. She is as magnetic and intense as even he could wish, but she has a strong streak of practicality and strength which he lacks. She will help him to make his dreams a reality and make sure he makes the best of himself and his prospects.

He puts love first every time in his life. So does she—so there is more than enough romance between them. These two are on the same wavelength. The moody Scorpio woman needs quite a lot of reassurance that she is really loved, and the sensitive, caring Pisces man, who notices the slightest change of mood in anyone, will understand her needs and give her no cause to be insecure.

Emotionally, therefore it is a good match. Physically, it is not so good. His extreme gentleness is not what she really wants in a lover. She is looking for a man who can match her own intensity and passion. She will instinctively try to draw this reaction from him, but it will just cause him to go back into his shell and he will become miserable if she persists. He is truly loving, but he lacks her tremendous passion—as, indeed, do most men, barring perhaps another Scorpio or a Leo. She will realize before long that he will make a loving friend, and that she should look elsewhere for a lover.

Pisces Man—Sagittarius Woman. An uneasy match. He is no match for the strong and self-willed Sagittarian woman. He will not attempt to argue or reason with her. He will let her go her own way, and lapse into moodiness and depression when her actions upset him.

She is a very strong character. She is a born fighter, and will provoke a partner into a quarrel in the interests of "clearing the air." These little ups and downs don't upset her; she forgets them five minutes later, but they do upset the Piscean man. He hates fights and angry upheavals and the more she does this, the more he will withdraw from her, sometimes leaving her without warning if things get too much for him.

She will quickly lose patience with the moods and silences that unhappiness brings to him. Her temper will often get the better of her as she tries in vain to make the Piscean man into a more equal partner. He won't do it. Although he may appear weak and indecisive, she cannot force him to live in a way he doesn't want to.

The Piscean man is emotional, the Sagittarian woman passionate, but they don't really hit it off together physically. He needs a softer and gentler partner; he finds her too demanding, while she finds his hyper-sensitive nature and emotional need for constant love and reassurance very draining. She has not the patience for this type of relationship. Not a very loving couple: they would do better to settle for friendship.

Pisces Man—Capricorn Woman. She hides her true feelings and her great need to love and be loved, for fear of

rejection. The Piscean man, with his depth of feeling and his understanding of women, can do a great deal to help her lower her defenses and discover her emotional potential. He is full of emotion and can show her how to love. In the short term, this could be enough for them; but in the long term she is looking to the future—and she doesn't like temporary love affairs.

He is a dreamer. He believes his own dreams can come true. He is loving and outgoing, sensitive and unworldly. He lacks ambition and will settle for the line of least resistance wherever possible.

The Capricorn woman is looking for an achiever, someone who will be ambitious, do well at their job, and give her the financial security she wants and needs. He makes her feel warm and cared for, but lacks the strength of purpose to suit her. She is hardworking herself and interested in her career, and she wouldn't be happy with a man who was not.

The instability in his character will bother her. She will not like his easy attraction for other women. He is a faithful lover when he feels securely loved, but he can stray if he feels unappreciated, and when he does he can cover his tracks amazingly well. This is part and parcel of his dislike of scenes and upheavals. He will always try to avoid them if at all possible. She may decide to leave him, to test him. He will let her go, not because he doesn't love her, but because it is not in his nature to fight.

Pisces Man—Aquarius Woman.
He is loving, sensitive and needs and gets a great deal of attention from those he loves. He is always looking for security, both financial and emotional, and it is this constant need for reassurance that gets on her nerves. She sees it as self-indulgence. She is independent and aloof herself; she asks nothing of anybody and doesn't like anybody asking of her. Clinging personalities scare her off—and no Aquarian woman values anything that comes easily. She likes a man to be unobtainable, so that she can worship him and dream about him—even when she later finds he has feet of clay.

The Piscean man is loving and will take care of her, so far as she will let him. He will give her absolute devotion and caring tenderness, but she will not appreciate it. It is not what she wants. She likes what she cannot have: the more unavailable a man is, the more she yearns for him. He is too loving and out in the open to suit her.

He is very emotional; his moods are ever-changing and he can turn against someone he has loved very quickly. If he feels unloved or unappreciated, he is likely to just walk out.

It is always easy for him to find another woman; he is very attractive to women and knows just how to handle them. If he does this, it may wake her up: once he is less available, she is likely to find her feelings for him rekindled, and go chasing after him again. This combination will never really work though; he is too loving and intense for her, she is too detached and cool for him.

Pisces Man—Pisces Woman. Perfect understanding between these two makes a near-perfect partnership. They will not let each other down, or hurt each other.

He needs love above all else: so does she. They have a wonderful and emotional love-life: both will sacrifice anything for love. Physically, they are well-matched. They instinctively know each other's needs and are sensitive to the smallest change of mood. They have a superb wordless communication. They give each other a deep security, and although they are both moody, nobody knows better how to soothe a Piscean than another Piscean.

The difficulty in this relationship is that she is looking for a strong protector to stand between her and the harsh realities of life—and so is he. She wants him to look after her—and he wants her to look after him. Neither wants to take responsibility, and both are impractical dreamers. They cannot give each other the material and financial backing they both need.

However, even if this is not a permanent relationship, it will be an exceptionally loving and rewarding one. Neither of them will ever forget the other and there will be a lasting bond between them.

They each give freely and completely to one another. When they do drift apart, each subconciously seeking someone stronger to give them the security they deperately need, they will remain loving friends.